Property

Mergers, Acquisitions and Alternative Corporate Strategies
Hill Samuel Bank Limited

Tax: Strategic Corporate Tax Planning
Price Waterhouse

Finance for Growth
National Westminster Bank PLC

Company Law and Competition
S J Berwin & Co

Marketing: Communicating with the Consumer
D'Arcy Masius Benton & Bowles

Information Technology: The Catalyst for Change
PA Consulting Group

Marketing to the Public Sector and Industry
Rank Xerox Limited

Transport and Distribution
TNT Express

Property
Edward Erdman

Employment and Training
Blue Arrow PLC

Audio cassette documentaries are available on each of the titles above, showing through case studies, and interviews with senior executives, how British companies can take advantage of new markets in Europe. The cassettes are available at £12.95 through bookshops or from Didasko Ltd, Didasko House, Wennington, Huntingdon, Cambs PE17 2LX.

Property

Edward Erdman

With a Foreword by
the Rt. Hon. Christopher Patten, MP
Secretary of State for the Environment

Published in association with
CBI Initiative 1992

MERCURY BOOKS
Published by W.H. Allen & Co. Plc

First published in 1990
by the Mercury Books Division of
W.H. Allen & Co. Plc
Sekforde House, 175–9 St John Street, London EC1V 4LL

Set in Plantin by Phoenix Photosetting, Chatham
Printed and bound in Great Britain by
Butler & Tanner Ltd, Frome, Somerset

British Library Cataloguing in Publication Data
Erdman, Edward L.

   Property.
   1. European Community countries. Real property
   I. Title   II. CBI Initiative 1992
   333.33094

   ISBN 1–85251–052–8

Contents

Foreword

Property stands apart from other business themes which featured in the CBI's Initiative 1992 in the sense that the single market programme does not address itself to property and has no Community measures relating to it. It is, none the less, entirely appropriate that property should have been included in the Initiative.

The Government fully supports the completion of this single market in goods and services, which will bring together the largest population in the industralised world. It will stimulate competition, increase cross-border investment, facilitate economies of scale and generate substantial cost reductions and efficiency gains. This should lead to accelerated economic growth, greater wealth, higher standards of living and more jobs. There are major implications in all this for the property sector, through increased demands for accommodation from new and growing businesses and through pressure for relocations within and across national borders.

1992 underlines one of the essential truths of corporate planning: that no company can afford to ignore the property implications of its business decisions. Specialist advice from property consultants will be all the more necessary where firms' accommodation requirements are increasingly dictated by European rather than national market considerations. This must be so, because any EC company establishing a business operation in another member state will have to get to grips with a property system that differs, sometimes radically, from what it is used to at home.

The opportunities presented by the single market are enormous. Many UK companies are already pursuing well-planned European strategies with great determination, which must be the right course if only because the EC already accounts for around half our exports. It also presents a vital challenge to the property and construction industries in particular: to respond to pressures for growth and expansion by developing to standards of design and landscaping that are sensitive to the natural and the existing built environment. It is no longer acceptable for growth to be achieved at the expense of our environment: businesses which recognise this will be the ones that prosper in the Europe of the 1990s.

This book focuses in considerable detail on the essential differences in property practices and procedures in each of the EC member states. I congratulate Edward Erdman and CBI Initiative 1992 and commend this book to the business community.

The Rt. Hon. Chris Patten, MP
Secretary of State for the Environment

Preface

The CBI's invitation to participate in the 1992 Initiative proved to be a most timely one for my company. We had resolved to pursue a wholehearted commitment to the single European market, having previously – like so many others – achieved various forms of association with companies in other member states.

The writing of this book coincided with the successful conclusion of negotiations with one of France's leading firms of property consultants and I was, therefore, able to announce at the CBI Initiative 1992 seminar on property in October 1989 that we were on our way to becoming a truly European company through an exchange of equity rather than through mere association.

Property, like the financial sector, is a truly international market, and we need to ensure that UK companies are not left on the sidelines. I hope that *our* commitment to the EC, as demonstrated in the seminars, this book and the accompanying tape, will encourage the reader to grasp more of the opportunities which 1992 promises to offer.

That is not to say that the European property scene is as simple and clear-cut as one might wish, and this book pulls no punches in pointing out the difficulties. Attitudes, traditions and regulations across the current national borders are markedly – and at times frustratingly – different. But with property assets now representing such a significant proportion of the total asset value of leading UK companies, no business with an interest in the future dare ignore the topic with which this book deals. The global nature of the property market will not diminish, and 1992 should act as a beacon encouraging further UK involvement in the single market.

Of course, Europe has continued to change. Indeed, much of this book was prepared before the dramatic events behind the Iron Curtain. In the face of such change, our task, in the property sector, is to use sound and reliable research to learn to interpret political and economic indicators and to encourage our clients to grasp the opportunities as they arise. I hope that this book will play some small part in helping to bring that process forward.

I would like to take this opportunity to express my appreciation of the efforts of those who have worked on this book, particularly

Jon Gooding, our International Director, and his assistant Astrid Jennewein, as well as those many others within the company who contributed both detail and constructive comment.

Charles M. Lee
Chairman
Edward Erdman

I
Overview

1. Introduction

From the UK perspective, it is entirely appropriate that the CBI should have included property on the list of key topics for its Initiative 1992. The UK property market is highly sophisticated and based on well-established traditions, customs and codes of practice, and it is widely recognised within the UK – as elsewhere – that every major business decision has a property dimension. Many of the opportunities, therefore, offered by the completion of the single market will, by definition, involve property concerns.

It may, then, come as a surprise to many to find that, for all its 279 directives, the Single European Act makes no direct reference to property. This is, perhaps, inevitable, in view of the very considerable disparity between custom and practice, tradition and ambition in the Community's approach to property matters. It is none the less regrettable, because it leaves the differences subject only to market forces and to the individual concerns of specific governments rather than to the persuasion of a common drive towards harmony.

Later chapters will demonstrate (at times all too painfully) the size of the disparity. They will also indicate some of the ways in which, despite its apparent relegation to the sidelines, the property market in various member states is beginning to develop.

To define the UK market as the most sophisticated is not arrogant. It is undeniable that, with the exception of the Republic of Ireland, the Netherlands and (to a lesser extent) Denmark, no other property market in the EC can compare in terms of liquidity, institutional involvement, transparency and ease of trading. As we look at areas such as professional practice, forms of tenure, finance and so on, the UK market's level of sophistication will become apparent.

Being the most sophisticated is, of course, no guarantee of future success. If UK commercial, retail and industrial organisations and investors – not to mention the professional property industry itself – fail to grasp the opportunities before other member states catch up (or before non-Community rivals, such as Sweden, the USA or Japan, increase their footholds), then all the expertise and sophistication in the world will be of little benefit.

This means, among other things, that organisations must continue to recognise that there is a property dimension to most major corporate business decisions and continue to develop a broader understanding of the role of property as part of a corporate strategy.

At the simplest level, all manufacturers need a factory, all secretaries need a desk, and all shopkeepers need a window in which to display their wares. At another level, every public company needs to understand – before it has to learn by its mistakes – the consequences of understating the true asset value of the company.

In corporate transactions over the past decade, property assets have been an increasingly important element, especially as US-style highly leveraged buy-outs have become the fashion. Indeed, property now represents 24 per cent of the total net asset value of the top 1,000 companies in the UK, and any company which fails to put its property assets to work effectively is not only failing to maximise an opportunity, but is also putting itself at risk.

One of the aims of this book is, therefore, to encourage every company – and not just those with immediate plans to make further acquisitions of real estate within the EC – to pause for a moment and take a long, hard look at its existing property portfolio, and to ask itself just where in the organisation, the responsibility lies for the informed and effective management of this key area.

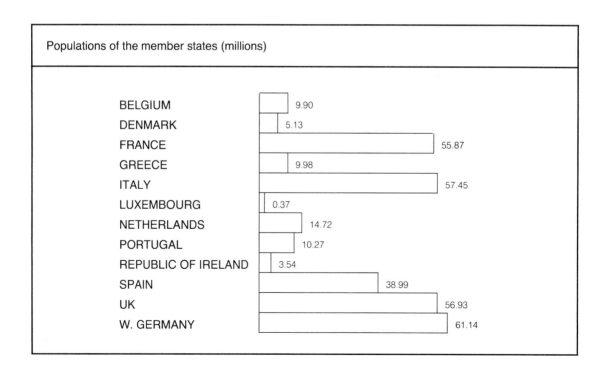

Populations of the member states (millions)

BELGIUM	9.90
DENMARK	5.13
FRANCE	55.87
GREECE	9.98
ITALY	57.45
LUXEMBOURG	0.37
NETHERLANDS	14.72
PORTUGAL	10.27
REPUBLIC OF IRELAND	3.54
SPAIN	38.99
UK	56.93
W. GERMANY	61.14

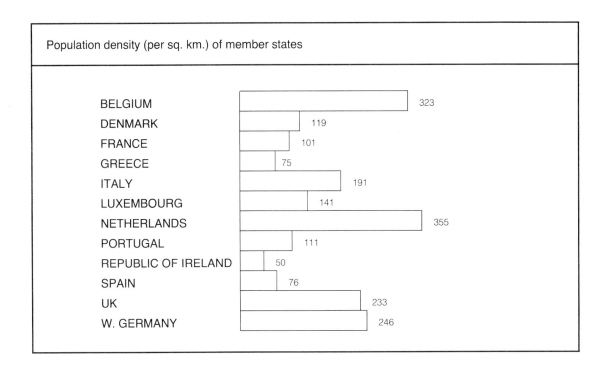

Population density (per sq. km.) of member states

BELGIUM	323
DENMARK	119
FRANCE	101
GREECE	75
ITALY	191
LUXEMBOURG	141
NETHERLANDS	355
PORTUGAL	111
REPUBLIC OF IRELAND	50
SPAIN	76
UK	233
W. GERMANY	246

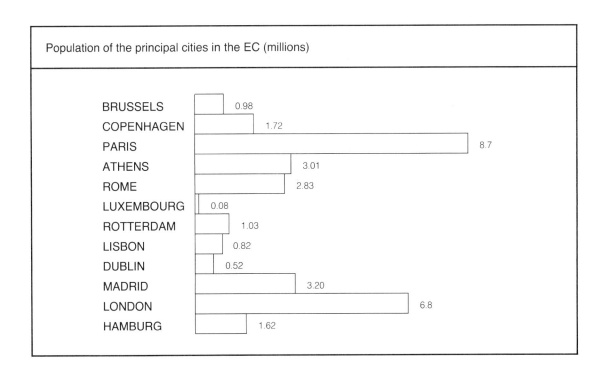

Population of the principal cities in the EC (millions)

BRUSSELS	0.98
COPENHAGEN	1.72
PARIS	8.7
ATHENS	3.01
ROME	2.83
LUXEMBOURG	0.08
ROTTERDAM	1.03
LISBON	0.82
DUBLIN	0.52
MADRID	3.20
LONDON	6.8
HAMBURG	1.62

This book also aims to assist companies that are expanding in Europe by way of merger or acquisition to be able to analyse and appraise the property assets of the target company or potential bedfellow. It is simply not good enough nowadays – and will become increasingly unacceptable – to view property as merely a factor of production to be held on the balance sheet at cost.

There are many companies which take the view – and their individual circumstances may make them right – that such local matters as real estate are best left in the hands of the local manager. But if this is the company view, it is essential that head office ask itself whether the corporate structure is one which provides local management with the incentive to ask a number of important questions: are the land assets being used efficiently? is any of the land within the portfolio surplus to present and future need? what is the redevelopment potential of land and premises within each local property portfolio? should the whole operation be relocated in order to allow the (beneficial) wholesale redevelopment of the site for alternative use? should the company consider releasing capital by refinancing or entering into a sale and leaseback arrangement? or, are there, in fact, good reasons why local management may consciously wish to avoid addressing such issues? Property knowledge and expertise need to be at main board or senior management level so that a view can be taken of the bigger picture. Local management recommendations can then be assessed in the context of the overall strategy.

This book seeks to provide sufficient information on the European property market to enable the reader to identify the key issues and to ask the right questions. It does not set out to provide a comprehensive gazetteer of European property; the subject is too large and too complex for such an approach. And, despite the best intentions, it has not achieved total comparability at all points; the available information – from primary and secondary sources – is uneven.

Part II, which covers each member state's property market individually, should be seen as an integral part of the whole. Indeed, for many readers Part II will be the more important part, because it provides a detailed guide to the peculiar complexities of each of the markets. But this brings us full circle: in a sector where diversity is the norm and harmony a long way off, there can be no substitute for detailed, specific guidance from professional advisers, be they lawyer, accountant or chartered surveyor.

2.   Today's market*

The EC consists of five kingdoms, six republics and one grand-duchy, and it uses eleven different languages. The extent to which a twelfth language – 'chauvinism' – is used varies, although each member state is to a greater or lesser degree prone to a protectionist response. In the industrial and commercial sectors, change is being thrust upon even the most recalcitrant by the recognition that failure to take a European view will probably result in extinction.

Property, perhaps, represents the ultimate national bastion: in most European countries, property law is at the very heart of the constitution; in the United Kingdom, it forms a key part of common law. Any attempt at interference by the European Commission or the European Parliament in such a fundamental area would be likely to meet with some resistance.

As a result, the Community's market is highly fragmented, with fierce competition not just between member states but even within member states. In many aspects, parochialism rules.

Regional competition

Throughout France, it is generally accepted that Paris and the Ile de France region occupy an overwhelmingly dominant position. Even so, a rapid extension of the high-speed rail system (Train à Grande Vitesse or TGV) is bringing a number of other major centres (including Lyon, Marseille, Nice, Grenoble, Dijon and Bordeaux) closer not just to Paris but also to the rest of the Community.

The German Federal Republic, by contrast, is a collection of semi-autonomous states – a fact which encourages direct competition between the country's major commercial and industrial centres. Whereas the northern sector used to be the dominant industrial region, there has been a definite shift towards the south. Although Bonn is, unquestionably, the capital of the national government, Frankfurt is West Germany's financial centre and also ranks fourth in

* This book was compiled with information current on 1 September 1989.

7

the world after London, New York and Tokyo. Düsseldorf, a major centre for general industry, is second only to New York in the number of Japanese companies which now trade within its boundaries. Munich is the nation's own 'silicon valley' and could claim to be the country's new technology capital.

In Belgium, of course, there can be no dispute as to which city is the 'true' capital. The difficulty here is one of language: with three in use in the country as a whole, the capital is officially bi-lingual, although around 80 per cent of its inhabitants speak French rather than Flemish.

In Spain, it is said that the Catalans of Barcelona will not speak other than grudgingly to the Madrilenos, and that neither will address the Basques freely! Whether or not this is any more than apocryphal, it does underline the traditional differences between the regions of Spain, differences which continue today in terms of commercial and especially industrial activity.

Equally apocryphal, no doubt, is the suggestion that in Italy the problem of pre-eminence was solved by the development of three capitals – one for business, one for politics and one for pleasure!

Denmark's membership of the Community is focusing more attention on its southern sector and the border with West Germany.

In the Netherlands, the southern region – strategically placed for access to the Community – has drawn attention away from the Randstad in the north, which traditionally took the lion's share of the nation's industrial and commercial activity.

The main conclusion to be drawn from these variations – in terms of the property market – is that the potential investor, purchaser, or party to a joint venture will be faced by a complex range of structural differences on a regional basis as well as nationally.

The differences between England and Scotland may not appear so extreme, but they do provide an indication of the situation to be expected in other parts of the new Europe. Nor should it be a surprise that these traditional differences – and antagonisms even – should so often relate to matters of property, when property is, as we have said, so close to the heart of the state and its constitution.

No doubt the passage of time and, in particular, the needs and requirements of multi-national companies will dictate the parameters of the market and bring about a greater harmonisation to the European property scene. Even so, political developments – notably the local success of the Social Democratic and Green parties in Frankfurt, and their joint opposition to further high-rise development in the city – suggest that a very rapid harmonisation in the European property sector cannot be counted on.

Part II of this book provides, in some detail, ample evidence of the different approaches to property matters in the various EC member states, but it may be helpful here to summarise some of the key areas of difference.

Forms of tenure

There is, of course, one major difference between the UK and most of its Community partners: beyond the Channel, there is a far greater tradition of sole ownership or co-ownership (condominium) than of leasing. Indeed, in some cases, the failure of a company to own the premises it occupies is seen as a reason to doubt the company's commercial success. This is one way in which the property market outside the UK and the Republic of Ireland seems noticeably less sophisticated. In West Germany, notwithstanding the long tradition of ownership, there is a definite move towards a broader approach, including an acceptance of the value of sale-and-lease-back transactions.

Leasing
Forms of leases and the legislation which governs them vary substantially across the Community. In Portugal, for example, the landlord and tenant legislation is such as to confer absolute security of tenure, with rental indexation at a rate below inflation. This has the effect of keeping rents low but generates a considerable trade in premiums or 'key money'. The Portuguese government is currently undertaking a review of the legislation, although it does not appear to view the issue as a major priority.

Until 1985, similar legislation existed in Spain, where fixed rents and absolute security of tenure also led to a valuable trade (between tenants) in premiums. The Spanish government's decision to change radically the landlord and tenant legislation has, however, led to absolute *insecurity* of tenure for tenants taking leases since that date.

These are extremes, and in between there is a spectrum of circumstances which does not lend itself to generalisation except to say that, in most cases, much greater security of tenure is enjoyed by retail tenants than other commercial lessees.

In Greece, for example, retail leases do not allow termination at the landlord's instigation, except where the landlord can prove that he requires the premises for his own use. A similar proviso exists in the Netherlands, except that retail leases are for a specified period (five years or a multiple thereof) and renewable unless the landlord requires the premises for his own use. In Denmark, where, as elsewhere, the tradition is to own the premises one occupies, a non-industrial lease may be 'for time and eternity', an ominous phrase which simply means that the lease, though subject to indexation, has no fixed period and will run until one or other party seeks to end it. In Italy, the minimum period of a commercial lease is six years with an automatic extension for the same period at the same rent. Rent reviews – permitted every two years but not during the first three years – may not exceed 75 per cent of the annual increase in the retail price index.

In France, as in Belgium and Luxembourg, there is a tradition of ownership, but in the rented sector much use is made of the 3/6/9-year lease where the tenant has automatic right to renewal and to rent review at the end of each three-year period (except for retail properties where the rent can be increased on renewal only in line with indexation). If the landlord does not wish to renew the lease, he or she must be prepared to compensate the tenant according to a number of factors, including the availability of comparable premises nearby and the impact on the tenant's business.

Belgium provides yet another peculiarity: a commercial lease is renewable no less than three times (so that a 3/6/9-year lease, where the tenant has the option to give six months' notice to quit at three-yearly intervals, can effectively run for thirty-six years, with no right of withdrawal by the landlord but a right for the tenant to withdraw at six months' notice).

Such is the complex and – to those accustomed to the UK retail, office and industrial market – unsatisfactory nature of some of the forms of tenure to be found within the Community.

Methods of measurement

Another of the more difficult variations within the Community is in the methods which different member states traditionally use to measure the area which is for sale or rent (see facing page).

It is important to avoid any comparisons between prices or rentals per square metre without being sure of the basis on which the given area is computed. In Denmark, for instance, the space given will refer to the gross internal area, including all common areas, staircases, lifts and service areas. In such a case, as much as 15 per cent of the quoted area may be made up of common space, with the net lettable area that much less. Other member states traditionally measure the gross internal space but exclude the staircases. Yet others, and this includes the UK, measure just the net lettable area.

International methods of measurement

1. Net lettable area
(i.e. exclusive of common
areas, WCs, etc.)

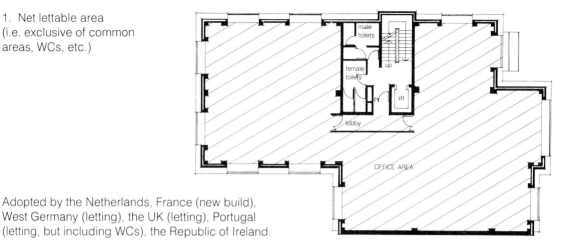

Adopted by the Netherlands, France (new build),
West Germany (letting), the UK (letting), Portugal
(letting, but including WCs), the Republic of Ireland.

2. Gross external area
(i.e. external face of wall by
external face of wall,
including all common areas)

Adopted by Portugal (selling), Belgium, Italy,
Luxembourg, the UK (new build), Denmark (new build).

3. Gross internal area
(i.e. internal face of wall by
internal face of wall, including
all common areas)

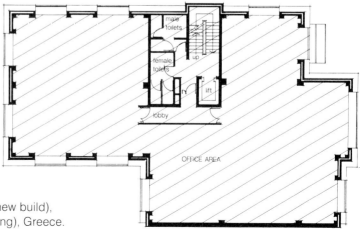

Adopted by Spain, West Germany (new build),
the Netherlands, Italy, Denmark (letting), Greece.

Custom and practice

Property values

We have already referred to the traditional preference throughout the rest of Europe for ownership rather than renting. To some extent, of course, the preponderance of ownership is a function of the relatively low value of property in other member states. Where real estate prices are high, it is not usually practical for companies to remain as owner-occupiers. It can, therefore, be assumed that, as the market in the EC develops and as property values increase, the traditional preference for ownership will gradually be replaced by a more mixed market before eventually, perhaps, following the UK example.

Condominium

However, in discussing the tradition of ownership, it is important to appreciate that this is not necessarily limited to sole ownership. There is a sophisticated use of co-ownership or condominium ownership, with quite complex arrangements to cover the common areas shared by the owners of individual floors or parts of a building. Because there is no history of the *co-propriété* or condominium-style ownership of commercial property in the UK, it is important for UK companies or investors looking across the Channel at a new market to take into account the strong history of such forms of ownership in the rest of the EC. In particular, much of Europe's office property is sold in units, often floor by floor.

Brokerage systems

With few exceptions, Europe has traditionally placed little value on property and property management. Consequently, there has often been no perceived need for a specialist professional property service and, with very few exceptions, there are no non-UK general purpose surveyors practising in Europe. Nor is there (except in the Netherlands and the Republic of Ireland) any organisation comparable to the Royal Institution of Chartered Surveyors (RICS) with a responsibility for establishing and monitoring standards.

Most people dealing with property in Europe – if they have any qualifications at all – tend to be qualified in law, accountancy or business studies of some sort. Their property training is gained largely through working alongside those who share a similar background but have had longer experience. With more opportunities for appropriate study, the situation is beginning to change. Even so, the range and volume of such opportunities fall well short of the pattern long established in the UK. The following two examples demonstrate a situation fairly typical throughout the Community (excluding the UK and the Republic of Ireland), although Italy, Greece, Portugal and Spain present a rather less sophisticated picture.

France

The surveying profession in France, although generally more sophisticated than in other member states, lacks structure and allows for the existence of many unprofessional intermediaries. Until quite recently, there was no formal training in property available; the small course now running covers subjects similar to those in the RICS examinations.

In the agency field, several large firms provide quite a comprehensive service; industrial and office agency is well established, but the retail side suffers from the attitude of the retailers who often see no use for an agent. The same is true in the residential sector, where services such as structural surveys are rarely required.

Investment services are provided by the larger firms, but not as comprehensively as in the UK. Private treaty predominates as a means of sale: auctions are usually restricted to special cases such as bankruptcy, and tenders generally used only for local authority sales. In the absence of any real structure or code applied to valuations, many commercial organisations will value their own property assets. In many areas, the need for valuation is not so great because of the tradition of indexing to fix rental levels.

Property management is covered quite comprehensively by French firms, although project management is more the responsibility of the architect and engineer. The larger firms also undertake development work, although many organisations prefer to use their own in-house teams because professional surveyors in France tend not to have a sufficiently wide overall knowledge.

West Germany

Despite its senior status within the Community, West Germany has not tended to show a great awareness of the value of its property assets. With no organisation akin to the RICS, little formal training and no real property profession as such, large West German companies have formed their own in-house teams to cover everything from investment decisions to management. The absence of property training limits the methods by which these in-house teams can acquire knowledge of the property market. The use of in-house teams restricts the availability of agency services: only a few firms offer investment services, and sales tend to be by private treaty, with very little use of auctions or tender.

Most valuations are undertaken by architects or engineers appointed by a court and tend to be mostly relevant to depreciated replacement cost. Rents, too, tend to be linked to indices, thereby obviating the need for an independent valuation.

The need for management services is recognised but still tends to be fulfilled either by a company's in-house team or, in multi-tenanted property, by one of the occupiers. Project management tends to be handled by the architect, although the involvement of surveyors is increasing. So too is their involvement in the area of development.

Surveyors
The surveying professions in Belgium and particularly in the Netherlands are, however, far closer to those that exist in the UK and the Republic of Ireland. The Netherlands has its national equivalent

of the RICS (the Nederlandse Vereniging van Makelaars) which lays down standards and sets professional examinations. As in the UK, entry to the profession is by way of a three- or four-year degree course, and the market is dominated by ten or so companies offering a full service with the remaining companies tending to specialise. In Belgium, members of the Union Belge des Géomètres-Experts are recognised professionals, qualified essentially as land agency surveyors, although many subsequently specialise. They carry out management tasks, act in an agent's capacity, produce schedules of dilapidations and may do some project management. None the less, there is still some scepticism within the market as to the need for these professional skills, and many businesses have their own in-house experts.

Brokerage fees

Brokerage fees throughout the Community tend to be substantially higher than in the UK.

Transaction costs for selling/freehold					
	Legal	Brokerage	Stamp or equivalent	Total	Other costs
Belgium	1%	3%	12.5%	16.5%	17% VAT on brokerage fees
Denmark	1%	1.6–3%	1.2%	14.6–16.6%	22% VAT on all fees
France	1%	5%	19%	25%	18.6% VAT on brokerage fees
Greece	1.25%	4%	12%	17.25%	6% VAT on all fees
Italy	0.5%	4%	10%	14.5%	19% VAT on all fees
Luxembourg	3%	3%	10%	16%	6% VAT on all fees
Netherlands	0.5%	2%	6%	8.5%	18.5% VAT on all fees
Portugal	1%	3.75%	0.5%	5.25%	8% VAT on all fees
Republic of Ireland	1% + IR£100	1.75%	1.6%	3.75–8.75% + IR£100	25% VAT on all fees
Spain	1%	5%	7%	13%	12% VAT on all fees
UK	0.5%	1.5%	1%	3%	15% VAT on all fees
West Germany	1.25%	3–5%	2%	6.25–8.25%	14% VAT on all fees

Transaction costs for letting					
	Legal	Brokerage	Stamp or equivalent	Total	Other costs
Belgium	0.5%	15% of first year's rent	12.5%	13% + 30% of first year's rent	17% VAT on brokerage
Denmark	1%	10–12%	1%	12–14%	22% VAT on all fees
France	1%	30% of first year's rent	16.6%	17.6% + 30% of first year's rent	2.5% marginal local tax; 18.1% VAT on all fees
Greece	1%	highly negotiable 3–4%	12%	(approximate) 16–17%	6% VAT on all fees
Italy	0.5%	one month's rent	10%	10.5% + one month's rent	6% VAT on all fees
Luxembourg	1–3%	one month's rent	10%	11–14% + one month's rent	6% VAT on all fees
Netherlands	1–11.5%	6% up to 3rd year; 1.5% up to 6th year; 1% up to 11th year	6%		18.5% VAT on all fees
Portugal	1% negotiable	one month's rent	0.5–10%	1.5–11.5% plus one month's rent	10–14% VAT on value of deed
Republic of Ireland	1–5%	10%	1–6%	12–21%	25% VAT on all fees
Spain	1%	10% of first year's rent	1–6%	2–7% + one month's rent	12% VAT on all fees
UK	0.5%	10%	1%	11.5%	15% VAT on all fees
West Germany	0.5%	16–24%	2%	18.5–26.5%	14% VAT on all fees

Rents and prices★

Not surprisingly, the cost of renting and of buying property varies considerably across the EC, as it does within the UK. More surprising – and sometimes frustrating – is the difficulty of establishing some logic or rule of thumb across the Community.

Taxation

Taxation, both direct and indirect, differs widely throughout the Community and has a considerable impact on property values. Not only is there a considerable range of VAT rates (from 1.6 per cent to 38 per cent), but the treatment of VAT in relation to property also varies. Stamp duty, another form of indirect taxation, ranges from a low of 1 per cent in the UK to a high of 18 per cent in France. This tax affects not only property values but also the liquidity of the market. The treatment of capital gains on property varies widely; some member states – including France – have wealth taxes on individuals which encompass property.

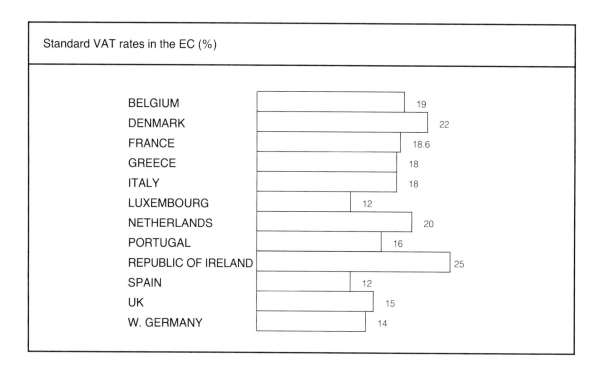

Standard VAT rates in the EC (%)

BELGIUM	19
DENMARK	22
FRANCE	18.6
GREECE	18
ITALY	18
LUXEMBOURG	12
NETHERLANDS	20
PORTUGAL	16
REPUBLIC OF IRELAND	25
SPAIN	12
UK	15
W. GERMANY	14

★ All rents given in this book are expressed as a sum per annum, unless otherwise stated.

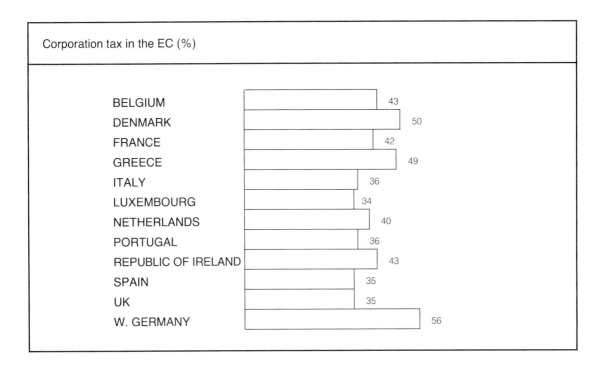

Corporation tax in the EC (%)

BELGIUM	43
DENMARK	50
FRANCE	42
GREECE	49
ITALY	36
LUXEMBOURG	34
NETHERLANDS	40
PORTUGAL	36
REPUBLIC OF IRELAND	43
SPAIN	35
UK	35
W. GERMANY	56

VAT rates in each member state can be found in Part II in the sections on the retail market. Also in each section is a brief outline of corporate income tax, VAT on property, transfer tax and other national, federal and local taxes. These tax details have been provided by Price Waterhouse, whose own publication in the CBI Initiative 1992 series – *Tax: Strategic Corporate Tax Planning* – deals with these issues in considerable detail. The various tax rates are unlikely to remain unchanged and they should be confirmed prior to any negotiations.

The result of such a great variety in rates and levels of taxation is, of course, that it becomes very difficult to make direct and straight-forward comparisons between property values in the different member states.

Planning

Planning regulations within the Community range between being *laissez-faire* and draconian with, somewhere in between, the French *redevance* tax, a fiscal measure designed to discourage inappropriate development by putting a considerable charge on office and industrial space in over-subscribed areas.

A number of member states operate systems in which some or most of the elements can be understood easily by those accustomed to the UK pattern. Apart from the Republic of Ireland, the system in Portugal is, perhaps, the most like that in the UK, except that it is extremely slow. In France the planning system is extremely complex, although many elements of it are quite similar to UK practice.

In Spain, Madrid is bound by absolutely inflexible regulations based on a master plan which divides the land into pre-determined uses, while outside the capital the regulations are far less restrictive. The Netherlands has a three-tier system in which the applicant may, if turned down by the local authority, appeal to the province and subsequently to central government. In Belgium, the route is from the local authority to the province and thence to the Minister of the Region. The Italian procedure is both multi-tiered and heavily bureaucratic – the planning laws of the regional governments must fit with the fundamental principles laid down by central government.

The West German regulations are detailed, but logical and coherent, while, in Greece, there is really no coherent legislation. The only restrictions are those built into the plot ratio (the area on which construction can take place, *pro rata* to the area of the site) and the obligation to protect and preserve any archaeological finds upon pain of severe penalties.

As with many other aspects of the property market, the potential investor, developer or purchaser could only benefit from greater harmonisation. It is unlikely, unfortunately, that any real unity of approach – beyond a certain basic understanding – will be in place for the foreseeable future.

Infrastructure projects

The suitability of a particular location for a specific use will be affected by a variety of factors ranging from price and quality through to labour costs and financial incentives. Obviously, access and services are fundamental and, undoubtedly, some of the major infrastructure projects now under way or at the planning stage will have an impact on the suitability or desirability of the areas which they serve.

The Channel Tunnel

From the UK standpoint, the construction of the Channel Tunnel is a development of major significance. While the politicians may have their own perspective, those concerned with the suitability of particular locations for the survival or expansion of their business will want to tap the benefits of the Channel Tunnel and avoid its disadvantages.

Of the two regions which will be instantly linked by the Tunnel, the Nord-Pas de Calais seems, on the face of it, to have gained an advantage over the south-east of England. With lower rental levels for both office and industrial uses, cheaper energy costs, an abundant supply of land and sites, more generous financial assistance programmes and fewer problems with labour shortages, the French side of the Tunnel has the definite edge. With a strong recovery under way in the region and with business conditions likely to be more stable in France than in the UK, the Nord-Pas de Calais seems to be offering a more attractive environment for inward investment.

However, whether these benefits outweigh the principal negative – that various on-costs, such as national insurance contributions, make average labour costs higher on the French side than on the UK – will depend upon the significance of labour costs to a particular company. Total labour costs are, on average, 40 per cent higher in France than in the UK and this may tip the scales in Kent's favour notwithstanding the other elements. Even so, situated at the strategic crossroads of a major European transport network, the north-east of France has already seen in the past ten years one in four of its newly locating companies coming from the UK.

In general terms, of course, the Tunnel provides an example of the way in which a unified market will encourage investment in more efficient communications. This, in turn, can only have a positive effect on the property market, by attracting new industrial and service investment and by encouraging development.

Other infrastructure developments

The bridge now being built in Denmark, between Zealand and the Continent, will significantly reduce travelling time between the capital, Copenhagen, and the rest of Europe.

There is also a proposal to build a bridge from Denmark to Malmö in Sweden and thereby to forge a direct link between the Community and the whole of Scandinavia. If the bridge is built, Denmark will cease to be on the far northern edge of the Community and will become instead a potential through-route for investment, goods and services.

At the south-eastern edge of the Community, a further bridge is planned, this time to the north of Patras in Greece. Though likely to be of major benefit to the rapid movement of freight between the ports and the mainland, the date of construction is uncertain.

The investment market

Liquidity

Property is an illiquid asset, although the degree of liquidity differs greatly from country to country. At one end of the spectrum, the UK – with its low transaction costs, high level of institutional investment, relatively large stock of high quality property and large number of participants in the market – enjoys substantial liquidity.

Elsewhere in the Community, particularly in the smaller member states, high transaction charges and a low level of institutional involvement can lead to a severe lack of liquidity, particularly for the larger lot sizes. Transfer costs affect liquidity because high costs erode a potential dealer's profit on 'a turn' (a rapid re-sale). As a result, the small dealing and trading companies, which in the UK effectively act as market makers by taking a short-term position, are themselves taken out of the market. Their absence removes liquidity and depresses the market.

Data

Another major factor which contributes to the lack of liquidity in many of the Community's property markets is the absence in other member states of good market information. The UK has become accustomed to a freely available supply of good quality market information and published research: elsewhere it is very limited.

This is not to say, of course, that UK investors have ignored the European market or that they will ignore it in the future. Their involvement can be traced back to the late 1960s and early 1970s, when investments were made in the Netherlands, France, West Germany and, in particular, in Belgium, where the UK's accession to the Community in 1973 exerted a strong influence on investment in Brussels. The aftermath of the oil crisis and, more specifically, falling prices and differential rates of inflation in the mid-1970s, however, resulted in almost no investment deals being concluded during the second half of the 1970s. The increase in activity in the early 1980s was a result not only of the lifting of the exchange controls imposed in the 1970s but also of a greater feeling of confidence among investors together with their identification of new opportunities.

Since 1982, the main influence on the market has been the internationalisation of debt, while deregulation, technological advance and the 1987 Stock Exchange crash have also played their part in encouraging investment in property in Europe. The increasing accessibility of all markets in Europe, including the property investment market, and the increasing importance of a higher number of individual cities in the Community should further stimulate the interest of investors.

3. The impact of 1992

The advent of the single market is providing a catalyst for change in the business environment. Corporate activity is on the increase, resulting in a growing number of cross-border mergers and acquisitions as well as other types of corporate alliance. Indeed, between 1984 and 1987, the number of cross-border acquisitions within the Community more than doubled, increasing by about 100 a year, from 209 in 1984 to 495 in 1987. Throughout this period, the business community of some member states – notably the UK's – has been consistently more active as a buyer; more recently others, including France and Italy, have increased their acquisition activity. As a result, individual companies in various member states have acquired a portfolio of property.

Past experience would suggest that, in many cases, these companies may be sadly ill-informed about the extent, content and value of such assets. However, the presence in the Community of this new body of owners will generate a demand for advice. Such advice will be provided in the main by a new generation of surveyors who have an international capability, including the ability to take a view over the European market as a whole. This body of internationally led professional firms will make strategic recommendations about acquisition or disposal on the basis of pan-European comparisons.

The result of all this activity should be – to put it simplistically – that a level will be found. However, taking into account all the structural differences which exist, the question must be asked: to what extent will there be any real harmonisation in matters affecting the property market?

Taxation

The way in which a cross-border investment is structured can significantly affect its post-tax return and any UK company undertaking a property transaction within the Community should consider a number of issues. A decision on whether to finance the venture with

UK or overseas borrowing, for instance, will be affected by local commercial taxes or exchange control constraints on the debt/equity ratio. In any event, it is important to optimise relief for interest costs, and this will depend on the source of the original loan.

A company will also need to know if it must obtain UK Treasury consents or local licences or consents, and it will also have to decide whether the investment should be made by a UK company, by a company resident in the member state concerned or by a company resident in a third country. This decision may well determine whether tax on the disposal of the property, or on the company owning it, is paid in the UK as well as in the country in which the property is located. Or, indeed, whether it is paid at all. It may, for example, be tax advantageous for a UK company to form a non-UK-resident holding company in a territory which has a tax regime favourable to overseas holding companies. Currently, the Netherlands and Luxembourg tend to be favoured locations for property holding companies, and they will probably resist harmonisation, which would dilute their advantages.

It may well be that, in the course of time, the disparity in the rates of taxes levied in the member states will decrease, perhaps under the influence of general economic forces. In the case of direct taxes, however, such a prospect is probably some way off.

Conveyancing and brokerage

In looking at brokerage as a profession in the Community, we commented on the disparities in terms of performance and status. There has, however, been a general trend in several areas towards merger and acquisition – a trend which has been driven largely by the increasing demands of the client and by fierce competition in the market place.

This combination of demand and competition is sufficient to squeeze profit margins at a time when costs are being driven upwards by the depth and breadth of service which the market now demands and expects. Today's client assumes that its professional advisers will provide detailed market research, marketing skills, financial services expertise and much more besides. It is this sort of expectation which has led, in the accountancy profession, to the emergence of a small number of very large firms.

A similar process is under way in the legal and surveying sectors, as firms position themselves for the impact of a larger single market. In view of the lead which the UK surveying profession is generally accepted as having over most of its European rivals, the opportunity for UK surveyors is clear.

Whether a firm chooses to develop in the EC by way of organic expansion, acquisition or association, one inevitable consequence of having international practices serving international clients is that **Fees** there will be some harmonisation of fees. Local professional bodies which have tended to act as a price-fixing cartel will no longer be able to regulate the scale of fees in the face of major pan-European groupings. This more competitive environment will drive the level of fees across the Community down, in much the same way that fees in the UK have been driven down over the past twenty years.

One outcome of increased competition which is more difficult to predict with such confidence is what role lawyers will play in the Community on matters of property. As will be shown in Part II, the line between the lawyer and the real estate broker is, in many parts of the EC, an extremely fine one. In some member states, notably Portugal, lawyers are the largest and most successful real estate brokers in the market. Quite how far this duality of function will decline in the face of pan-European competition and the presence of major international surveying firms is still a matter for speculation.

Lease structures

In this general overview of the current property market, the pattern of lease structures has been shown to be largely unsuitable and unacceptable to the institutional investor. This will become more evident in the chapters following.

One direct consequence of the Single European Act is the increas-**Investment patterns** ingly international view being taken by pension funds and insurance companies. Member states are progressively removing restrictions on their domestic funds to enable freedom of investment within the Community. Pension funds and insurance companies are taking full advantage of the opportunity.

Although in 1989 the top twenty UK property companies (in terms of market capitalisation) had only around 3 per cent of their total holdings in Europe (a ratio which is almost identical to the 1987 ratio), a number of major companies have announced their intention of increasing their level of European investment as part of their development programme. It should also be noted that institutions from outside the Community are investing heavily inside. This is especially true of Swedish institutions, following the removal of their own domestic regulations, and of the Japanese who, having grown accustomed to the UK market, are now turning their attention to other parts of the Community.

The effect of so much cross-border or international investment is to focus the minds of local developers upon the requirements of these institutions. As a result, there have been, within the legal confines of each member state's own system, indications of some early movement towards a more institutionally acceptable form of lease. While this does not even approach the twenty-five-year lease with five-yearly rent reviews which the funds have insisted on in the UK, the institutional investors in the EC do seem more prepared than formerly to accept a degree of management and a shorter lease, provided there is some mechanism for a review of the rent to an open market level at intervals no longer than five-yearly.

Even so, however helpful this degree of harmonisation proves to be, there remain significant differences which will not be removed without major constitutional changes.

The office market

London

London is an increasingly popular location for overseas companies. These companies, however, have acutely conservative attitudes: they tend to choose almost exclusively the traditional areas of London and to cluster together closely. Nor are they noticeably interested in areas of the UK outside London and the South East. Of the top 1,000 overseas-owned companies in the UK, no less than 739 are located in London or the South East, and 44 per cent are located in the capital itself. London's role as Europe's most important 24-hour financial

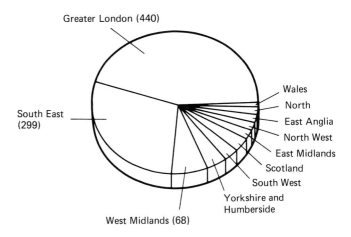

centre is a combination of long tradition and the effects of deregulation, and its supremacy is supported by the presence of over 500 foreign banks. There is likely to be continuing demand from the Far East, Australia and North America as such organisations seek to expand their presence as a platform for further activity in the Community at large.

There are, however, two conditions which are likely to influence future patterns: on the one hand, serious doubts have been raised about London's ability to continue to respond to the demand for office space, and on the other hand there is a determined effort by other cities in the Community to raise their own profile in the office sector.

Paris

France is, of course, committed to the single market concept and is, geographically, ideally located to obtain maximum benefit from its creation. Paris, in particular, is likely to become a major office centre, benefiting from stronger tenant demand, which in turn is likely to lead to an increased rate of growth in office rental levels. The current high rate of tax on the sale of buildings will, however, act as a disincentive to investors wishing to sell properties and rationalise their portfolios.

The West German office market is characterised by imbalances between supply and demand, resulting in major shortages of space limiting investment opportunities. Research by the Office Network indicates that office vacancy rates in the five largest West German cities were below 4 per cent in mid-1988, and that Stuttgart, with a vacancy rate of 1.1 per cent, had the least office space available in any of the forty-one cities monitored worldwide.

Frankfurt

The high – and still rising – rental levels in Frankfurt are mainly the result of demand by international companies attracted by the world's fourth most important financial centre. Although rental levels are high by comparison with other West German cities, they are still – by international standards – relatively low. Currently, 185,000 square metres of new space is under construction and is expected to be pre-let before completion.

Dublin

In Dublin, a major development on the banks of the River Liffey will provide 69,000 square metres of offices targeted specifically at the financial community. This single scheme will provide two-and-a-half times the total annual absorption of office space in the city.

Brussels

The office market in Brussels, where top office rents are now lower than those in most other European capitals, is expected to perform well in coming years. 1992 is likely to affect the demand for office space in Brussels significantly, and official estimates put the total number of additional jobs which will be created by Brussels' increasing importance as the administrative capital of the EC at between 15,000 and 60,000.

The supply of office space in the Netherlands has increased

significantly: nevertheless, a rental record was reached towards the end of 1988 for the fifth consecutive year. A whole new business district has been created over the past five years in the south-east of Amsterdam, largely as a consequence of the development constraints in the central area of the capital.

Despite, then, the very strong position which London still holds in the office sector, it will find itself under increasing pressure from rival cities. Most noticeable will be the tendency for Frankfurt, Paris and even Madrid to look increasingly attractive to corporate occupiers.

The retail market

Individual retailing industries have developed largely in response to local, regional and national requirements and, of all the property sectors, the retail property market will be the least directly affected by the advent of a single market. None the less, as will be seen in Part II, the retail sector is due for change and provides a number of threats to and opportunities for the various traditions. There are several lessons to be drawn for UK-based retailing organisations, not least that the UK industry's strength in the multiple chain sector gives it a degree of expertise which outweighs the apparent advantage of size that some of the larger French and West German retailers might claim.

The UK retailing industry leads the Community in its innovation both of forms of retailing and of variety of product. With much of the EC close to saturation in terms of mainstream retailing, the niche marketing successes of UK operators are ideally suited to the new market. Indeed, retailers such as the Body Shop have already moved into several of the major European cities. As well as its capacity to innovate, the inherent energy and drive within the UK retailing industry are characteristics which suggest that the single market will offer a major opportunity to UK retailers who can tailor their natural talents to the particular restrictions of the individual retail centres.

In its recent report 'Retailing and 1992 – the impact and the opportunities', the Corporate Intelligence Group listed a number of key lessons, including the fact that the single market will 'fundamentally change the environment' in which UK retailers will operate. It also encouraged UK retailers to see the EC as 'the equal of the United States in terms of potential for acquisitions, mergers and, especially, joint ventures'. While drawing attention to the north-west of the Community as a major 'growth consumer market for UK retailers', it emphasised the fact borne out in Part II that Spain and Italy are under-developed retail markets with strong potential. Warning that some

European operations are 'potentially dangerous predators', it urged UK retailers to take advantage of 'their high quality advertising and publicity' and not to restrict their interest to the existing member states, but to anticipate the addition of Austria, Norway and, perhaps, Sweden within five years.

In the retail sector, of course there has long been an international flavour to European high streets. Even so, in recent years the volume of two-way traffic has increased, with outlets such as Benetton, Stefanel, Louis Vuitton and Yves Saint Laurent well established in the UK, and other outlets, including Mulberry, Laura Ashley and Body Shop, equally visible in Continental cities. Unfortunately, restrictive legislation and security of tenure provisions, in addition to the hostility of planning authorities (influenced in some places by powerful lobbies of small shopkeepers), continue to limit retail investment opportunities.

The industrial market

Of the three markets, the industrial sector is the most difficult to assess as a whole, given the range and variation of activity it contains. What is clear, though, is that the single market – and, in particular, some of the major infrastructure initiatives – will have an impact on the way in which the industrial companies perform. The increasingly universal product line will lead to the removal of duplication and the greater standardisation of units. Factors such as accessibility, labour and raw materials in the Community will grow in importance, while access to the increasingly sophisticated network of road and rail systems and to seaports and airports will remain a key element.

Rationalisation

The size of the market encourages economies of scale and may result in production being concentrated on a regional basis. At the same time, there is a demographic shift apparent throughout the EC, in which workers are no longer dependent on traditional industries fixed by the location of raw materials or their ports of access. The tendency to produce more expensive 'sunrise' products, as well as services which, by their nature, can originate almost anywhere, may also be accelerated by industry increasingly withdrawing from corporate employment and providing a sub-contractor rather than employee service.

One specific danger facing the UK – and, therefore, potentially influencing UK operations and investors in their view of the future European market – is that the demand from the expanding market will lead to the increasing use of warehousing facilities wherever the

Science parks

transport network offers the best access to the greatest number. The danger for all member states on the geographical periphery of the single market is that an increasing number of organisations in the manufacturing and distribution industries will locate their major facilities in the heart of the Community, with only localised servicing and storage in places such as the UK. Certainly, there has been major and rapid growth across the Continent in the science park sector. (A science park is a group of usually modern industrial units arranged and located to form an attractively laid out campus, often near a university or similar educational institution.) With eighteen science parks already operating, fourteen more under construction and a further twelve at the planning stage, France has set its sights highest among the member states.

But it is not only in terms of numbers that France is the most energetic advocate of this comparatively new form of development. The eighteen parks already active in France contain a total of 1.87 million square metres of space; the UK's thirty-eight such parks offer a mere 300,000 square metres by comparison. The West German parks are closest in style to the UK model and sixty-eight 'innovation centres' have appeared during the 1980s. The movement has also begun to spread to Austria and Switzerland. Belgium and the Netherlands too now have their first few such centres, although in Belgium the aim, as in France, is to attract established research-based corporations. Italy, with only limited development so far, has plans, none the less, for considerable expansion over the next few years, while in Spain six of the seventeen regions now have parks along the French lines.

A number of those attempting to gaze into their crystal ball have predicted a gradual move away from the northern part of Europe towards the sun and the South. The suggestion is that, as communications and information technology make Europe even smaller than it is already, those involved in the leading edge industries will be able to move into 'centres of excellence' wherever it is most pleasant to reside. Many people would, doubtless, exchange the dull grey skies of northern Europe for the blue skies of the South, especially if the current skills shortage puts a premium on those talents most in demand. We are still some way from knowing what the final picture will be, and major centres such as London, Paris, Brussels and the cities of West Germany are continuing to hold their own and to attract an increasing proportion of the investment market.

4.   Developing a property strategy

To paraphrase the old adage: 'Some companies are born with property, some acquire property, and some have property thrust upon them.' In every case, there has long been a tendency to treat real estate, however obtained, either as just a factor of production or as an inevitable by-product of the principal manufacturing or trading activity. In fact, as has been said already, the impact of real estate upon the company's balance sheet is such that, in whatever field it operates, a company must have a clearly defined policy in respect of its property assets. The company's property needs, moreover, should form part of the corporate plan.

The impact of the single market for many companies, with its proliferation of mergers, acquisitions and joint ventures, means that an increasing number of organisations now need to take full cognisance of their property portfolio. At the same time, though, many of the individual components of these portfolios are managed by people with a limited property expertise. It is important, therefore, for any company or group – whether it already has a European property portfolio or is simply anticipating one – to begin by looking carefully at its attitude to property. Does it, for instance, believe that it owns property solely to use it or does it also own it for profit? Is property seen by the company as a cost or as an asset?

In earlier chapters, it has been suggested that the UK property market is significantly more sophisticated than the market elsewhere in the Community; many – if not most – UK companies now accept that every major business decision has a property connotation and this presupposes a recognition of the profit aspect – and a view of property holdings as more than dead money on the balance sheet. One effect of the general process of harmonisation before and after 1992 will undoubtedly be the gradual raising of the standard of the European property market. This will go beyond the harmonisation of practice to include a greater awareness of the true or potential value of the property portfolio.

Property as part of the strategy

It has already been suggested that property planning needs to be undertaken at the same level as the overall strategic planning of a business. It follows, therefore, that a company needs property expertise either at main board level or at a level which feeds directly into the main board.

Far too many companies (including some of the largest and most successful) still take the view that property and premises are just a local issue which should be dealt with by the local board of directors or by a management committee. In terms of day-to-day repair and maintenance, this is perfectly sensible. What matters is that a view is taken of the entire portfolio of property held by the company and that it is periodically reviewed at the highest level by someone with the necessary expertise. Many of the decisions which the company can take with regard to each element of the portfolio require a certain distance from the premises (even from the country in which they are located) to permit a measure of objectivity. Decisions on where to locate and on whether to relocate will depend on both local and corporate positions. So, too, will any decision about changing the existing use of specific premises.

Those with responsibility for the portfolio must also be prepared to ask questions about the possible restructuring of the existing holding. If a particular property is a freehold asset, there are various options to be considered, including disposal, sale-and-lease-back, mortgage, sub-letting all or part, developing the site for letting or for selling, and letting short term in anticipation of future need. Any one of these options could well maximise or make better use of the property assets.

The same considerations will influence decisions when the property is leased. Should you buy the freehold? Re-gear? Assign the lease or sell it? Or perhaps sub-let? Whatever the choice, you must also, of course, take into account the potential tax advantages of each option.

Valuation

But before any such decisions can be taken, those with responsibility for property need to be able to assess the true value of such property to the company. The valuation will include the utility value – is it in the best and most suitable location? is it able to function in the most efficient way? and (though this is more complex), does it provide the most acceptable environment for its purpose? The answers to questions about the physical qualities of the premises can then be set against cost factors, so that the company can seek to minimise the negatives and maximise the positives. In assessing the true value of the property in question, there is always an underlying balance to be made: the balance between the cost of the property as it now is and the cost of *not* developing the site. Exploring this balance is one of the ways in which a company can take a dynamic view of its property portfolio.

Equally dynamic must be the viewpoint underlying any decision on whether to buy, rent, or build new premises. The decision to buy must involve an evaluation of the tax implications and of the exchange risk, as well as of the potential growth in value of the property as an asset. This can then be compared with an analysis of the benefits and drawbacks of leasing. A decision to rent must include a careful analysis of the length of lease, the landlord and tenant legislation in the market in question, the custom and practice on the indexation of rents, the level of premiums or 'key money' likely to be demanded (and perhaps later received) and the frequency of rent reviews.

The impact of a more general harmonisation of practice, however rapidly or slowly, will eventually lead to a reduction in some of the most blatant anomalies, including such problems as landlord and tenant legislation, historic rents and rent reviews.

An accurate valuation

In any company with a property portfolio, head office must be provided with accurate valuations of the real estate on a regular basis. Only in this way will it be able to make a true assessment of the profitability of a trading operation in relation to the capital employed. Such a valuation is essential for balance sheet purposes and in order to assess the 'opportunity cost' of occupying the site. While the balance sheet takes account of the property in terms of its existing use, the opportunity cost reflects the redevelopment value. As we have seen, it is important for a company to look at the possibility of relocating an existing business, both in order to maximise the efficiency and productivity of the operation and to release inefficiently used assets *pro rata* to their value.

Of course, all this applies just as much to a UK portfolio as it does to a European one. But when the range of opportunity extends over twelve member states with as many different tax regimes, grant aid and financial incentives, accounting procedures and methods of treating property for balance sheet purposes, a dynamic rather than *laissez faire* approach is demanded.

The case for expansion

A decision to expand in Europe by way of direct acquisition must begin with ascertaining the business need which is to be satisfied. The expansion may be aggressive or defensive, but it will usually be the business need which will dictate both the location and the available budget. In short, the macro location decision will not normally be property driven, but as part of the macro decision-making process, companies should properly evaluate the alternative property options. To do this effectively, the examination of cost must include an assessment of both the buying and leasing options, and of the exchange-rate risk.

Recent figures show that between 1968 and 1988, prime office rents in various key centres increased at substantially different rates:

Centre	% increase (1968–88)
London (City)	680
London (West End)	480
Paris	390
Brussels	312
Frankfurt	252
Amsterdam	210

Source: Martin Myers, Imry Merchant Developers, *Estates Gazette*, 1989

If one considers, however, the gross value in pounds sterling of a prime office building located in each of these centres adjusted for currency fluctuations, the variation in the level of appreciation of investment values provides a different sequence:

Centre	% appreciation
Frankfurt	1,070
Paris	1,020
Brussels	1,020
Amsterdam	780
London (City)	750
London (West End)	530

Source: Martin Myers, Imry Merchant Developers, *Estates Gazette*, 1989

For the high street retailer, of course, the parameters affecting their choice of location are far simpler. An experienced retailer or retail agent can identify by simple observation the best location in a principal shopping street or shopping centre. The depth of the retailer's pocket will then dictate how close to or far from this point to choose the site. As is indicated in Part II, the retailer's difficulties tend to be the lack of suitable units in suitable locations, together with (and often caused by) archaic landlord and tenant legislation in some European countries, leading to low rents and outrageously high premiums.

Although they have greater flexibility, office users are driven primarily by employment issues such as the availability of skilled labour, and labour costs. These, in turn, will be influenced by communications, the quality of the environment, tax regimes and so on.

The industrial and distribution sectors enjoy, perhaps, the greatest flexibility of all the sectors. Access and communications are of great importance, as is the availability of a skilled, semi-skilled or unskilled workforce. But with increasing mechanisation reducing the labour force requirement, and the speed and ease of distribution allowing more flexibility in terms of location, financial issues including tax relief and grant aid are becoming an ever more critical factor.

This has clearly been recognised by all members of the Community who, without exception, have set up a range of tax reliefs and financial incentives designed to attract foreign companies. Indeed, any manufacturing company looking for a base in the EC – as Toyota and others have found quite recently – will not be short of suitors.

Taking all the factors into account

Any decision on expansion in Europe will, then, need to take account of a wide range of important variables so that an accurate assessment of each possible location can be made. These factors include: the projected growth in rental value, including any legislation which inhibits that growth or any changes in legislation which may affect it; the current capital values and their projected growth; inflation rates; the exchange rate risk; taxation; liquidity; and transaction costs.

But there are also less quantifiable factors which may affect the decision: image, fashion, language barriers, religion and business culture. Although, for the most part, not directly related to property *per se*, they can have an impact on the investment value. It should not be forgotten, for instance, that it is only some thirteen years since the Portuguese Revolution, during which the authorities seized all foreign property without compensation. Spain is currently proposing the expropriation of some foreign and residential property on the coast where the necessary permissions were not obtained. At the same time, the increasing prominence of Green politics in Europe may lead to some fairly significant shifts of local or national policy in relation to land use and planning.

By being aware of the variety of factors that need to be taken into account, and by setting them out in a coherent order of importance, the company will be able to assess the business priorities which should dictate its property needs. From this it should be able to draw up a 'model' portfolio: one in which the spread of properties will be capable of fulfilling both the property investment and the corporate business requirements, and will, as a result, enhance corporate profit levels. Against this model portfolio the existing property holdings of any organisation can be tested and decisions made on such matters as expansion in certain holdings, redevelopment in others, reduction or selling off of unwanted elements of those holdings, complete disposal of some holdings and, of course, the purchase of new assets, not only to replace space lost from the disposal of inadequate facilities, but also to accommodate the challenges which the single market will present for increasing production. The model portfolio should be used as a template against which an existing portfolio can be measured and from which a brief can be written for the future.

II
The member states

Belgium

Geography

Land area	30,514 sq. km.
Population	9,900,000
Density	323 per sq. km.
Main towns	Population
Brussels	980,000
Antwerp	976,000
Liège	591,000
Gent	484,691

A small country with its two most remote points no more than 330 kilometres apart, Belgium is centrally located in Europe, sharing borders with four of its trading partners: the Netherlands to the north, West Germany to the east, and Luxembourg and France to the south.

The north and west of the country are flat; the land scarcely rises above sea-level and there are a great number of navigable rivers and canals. To the south stand the forest and wooded hills of the Ardennes.

Of the three linguistic communities, the Flemish-speaking Flanders region in the north contains the towns of Antwerp (one of the world's largest seaports) and the province of Limburg, as well as around 60 per cent of the country's total population. To the east, including the towns of Eupen, Malmédy and Sankt-Vith, the principal language is German. French is spoken in the provinces of Hainaut, Namur, Liège and southern Brabant. Though the capital, Brussels, is officially bilingual (French and Flemish), 80 per cent of its inhabitants speak French.

Transport and communications

Communications within Belgium and with its neighbours are excellent, and include 1,500 kilometres of illuminated motorways and

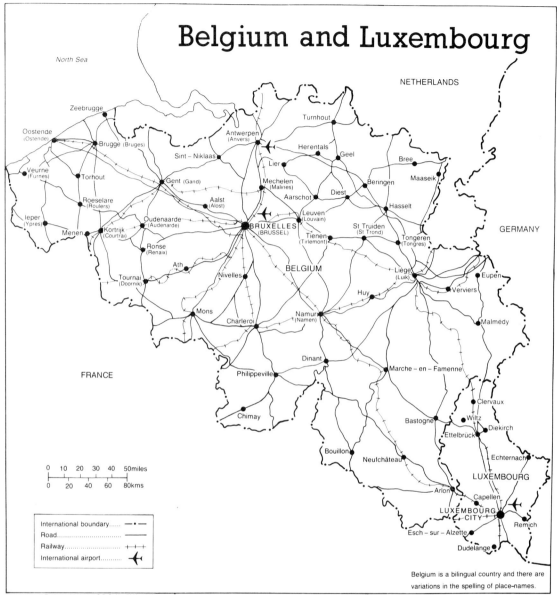

Belgium and Luxembourg

North Sea

NETHERLANDS

GERMANY

FRANCE

BELGIUM

LUXEMBOURG

Zeebrugge
Oostende (Ostende)
Brugge (Bruges)
Turnhout
Antwerpen (Anvers)
Herentals
Geel
Bree
Maaseik
Veurne (Furnes)
Torhout
Sint – Niklaas
Lier
Mechelen (Malines)
Beringen
Gent (Gand)
Aalst (Alost)
Aarschot
Diest
Hasselt
Roeselare (Roulers)
Ieper (Ypres)
Oudenaarde (Audenarde)
Leuven (Louvain)
St Truiden (St Trond)
Tongeren (Tongres)
Menen
Kortrijk (Courtrai)
Bruxelles (Brussel)
Tienen (Tirlemont)
Ronse (Renaix)
Ath
Nivelles
Liège (Luik)
Eupen
Tournai (Doornik)
Huy
Verviers
Mons
Charleroi
Namur (Namen)
Malmédy
Dinant
Philippeville
Marche – en – Famenne
Chimay
Clervaux
Bastogne
Wiltz
Diekirch
Ettelbrück
Bouillon
Echternach
Neufchâteau
LUXEMBOURG
Arlon
Capellen
LUXEMBOURG CITY
Remich
Esch – sur – Alzette
Dudelange

0 10 20 30 40 50miles
0 20 40 60 80kms

International boundary......	— · —
Road...........................	———
Railway........................	+++
International airport...........	✈

Belgium is a bilingual country and there are variations in the spelling of place-names.

Department of Trade and Industry C.D.O. No. 7352, 1988

3,750 kilometres of rail network. Belgium's principal airport and the operating centre of the state-owned airline, Sabena, is at Zaventem, on the north-eastern outskirts of Brussels.

General economic

A mature industrial economy heavily dependent upon international trade, Belgium imports almost all of its raw materials, and its exports account for nearly 60 per cent of its gross national product (GNP). Like most European countries, the economy has experienced difficulties since the mid-1970s, with unemployment reaching a peak of approximately 13 per cent of the working population. Since the early 1980s, government policy has been directed towards curbing the public sector deficit and improving the balance of payments. Suspending the indexation of wage increases for part of the 1980s has reduced wages in real terms and improved industrial competitiveness.

Industry

The declining importance of Belgium's traditional coal and metal industries (established in the south of the country in the 19th century) means that the old style heavy industry now accounts for less than 20 per cent of total manufacturing output.

At the same time, new industries, including chemicals, food, drink and light engineering, have been attracted to the northern Flemish region, where the traditional textile activities continue to flourish.

Forms of tenure

Of the two principal types of lease defined by statute and relating to commercial property, one (commercial lease) applies to any commercial premises with free access to the public for the purpose of entering into commercial transaction. This is intended to include all forms of retailing. The other (civil lease) covers all forms of commercial and residential property, including offices and industrial premises. The significant difference between them is that a commercial lease confers substantial security upon the tenant, whereas a civil lease confers none.

Commercial lease

Any tenant of property subject to a commercial lease is entitled to three lease renewals, each for a period equal to the duration of the original lease. A nine-year lease, for example, will entitle the tenant to occupation for a maximum of thirty-six years. Although the landlord has no rights to recover possession during this period, the tenant may – at three-yearly intervals – give six months' notice to quit. Not surprisingly, this one-sided arrangement makes retail property unpopular with institutional investors in Belgium.

Civil lease

A civil lease granted for up to twenty-seven years is not regulated in any way other than by the terms of the lease itself. A lease granted for more than twenty-seven years is deemed to be a long lease and is subject to separate legislation (*au emphytéose*).

A civil lease is made by agreement between the parties. It can be struck on whatever terms the parties choose, although the majority tend to be 3/6/9 leases, where the tenant has the option to give six months' notice to quit at three-yearly intervals. There is also an opportunity for both parties to reconsider the level of rental at the same intervals, as well as annual indexation. Landlords' concern about the tenants' right to break the lease has led more recently to leases being granted for longer terms (nine and twelve years), but with the landlord relying on indexation alone with no option to review the level of rent. (Indexation is by reference to the cost-of-living index – l'Indice des Prix de Détail à la Consommation.) On expiry of a civil lease, the tenant has no automatic right of renewal.

The investment market

In the mid-1960s, the Belgian property market, previously dominated by local investors and by domestic funds and insurance companies, was entered in force by UK investors and developers, then by Dutch and later Arab and Japanese companies. What had been a very strong investment and development market from 1968 onwards was seriously affected by the oil crisis and subsequent depression of 1975.

A serious over-supply of space and exceptionally high mortgage rates, which reached 15 per cent (three times the early 1960s rate), meant that prime rents in the central business district fell by more than 30 per cent from their 1974 peak of BFr 3,500 per square metre. Rents did not recover to their pre-crash level until 1983, and within two years the over-supply had been absorbed. The cost of money also fell from its peak to 9 per cent, and since 1986 the market has seen substantial investment by Belgian, Dutch and Scandinavian companies, especially those from Sweden (more than £300 million in 1988).

In the early 1980s, prime office investment yields (as low as 7.5 per cent before the 1975 depression) climbed to 10 or 11 per cent, but by 1986 had returned to the pre-crash level. Foreign confidence is now such that overseas investors are today accepting yields as low as 5 per cent, although local investors are slightly less optimistic.

Taxation

A real estate tax (*précompte immobilier*), based on the estimated rental value of a property, is reviewed every ten years and contains no indexation. Although the bulk of the tax is passed to central government, a small proportion is given to the commune (the local authority). This element may be increased, thereby resulting in a very small percentage increase in the total tax payable.

Each sale or exchange of real estate located in Belgium requires registration and is subject to a tax of 12.5 per cent of the price or market value. On resale within three months of the first acquisition, the vendor can reclaim 80 per cent of the registration duty; on resale within two years of the first sale but after the initial three-month period, only 60 per cent can be reclaimed. The duty is reduced to 5 per cent on sales made to registered real estate brokers, provided that the resale is within ten years of the purchase. Leases, sub-leases and transfers of leases are subject to a tax of 0.2 per cent of the cumulative amount of rents and charges for the duration of the lease or, if this is indeterminable, of ten times 0.2 per cent of the annual amount.

Grant aid and investment incentives

Aid is available to enterprises choosing to set up within the Greater Brussels region, and varies according to the size of the company and the nature of its business.

Small and medium-sized companies (i.e. commercial businesses with up to forty employees, and industrial, craft, tourist or service companies with up to seventy employees) are eligible for help with interest payments on loans and/or capital grants for investment as well as for accelerated depreciation rates. Some exemption from tax on income generated by investment in real estate is also available, as are grants for job creation.

Large companies are eligible for similar benefits as well as for a range of special grants linked to research and development, high-technology activities and technical innovation.

The Ministry of Economic Affairs (Square de Meeus 23, 1040 Brussels) has set up a department to provide information and assistance to foreign investors.

Planning regulations

For all material development, planning permission is required from the commune and from the province, which is required to make a decision within seventy-five days. In certain cases, the province may wish to negotiate for a longer period. In the event of planning refusal, the applicant has the right to appeal to the provincial planning authority and, should this fail, an appeal can be made to the Minister of the Region.

Every commune has its own particular fire regulations, and each new development requires consent from the local fire officer.

Brokerage

Letting fees are charged at 15 per cent per annum of the first year's rent (plus VAT at 17 per cent) although, in cases of pre-letting, a further premium of 5 per cent of the first year's rent may be payable by the landlord (unless a special arrangement has been made). Fees on purchases and sales are prescribed by the estate agents' national association (La Confédération des Immobiliers de Belgique) at the rate of 3 per cent plus VAT.

Conveyancing

Conveyancing is undertaken by a notary, whose charges are generally 1 per cent of the value of the transaction. The law requires the appointment of a notary to resolve the demise of a lease for any term of more than nine years.

The construction industry

(See under the Netherlands, pp. 147–9).

The retail market

Estimated value of retail sales	
1984	BFr 1,531bn (£23.5bn equivalent)
1985	BFr 1,637bn (£25.2bn equivalent)
1986	BFr 1,824bn (£29.4bn equivalent)

Estimated volume of retail sales (1980 = 100.00)	
1983	95.3
1984	95.2
1985	96.7
1986	97.3
1987	96.4

Estimated number of retail outlets	
1984 (Census)	124,000 total outlets
	38,000 food outlets
	86,000 non-food outlets
1987 (Comité Belge de la Distribution)	117,600 total outlets
	1,830 supermarkets
	92 hypermarkets

Shop hours	
Department stores	Mon. to Sat. – 09.15 to 18.00 (Friday until 21.00)
Super/hypermarkets	Weekdays – 09.00 to 20.00 (Friday until 21.00)
Small retailers	Mon. to Sat. – 08.30 to 20.00 (Sunday opening for many large and small outlets)

VAT rates		
	Lowest	1%
	Lower	6%
	Standard	19%
	Higher	25%
	Special	25.48%

Source: Corporate Intelligence Research Publications Ltd

Retail activities in Belgium have followed the European tradition, with a large number of small owner/proprietor-occupied units and out-of-town/edge-of-town hypermarkets in the French style. In Brussels, the edge-of-town shopping centres developed over the past ten to fifteen years have become increasingly important and now rival the principal downtown shopping area.

Brussels

Rue Neuve

Rue Neuve is a pedestrianised shopping street running from the Place Rogier at its northern end to the Place de Brouckere. The capital's principal downtown retail area, it incorporates City 2, a large shopping centre on three floors with a metro station at the lowest level. With a food court of some thirty retailers and more than 100 other retailers, including Yves Rocher, L'Herbier de Provence, Baskin Robbins, Daniel Hechter, Bata and Manfield, City 2 offers units of between 50 and 150 square metres on average although there are a few at 200 to 250 square metres.

A tunnel links the complex with the Inno department store – at 25,000 square metres over four floors, it is Belgium's largest. Inno is part of the GB-Inno-BM Group, one of the largest retailing groups in Belgium, with twenty-one department stores, fifty-five hypermarkets and hundreds of other outlets.

The buildings in Rue Neuve are period properties on three or four floors and have residential or minor commercial occupation above the retail space. With international traders such as McDonalds, Sock Shop, Scholl, Bata, Pizzaland and C&A (more than 3,000 square metres over three retail floors) and a large three-level Marks & Spencer unit nearby, demand for space is high. Rentals have risen steadily from BFr 30,000 per square metre in 1986 to more than BFr 48,800 per square metre in 1990.

Avenue Louise

On the east side of the city, close to the business district and to the fashionable office and residential area around the Avenue Louise, stands the capital's principal luxury shopping centre. The Avenue itself consists mostly of five-storey Victorian buildings with retail on the lower floor. The significant retail section, including traders such as Cartier, Valentino, Louise Fontaine, Burberry, Gucci, Chanel, Maxmara, Louis Feraud, Louis Vuitton, Céline et Cie and Bally, is no more than 350 metres in length. Beyond this, the Avenue opens out into the Place Stéphanie and is then dominated by offices and residential property with no significant retail trading.

Behind the Avenue, on the east side running down to the junction with the Boulevard de Waterloo, a shopping mall known as Galerie Louise – an attractive old-style arcade – offers units as small as 50 square metres, and includes traders such as Yves Rocher, Lacoste, Stefanel, Benetton, Rosenthal and Baume et Mercier as well as a café-restaurant. The arcade's visibility is enhanced because some of the units have access from both the Galerie and the Avenue.

At the northern end, where the Avenue meets the inner ring road (the *ceinture*), a number of luxury traders, including Yves Saint Laurent, Pierre Cardin, Hermès, Rolex and Giorgio Armani, have chosen to locate in the Boulevard de Waterloo close to the Hilton Hotel. Surprisingly, shopping on the south side of the road, adjoining the Avenue and the northern entrance to the Galerie Louise, is much inferior, consisting only of local traders and restaurants.

Prime rents in the Avenue Louise are now in excess of BFr 30,000 per square metre.

Edge of town

Le Basilix

An extensive out-of-town development in the Ganshoren district on the west side of Brussels close to the intersection of the motorway ring and the E40 Autoroute to Gent, Le Basilix includes a 25,000 square metre GB-Maxi supermarket and cafeteria. Next to it is a shopping centre on two floors, with some small mezzanine levels, containing around seventy retail units including tenants such as C&A, P&C (Peek & Cloppenburg, Netherlands), Bally, Manfield and Bata.

Woluwe

A most unimpressive building from the outside, the Woluwe Centre – on the Boulevard de la Woluwe to the east of Brussels – is none the less the capital's most important out-of-town retail development. Set on one level, with a speciality food court at the southern end, a metro station and extensive car parking, the centre includes a large Inno department store of approximately 7,000 square metres, large C&A and Habitat/Mothercare units and fifty or so other units. Work is now under way to extend the centre on the same level.

The office market

Trends

Belgium's strategic location in Europe – both in terms of geography and as host to so many of the Community's offices – provides good reason for the property sector to be optimistic. Just three hours by road from Paris, two from Luxembourg, one-and-a-half from West Germany and just one from the Netherlands, Brussels is forty minutes by air from London Heathrow and will soon be only four hours from Lyon on the French TGV (Train Grande Vitesse). With only 150,000 square metres of office space currently available in Brussels and a similar amount under construction, the supply of office space forecast to increase by just 5 per cent, and a current annual absorption of over 200,000 square metres, rental levels are likely to increase significantly.

Brussels

Of Belgium's total of 8.25 million square metres of office space, some 6 million are within the nineteen communes of the capital, and offer a full range from high-rise blocks to converted period property. Ease of access and movement through the city's extensive network of roads and tunnels means that there are many alternative locations from which to choose. Demand is sustained not only by the local community, but also by the direct and indirect activity generated by the EC and North Atlantic Treaty Organisation (NATO).

Brussels has, of course, traditionally benefited from its nineteen communes' status as the only official bilingual areas in the country. Elsewhere, all official correspondence must be filed in the official language of the commune (French or Flemish). Although there has been some prejudice against the Flemish communes for cultural and administrative reasons (the majority of the capital's inhabitants speak French), reticence about locating beyond the city boundaries is increasingly rare.

Quartier Léopold The old city of Brussels is defined by the ring road running from the canal on the west side to the Parc de Bruxelles on the east. The city's prime business district – the Quartier Léopold – is close to the Parc, around the Avenue des Arts and immediately to its east; the Square de Meeus and the Square Frère-Orban are its most prestigious addresses. The western end of the Avenue is the traditional banking centre and contains many French, Dutch, Swiss and American banks and insurance companies.

Public organisations, government bodies and ministries occupy more than 2.5 million square metres of office space in Brussels, and the EC – with its principal offices at the eastern edge on the Rue de la Loi – has taken a further 800,000 square metres. Until recently both the government and the EC leased all their office space, but they now have a policy of acquisition, arranged in some cases on a lease purchase basis through a financial institution. With some 3.5 million square metres, the Quartier Léopold provides rather more than half of the capital's total office space. Rents have now reached BFr 7,000 per square metre – a one hundred per cent increase since 1985.

Avenue Louise

With its mixture of office and residential buildings and, at the northern end, high quality retail outlets, this long and handsome street runs south-east from the inner ring road to the Bois de la Cambre. Several major insurance companies have their offices on the Avenue; the 27-storey ITT building at the junction with the Avenue Emile Demot is currently on offer in single floors, with rents of BFr 7,200 per square metre being achieved.

Gare du Nord

Immediately to the north of the city and incorporating the Gare du Nord, a 53-hectare development includes the World Trade Centre, the Manhattan Centre, the Sheraton Hotel and the 60,000 square metre Flemish Administration centre. Parts of this development (begun in 1970) are still under construction and the planning brief encourages buildings to be no less than twenty-five floors and to offer a minimum of 20,000 square metres' space. Rents are presently around BFr 5,000–5,500 per square metre according to specification.

Southern and eastern periphery

A popular edge-of-town location for major headquarters buildings, the Chaussée de la Hulpe runs around the Bois de la Cambre and links up with the Boulevard du Souverain.

Woluwe

Known as the mini-silicon valley of Brussels, following the arrival of Hewlett-Packard, 3M, Sperry Univac and others, an area linked to the airport and the motorway by the Boulevard de Woluwe has seen the development of more than 150,000 square metres of office and high-tech space in the past ten years. The Boulevard meets the Avenue de Tervuren at its southern end and this too is a popular location for headquarters office buildings.

Boulevard Léopold III

With its concentration of high-tech activities and such companies as SKF and Wang, the Boulevard Léopold III runs north from the city towards the airport and feeds directly into the motorway network, with connections to Antwerp, Cologne, Liège and Amsterdam.

Rue de Stalle

On the south side of the city, close to the junction with the E19 Paris–Brussels motorway, the Rue de Stalle contains a concentration of office buildings, and numbers among its tenants Siemens and Erickson. As much as 60 per cent of the construction here has been undertaken by Swedish developers.

Out of town

The only significant office developments outside the Brussels area are at La Hulpe, to the south-east of the capital. Here, in open parkland, a number of training centres and offices have been located, including the Swift world headquarters – 15,000–20,000 square metres of space in two buildings occupied by IBM – but, in view of the local authority's concern to maintain the parkland, there is no real prospect of extensive office development.

Specification

The current trend in Brussels is towards central heating and ventilation systems, rather than full air-conditioning, although many of the office buildings do provide this facility. Insulation standards for heat and sound are considered important and, more recently, raised floors are being included in new buildings, though many of the older speculatively built office premises have inadequate trunking and servicing. Local authority regulations require one car parking space to be provided for every 50 square metres of office.

Service charges

With very few full repairing or proportionally full repairing leases, care of the structure and exterior of a building (defined by the Napoleonic Code as 'gross repairs') remains the responsibility of the landlord. 'Common charges' cover only such items as lifts, security, air-conditioning, heating, internal decorative repairs and the lighting and heating of common parts divided *pro rata* between the tenants on a floor area basis. An average charge for a building without air-conditioning would be around BFr 700 or BFr 1,000 per square metre per annum, and for one with air-conditioning around BFr 1,200 or BFr 1,500 per square metre.

The industrial market

Brussels

With the decline in importance of the capital's traditional industrial areas – Vilvoorde in the north and Anderlecht in the west – the emphasis has shifted to new industrial estates on the north-east side, close to Brussels Airport. Although a large number of small and large factories remain in the traditional areas, some of the obsolete buildings have been converted as living/working units for use by craftsmen and artists.

Keiberg Estate   Between Zaventem Airport and the centre of Brussels – and not more than ten minutes from either – stands the Keiberg Estate, the country's best-known speciality and high-tech industrial location. Close to the outer ring road for access to the European motorway network, the estate is well landscaped and the buildings – especially those built more recently – are of a high standard.

Zaventem Estate   Immediately to the east of the outer motorway ring, still close to the airport yet no more than fifteen minutes from the city centre, lies the nearby Zaventem Estate. Rank Xerox, Bull, Subaru, Bosch, Michelin, Black & Decker, Pfeizer, Duracell and Asea are already on site, and new developments are increasingly in the high-tech sector. There are now some office buildings with no industrial content at all.

The speculatively built sheds have, on average, 6–7 metres free to the eaves, although some tailor-made units have an eaves height of up to 11.5 metres. The specification is generally high, with electric doors and dock levellers, double-skin insulated roofs with fan-assisted water heating throughout, and double-glazing to the office element. The sheds usually provide strip lighting up to 200 lux and standard floor loadings of 2.5–3 tonnes per square metre.

Regulations demand one parking space per 100 square metres of warehousing (as well as one parking space per 50 square metres of offices), but in many cases the provision will exceed this minimum requirement. Many of the new high-tech buildings have a high office content, often as much as half.

Rents

At Anderlecht and Vilvoorde, the old-style industrial stock is let at rents of less than BFr 1,000 per square metre per annum, but demand for the limited supply of high quality modern buildings available is considerable and rentals of between BFr 2,500 and BFr 3,000 per square metre are being achieved for traditional sheds.

On the high-tech estates at Keiberg and Zaventem, industrial space is let at BFr 2,000–2,500 per square metre, with some of the high-tech developments letting at BFr 3,500–4,000 per square metre. Office space there is now letting at BFr 4,500–5,000 per square metre.

Leases

As with other commercial property, a lease is usually internal repairing only, and the landlord retains full responsibility for the structure and exterior maintenance, although the leased area is calculated on a gross external basis.

Traditionally leases have been for three, six or nine years, but industrial leases now tend towards longer fixed terms in order to avoid the tenant's option to break. Where sheds are tailored to a tenant's requirement, terms as long as twelve to fifteen years may be granted, with the landlord relying solely upon indexation for any increase in the rent. Surprisingly, investors are prepared to acquire such property on the basis of initial yields as low as 8 per cent.

Antwerp

The industrial market in Antwerp is divided into two separate geographical locations – the north which is dominated by the harbour activities, and where the emphasis is upon larger depots of more than 10,000 square metres, and the south, which is the location for distribution activities. Rentals for sheds are in the region of BFr 1,000–1,500 per square metre and for ancillary office space around BFr 2,000–2,500 per square metre.

Denmark

Geography

Land area (excl. Greenland and Faroe Islands)	43,092 sq. km.
Population	5,130,000
Density	119 per sq. km.
Main towns	Population
Copenhagen	1,715,000
Århus	258,000
Odense	174,000
Ålborg	155,000
Esbjerg	81,000
Randers	61,000

Denmark consists of three major pieces of land separated by two parallel sea belts: Zealand to the east, the Jutland peninsula to the west, and the island of Funen in between. Of some four hundred additional small islands, only ninety are inhabited. The land is generally flat, nowhere exceeding 172 metres above sea-level.

Transport and communications

With 70,000 kilometres of first class roads, including 600 kilometres of motorway, 2,500 kilometres of railway, international airports and major seaports – at Copenhagen, Århus, Esbjerg, Ålborg, Vejle, Randers, Kolding and Odense – Denmark has a highly developed transport and communications infrastructure.

Although the capital, Copenhagen, is strategically located at the entrance to the Baltic Sea, only a short distance from the coast of Sweden, it is remote from much of the country's industry and the only

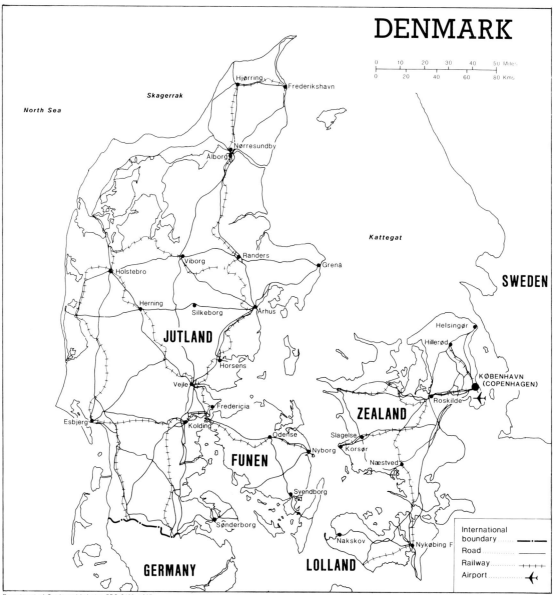

DENMARK

Department of Trade and Industry CDO 6489, 1987

rapid means of transport serving it is air. Kastrup International Airport – for intercontinental, European and domestic flights – is situated on an island immediately to the south-east of Copenhagen, just fifteen minutes from the city centre, and the airports at Ålborg, Århus, Odense, Esbjerg and six other provincial towns provide frequent daily services to the capital as well as flights to other European centres. No Danish town is more than two hours by road from its nearest airport.

The construction of a bridge from Nyborg to Korsør – due to begin in 1990 – will link Zealand with Jutland and the Continent and reduce travelling time between Copenhagen and Århus to three hours. There are also proposals to build a bridge to Malmö in Sweden within the next few years.

General economic

The present government (a centre right coalition) has sought to restrain domestic demand through restrictive fiscal and incomes policies. During an investment and consumer boom in early 1986, the domestic economy flourished, but by the autumn of the same year growth had been restricted by a credit squeeze and tax reforms introduced to tackle a current account deficit of 5 per cent of gross domestic product (GDP) and inflation of over 5 per cent.

By the beginning of 1987, as domestic consumption dropped, investment weakened and exports flattened, Denmark was heading for a steep recession, which continued throughout 1987 and into the first half of 1988. By August 1988, although the government's deflationary policies precluded any rapid recovery in the GDP growth rate, the economy seemed to have bottomed out. GDP was expected to have grown by 3 per cent in 1989.

Industry

Sixty-five per cent of the total land area is dedicated to agriculture, and farmland has traditionally been the most important of Denmark's very few natural resources. None the less, manufacturing accounts for some 20 per cent of GDP, one-third of it generated by a large number of small companies in the iron and steel industry, which produce a wide range of products. The second largest sector is food and drink – mainly food processing and brewing. In third place is the chemicals sector – producing principally fertilisers and pharmaceuticals.

Although more recent oil and gas finds in the North Sea have produced some new activity, Danish industry is, for the most part, based on the importation of raw materials and semi-manufactured goods which are then converted into products with a high value-added content. Shipbuilding, one of the few heavy industries in Denmark, is rapidly dwindling in importance.

Forms of tenure

Owner-occupation

A long tradition of owner-occupation by Danish companies created a stable borrowing basis for investments in plant, for debtors and for the financing of operating expenses. The economic crisis in the late 1970s broke this pattern and left many buildings empty. As property values dropped, the basis for many operating loans declined. Even so, although many companies decided to capitalise their property equity through sale and leaseback agreements, many large buildings and some business apartments are still owner-occupied.

Leases

Unlike leases in most other countries, including the UK, the terms of leases in Denmark, once made, are for 'time and eternity' (i.e. until either the tenant or landlord chooses to terminate). When a lease is granted, there is an initial fixed period during which the landlord cannot recover possession under any circumstances and the tenant cannot give notice to quit. Thereafter, the tenant can terminate the lease on giving suitable notice, but the landlord can only do so by demonstrating that he genuinely wishes to occupy the property or (within very strictly controlled parameters) use it for redevelopment purposes. Most terminations are therefore initiated by the tenant.

Although sub-letting of space may be permitted, landlords generally prefer to grant new leases in the interest of good estate management.

Rent review The lease usually contains provision for rent review and for indexation, with the rent rising annually to cover proven increased running costs or increased taxes payable by the landlord. The lease may also provide for an annual increase against the 'Regulation Index' (effectively a cost-of-living index based on a basket of commodities) and may also stipulate that the annual increase will be no less than a given percentage. It may also provide for a review – upwards or downwards – at specified intervals. Even so, government legislation exists which allows for such a review at four-yearly intervals.

In the one-in-ten cases where landlord and tenant fail to reach agreement at review, either party may apply to a special court presided over by one judge and two lay judges. One of these will have been nominated by the landlord's representatives and the other by the tenant's. First, the two lay judges inspect the premises, consider submissions and seek to agree a verdict between themselves. Because the law requires the review to bring the rent into line with others in the immediate area, the two judges agree in most cases, their verdict is published and the case proceeds no further. In a minority of cases, they fail to agree and then refer to the court for settlement by the third judge. The costs of referral are paid by both parties.

Industrial leases   Although, in view of Danish Landlord and Tenant Law, the original lease length is of little consequence, most industrial leases are for quite short periods, often between three and five years. In certain circumstances (where, for instance, the tenant has installed special equipment), a lease may be granted for ten or fifteen years.

As with commercial leases, the terms generally include indexation of the rent based on the Regulator Index, often subject to a minimum increase of around 4 per cent and with increases in line with the increase in taxation or proven servicing costs incurred by the landlord. An industrial lease may even provide for the tenant to contribute annually towards the depreciation of plant and machinery (such as heating systems).

Irrespective of the terms of the lease, both landlord and tenant are at liberty to request a rent review other than every fourth year, since any attempt to derogate the tenant's rights under existing legislation is null and void. It is, however, quite acceptable for the landlord's rights to be precluded by the lease!

Financial

Bank loans, negotiated on either a fixed or floating basis, are one of the two principal sources of property finance. In theory, they should be granted only for the short term, though in practice they are granted for medium terms with the right to terminate the commitment at short notice.

Finance for house building and house purchase, as well as loans to business for the purchase of buildings, machinery and so on, is provided by mortgage credit institutions.

Taxation

Corporate income tax

Rental income		50%
Realised gains	Rate	50%
	Basis	Proceeds over cost less depreciation (as indexed)
	Indexation relief	Yes
Relief for rentals		Yes
Relief for capital expenditure	Land	Nil
	Factories	6% p.a. (2% when accumulated depreciation amounts to 60%)
	Warehouses	6% p.a. (2% when accumulated depreciation amounts to 60%)
	Offices	Same rates as the qualifying buildings (if any) to which the offices are connected and service
	Special rates	Hotels, restaurants, etc.	4% p.a. (1% when accumulated depreciation amounts to 40%)

VAT

Land	Exempt
New buildings	22% (first sale by person constructing building taxable)
Old buildings	Exempt
Construction services	22%
Professional fees	22%

Transfer taxes

Tax on transfer of property deeds	1.2%

Other national/federal taxes

None significant.

Local taxes

Land tax based on value of land	Various from 0.6% to 2.4%

Grant aid and investment incentives

The northern, western and southern parts of Jutland and the islands of Bornholm and Lolland have been designated development areas. Grants can be obtained for 25–35 per cent of total capital investment for establishment, removal, expansion, rationalisation, change of production and so on.

Further information is available from the regional development board: Direktorate for Egnsudvikling, DK 8600 Silkeborg, Denmark (Tel. 06–82 56 55).

Planning regulations

In Denmark there are about fifty planning systems which have some degree of relevance to land use. The overall system of land-use planning and regulation is also controlled by numerous statutes, which are frequently amended and involve various authorities. There is no doubt that the system is extremely complicated and in recent years there has been a debate on simplification. At present, Denmark has a non-socialist minority government consisting of four parties. The Minister of the Environment, who has responsibility for comprehensive physical planning, is the only member of the Christian Popular party to hold ministerial office, and it seems highly unlikely that the political parties will be able to come to an agreement within the next few years.

The Planning Law reform of 1970 introduced a hierarchical framework in which national planning forms the framework of regional planning, which in turn forms the framework of municipal structure planning, which finally forms the framework for local planning. The Minister of the Environment, on behalf of the government, is responsible for national planning. Regional plans must be submitted to the Minister for approval, whereas municipal structure plans and local plans can be finally adopted by the council, provided they are in accordance with the superior planning framework.

In the first instance, a planning application will be made to the local council. The council will draw up a proposed local plan which will have to be published together with a brief description of its content and legal effects. Within a period of not less than two months from publication, objections to the proposal may be made or proposals for amendment submitted. Simultaneously with the publication of the proposal, the council must give notice in writing to (among others) the owners of the properties covered by the plan, the Ministry of the Environment and the regional planning authority. Notice in writing must also be given to any state authorities which have special interest in the plan (the Ministry of Agriculture or Forestry, for example). If a state authority vetoes the proposal, the council cannot finally adopt the proposal until an agreement has been reached. If such an agreement is not arrived at, the dispute may be brought before the Minister of the Environment. The majority of disputes, however, are settled by negotiations.

As far as appeals are concerned, the Municipal Planning Act states that only decisions involving 'legal problems' may be brought before the National Agency for Physical Planning for final decision. In practice, however, it is accepted that there is a wide range of reasons for appealing, that there is no time limit for appeals and that the appeal does not immediately effect a suspension.

Immediately after the final adoption of the plan, the council must publicise the adoption. The local plan must be entered in the land register of the local court for the properties covered by the plan.

Brokerage

Under Danish law, estate agents must operate independently and personally, to the exclusion of any commercial company. They must pass a Ministry of Commerce examination, maintain professional secrecy, have no personal interest in the transaction and have their financial affairs in order. Although occasionally acting as consultant to a purchaser, they generally represent the vendor, providing advice through to the point of agreement (*Slutseddel*). Even so, they owe a duty of care to both parties.

The maximum fee is controlled by law and is presently set at 3.09 per cent excluding VAT, but in reality the state of the marketplace means that on large transactions it will be in the region of 1.5–1.7 per cent. Letting fees are currently between 10 per cent and 12 per cent of the first year's rent.

Conveyancing

Though similar to the system in the UK, conveyancing in Denmark has an additional stage, similar to the conditional exchange of contracts. Once an acceptable offer has been made, both parties, together with lawyers and agents, agree heads of agreement (*Slutseddel*), which set out the principal terms of the deal. Though binding, *Slutseddel* are conditional upon such factors as survey or finance. When these are satisfied, the final agreement stage (*Skoede*) is reached. The fact that all land in Denmark has registered title should (but appears not to) hasten the preliminaries.

Although, like agents, lawyers will negotiate on larger transactions, the official scale of fees is:

On the first DKr 500,000:	0.1%
On the next DKr 500,000:	0.8%
On the next DKr 1,000,000:	0.6%
On the remainder:	0.4%

Stamp duty at 1.2 per cent on all transactions is, in Copenhagen and Zealand, payable by the purchaser and, in Jutland and the rest of the country, split between both parties.

The construction industry

Capacity

The industry has a small domestic market, with few large contractors competing in the international market. As a result of the country's limited natural resources, a large proportion of both materials and components have to be imported. Relatively high labour costs have led to a significant use of system building, with several system designs being imported from Scandinavia and West Germany.

In terms of turnover, the major companies are:

Monberg Thorsen	DKr 4,273 million
Rasmussen & Schiotz	DKr 2,462 million
Hojgaard Schultz	DKr 2,022 million

There is no national system of classification of contractors.

State of the industry

Following the recession of the late 1970s and early 1980s, the industry experienced strong domestic growth between 1983 and 1986. 1986 was an exceptional year, with almost 20 per cent more construction activity than in 1985. Currently rather depressed, the industry is not expected to recover again until 1991. The problem of demand is aggravated by the country's declining population.

Structure

Although on-site supervision is often the responsibility of a resident engineer, the architect acts as lead consultant, with design responsibility for a building project and cost control as part of his duties. Independent quality control consultants are not generally used.

On the contracting side, strong trade organisations used to play an important role monitoring and checking bids for the contractors, but this form of restrictive practice has now been prohibited by the government.

Design considerations

Denmark has no mandatory national technical regulations, and the codes of practice issued by the Danish Standards Institution are for guidance only.

Approvals

Prior to construction, approval must be obtained under the National Planning Acts and also the Technical Regulations. There is no legal timescale for the determination of an application by technical officials of the local authority; approval may take a few days or several months.

Programme considerations

As in most other countries, obtaining the necessary statutory approvals dictates the pace and duration of the design process. Once planning approval has been granted, the timescale for the preparation of the project and for bidding is usually about six months.

The widespread use of system building does, of course, lead to a shorter construction programme, but on conventional *in situ* structures, the construction programme is similar to that in the UK.

Placing the building contract

Most projects are tendered for on the basis of specification and drawings, using a standard form of building contract (*almindelige betingelser for arbejder og leverancer*), and contracts are usually drawn up on a fixed-price, lump-sum basis. On small and medium-sized projects, main contracting is the standard procedure but, on major projects, separate trades contracts are drawn up. Co-ordination of the trades is the responsibility either of the supervising architect/engineer or of a specially appointed co-ordinator.

Cost comparison

The level of professional fees in the Danish construction industry is lower than in the UK. For example, for a new build project of DKr 35 million (about £3 million excluding VAT), the total fees for architects and engineers would be in the region of 10 per cent. Construction costs are also lower than in the UK: an air-conditioned speculative office building on the outskirts of Copenhagen, for instance, will cost around DKr 7,500 per square metre (about £55 per square foot).

The retail market

Estimated value of retail sales	
1985	DKr 157.0bn (£12.1bn equivalent)
1986	DKr 167.8bn (£14.5bn equivalent)

Estimated volume of retail sales (1980 = 100)		
	1983	102.7
	1984	105.8
	1985	107.0
	1986	109.9
	1987	106.2

Estimated number of retail outlets	
1981 (Census)	50,800
1987 (DOD)	7,400 outlets in major chains and buying groups
1987 (Per Press)	765 free-standing supermarkets
	13 hypermarkets
	266 discount food stores

Shop hours	
By law the maximum shop trading hours are:	Mon. to Thur. – until 17.30 Friday – until 20.00 Saturday – until 14.00 Sunday – trading prohibited
After 1 October 1989, there will be an additional ten trading hours to be spread over the week, excluding Saturday.	

VAT rate
Standard 22%

Trends

Although the luxury market in Copenhagen remains strong, partly as a result of the influx of Swedish and other international visitors, the present state of the economy and the government's commitment to restricting consumer spending leaves little real prospect for significant growth over the next two to three years.

There is, however, considerable demand for more extensive out-of-town retailing facilities and retail parks and a noticeable increase in the number of businesses sold to immigrant traders keen to improve their returns by opening for longer hours. The combination of out-of-town facilities and increased shop hours will mostly damage the small, inefficient suburban shopkeeper, while Saturday afternoon and Sunday trading would be of substantial benefit to traders in Stroget and the central area in general.

Copenhagen

Copenhagen is the most important shopping centre not only for Denmark but for much of southern Scandinavia. Copenhagen's main retail area is pedestrianised, its four principal streets known collectively as Stroget. At the eastern end, Østergade is the prime section and the equivalent of London's Bond Street; it contains the largest number of international multiples, including the Body Shop, Benetton, Mulberry, Louis Vuitton, Gucci, Yves Saint Laurent, Chanel, Bang & Olufsen and Royal Copenhagen. At the western end, Frederiksberggade, with its many fashion shops, caters more for young people. There are, in addition, several department stores and other pedestrian streets (including Købmagergade) running out of Stroget.

The shape and size of the old buildings limit most units in Stroget to 100 square metres or less on the ground floor. In the side streets, occupied by many different trades including antiques, jewellery, books, fashion, arts and crafts, the units are even smaller.

On Østergade, prime rents – as high as DKr 10,000 per square metre per annum overall – produce an annual rental per unit of up to DKr 1 million. In the immediate side streets, however, rents can be as low as DKr 1,000 per square metre per annum.

With a low turnover of properties – perhaps no more than twenty in a year, and even fewer in Østergade – premiums as high as DKr 2 million have been paid for possession. However, the present economic climate and the lack of anticipated growth in the retail sector suggest that this record will remain unchallenged in the foreseeable future.

With the arrival of an increasing number of international traders, most landlords are looking at the quality of the covenant and the impact upon the investment value rather than any short-term rental profit.

Out of town

Since the early 1960s, about ten suburban shopping centres have been developed on the outskirts of Copenhagen, each with one or two major supermarket tenants and twenty to thirty additional retail units, including, in some of the better centres such as Lyngby, international multiples such as Benetton, Jacadi, L'Herbier de Provence and Fil à Fil.

Though not competing with the central area in the fashion and luxury goods sectors, these centres perform a useful function and provide an alternative to the suburban high streets where individual traders often perform relatively inefficiently but are protected by the restricted shopping hours and the prevailing landlord and tenant legislation which prevents new traders from entering the market and trading more aggressively.

An extensive edge-of-town centre at Hoje Taastrup includes a large office campus as well as retail units. Known as City 2, it contains around 100 retail units (including a 15,000-square-metre supermarket) on two levels, with a central food court and multi-level parking.

Retail warehousing

A number of one-off retail warehouses around the outskirts of the capital accommodate carpet stores, DIY centres, furniture stores and so on, but difficulties in obtaining consent from the planning authorities for any more coherent development means that there are no retail parks. Under existing regulations, local district authorities cannot give consent for retail warehouses larger than 2,300 square metres.

Anything larger must have permission from the Greater Copenhagen Planning Authority, which is lobbied heavily by small retailer pressure groups seeking to prevent any increase in out-of-town shopping or retail warehousing.

The retail market in the rest of Denmark

With most of the principal shopping streets in Danish towns now pedestrianised, retail activities are generally restricted to a compact and well-defined centre.

In Denmark's second city, Århus, prime rents on Sondergade (the main shopping street) are around DKr 2,200 per square metre per annum.

The office market

Trends

In theory, Denmark has little to lose from the advent of the single market: a small trading nation endowed with fewer raw materials and natural resources than most, it has a long history as an exporter of a variety of products to markets worldwide. With few barriers to international trade and quite used to doing business with the rest of Europe, Copenhagen is being seen as a natural financial centre in a unique position to act as a bridge between EFTA and the EC – a fact which should generate a demand for office space. The lack of space in the central business district is bound to encourage a shift to edge-of-town sites, especially Hoje Taastrup, although the present over-supply in these locations will probably preclude a significant growth in rents.

The only significant problem posed by 1992 is that the Single European Act will require Denmark to bring its taxation and VAT rates into line. For a government already carrying a national debt equal to almost 40 per cent of GNP, this could present major economic difficulties and, given its dependence upon domestic space users and government, could depress the office market.

Copenhagen

Local planning regulations jealously protect all buildings in the central area. No demolition is permitted within the city, nothing higher than seven storeys can be built and no increase is allowed in the square meterage provided at present. The central area is defined by the old ramparts and walls of the medieval city, and many of the buildings now used as offices were formerly industrial, printing and factory premises.

A 17th-century section to the immediate north (Frederiksberggade) now forms the central business district. Although the regulations still apply, the layout – designed to accommodate the original palaces – provides relatively large sites and substantial internal floor areas, so it has been relatively easy to adapt buildings to match today's needs.

Fifty-four of Denmark's largest companies have their headquarters within the Greater Copenhagen area, major exceptions being Danfoss, Grundfoss and Lego which all occupy freehold sites on the Jutland peninsula.

Central business district

The central business district is situated to the north of Kongens Nytorv and most office space within it is refurbished; tenants include lawyers, accountants, government agencies and trade unions, as well as banks and insurance companies. Specification within the district is poor by UK standards because the buildings are low-rise period properties, and prime rents are just under DKr 2,000 per square metre per annum. Air-conditioning, for which there is no local demand, is prohibited (except in computer rooms) by a law passed during the oil crisis and not yet repealed. Raised flooring, though now usually included in new developments, is not yet standard.

Many banks, insurance and oil companies have offices in Copenhagen, which views itself as the financial capital of Scandinavia, but some – including BP, a major insurance company, and the back-office and computer operations of several banks and insurance companies – have relocated out of town, leaving some large units available.

With little demand from major space users, a large unit falling vacant will tend to be let floor by floor. What little space is to let in the district is mostly between 100 and 1,000 square metres, with very few units larger than 2,000 square metres.

Edge of town

At around DKr 1,000 per square metre per annum, rents in the three principal out-of-town centres are approximately half those in the central business district. Rental values were held back by a short-term over-supply: prior to 12 March 1986, institutional investors were exempt from all tax on income and capital gains from property, and this resulted in a substantial volume of speculative development. Though now largely absorbed by subsequent demand for space, the scale of the development at Hoje Taastrup is such as to preclude any sharp rise in rental values.

Århus

The centre of the dairy industry and Denmark's second city, Århus has not been inhibited by the constraints of a medieval city or by any ban on demolition. A mixture of old, refurbished and modern specification space achieves a maximum rental for prime space of around DKr 1,050 per square metre per annum.

The industrial market

Background

West Germany is Denmark's most important trading partner and some major industries have chosen to locate on the Jutland peninsula for ease of access to the West German border and the European market.

Århus, Denmark's second city, has seen the strongest development in the past four or five years; more recently the 'Golden Triangle' formed by Kolding, Vejle and Fredericia has seen substantial rental growth, some of it in anticipation of the proposed new bridge between Nyborg and Korsør which will connect Zealand with Funen and Jutland.

Trends

Although Copenhagen, as the capital, will remain the administrative and financial centre of Denmark, the industrial and commercial sectors are clearly envisaging a shift towards the Jutland peninsula. The new bridge may improve the situation but the proposed completion date (1994) may be too late to halt the movement of industry to locations with better access to the European market.

Kolding, Vejle and Fredericia should see strong growth in the next few years, as should Odense, in anticipation of the completion of the bridge.

Copenhagen

Except for two major breweries, most of Copenhagen's industry is in the light industry or distributive sectors. In recent years, many electronics companies have relocated to Kongens Lyngby, an area to the north of the capital chosen by IBM many years ago.

Other industries have preferred the south-west side of Copenhagen, including Taastrup and Hoje Taastrup, where the intersection of motorways and ring roads combines with the new rail terminal to provide a first-class communications system.

Although some pension funds have built for letting and some developers have built speculatively with a view to selling units to investors, much of the new development – perhaps around 75 per cent – is owner-occupied. The new developments generally provide 40–50 per cent site coverage, with an office content of up to 25 per cent. Rentals are modest at around DKr 400–435 per square metre for the industrial element and DKr 650–760 per square metre for the office space. In general, specifications are basic – a simple two-storey office unit fronting a steel or concrete-framed single-storey shed, with an eaves height of 4–6 metres and one car parking space for every 50 square metres of lettable premises.

With building costs for an average specification standing at approximately DKr 4,330 per square metre and land values at a ceiling of DKr 1,620 per square metre further development seems unlikely, although substantial tax advantages from investment in property have provided attractive net returns to investors.

Hoje Taastrup

Hoje Taastrup is strategically located to the south-west of the city at the intersection of motorways South and West, and includes the capital's new main rail terminal, which has a rapid link to the old city centre station.

Up to 100,000 square metres have already been built or are under construction, and the development includes offices and the City 2 shopping centre, as well as a hotel and some limited retailing designed to service the local employees.

Ballerup

Favoured by banks and insurance companies relocating from the central business district, Ballerup (to the west of Copenhagen) has, in recent years, seen many speculative office schemes, largely as a result of tax incentives provided by the government. There is now a substantial volume of space awaiting tenants.

Birkerod

Birkerod is situated within the fashionable northern residential suburbs of the city, and is favoured by computer and other high-tech companies. IBM has been located in this area for some years.

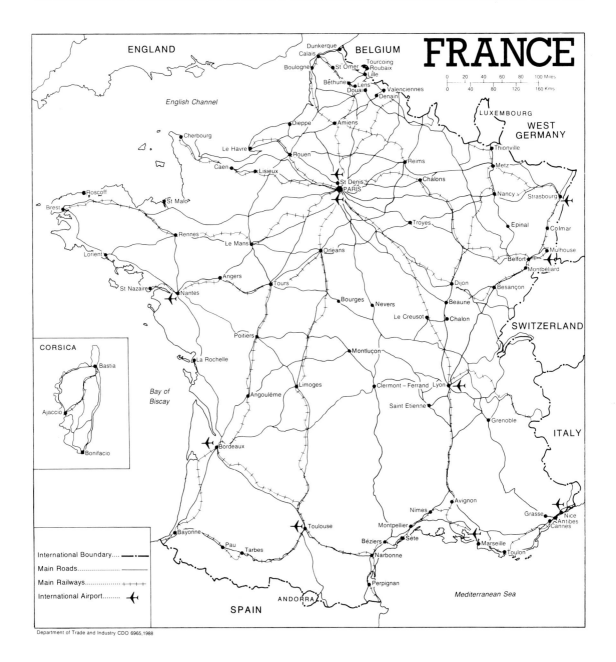

FRANCE

France

Geography

Land area	547,026 sq. km.
Population	55,870,000 (at 1.1.1987)
Density	101 per sq. km.
Main cities	Population
Paris	8,707,000
Lyon	1,221,000
Marseille	1,111,000
Lille	936,000
Bordeaux	640,000
Toulouse	541,000

France occupies a central position in western Europe and borders on six countries. To the north are Belgium and Luxembourg, to the east West Germany, Switzerland and Italy and to the south, Spain. France is the largest member state in the Community, slightly larger than the UK and West Germany combined, but with a little under half their total population.

Metropolitan France (which includes Corsica) is divided into ninety-six departments (*départements*). In 1972, twenty-two regions were created, each of which encompasses several departments. There is a directly elected regional council and an economic and social council in each region. The new regions serve chiefly as focal points for channelling government funds to the different departments and, increasingly, to encourage inward investment in their area.

Transport and communications

The French road system is a co-ordinated network radiating from Paris. The motorway system is continuing to expand and, at present, covers more than 6,000 kilometres.

There is an impressive, efficient, electrified railway system, which is currently being extended to increase the network for the high-speed TGV trains.

Air France, together with the two other French airlines, carried 24 million passengers between them in 1985.

Major ports are Marseille, Le Havre, and Dunkerque. There are 6,400 kilometres of navigable inland waterways, which are used to carry heavy goods, combustible minerals, petroleum and construction materials. Paris is the most important inland river port.

General economic

Two major factors have conditioned the development of the French economy, namely European integration, which has affected both the agricultural and industrial sectors, and the dismantling of trade barriers within the EC, which has greatly expanded the French motor industry while adversely affecting French consumer durables manufacturers.

The government's adoption of more restrictive policies aimed at reducing inflation and the public sector deficit, and improving the balance of payments has resulted in a modest growth at an average of 1.7 per cent per annum. GDP growth in 1987 realised 2.2 per cent due to the combined effects of lower oil prices, strengthened demand and increased spending power. Since 1987, the French banks have pursued a policy of monetary control based entirely on interest rates and changes in minimum reserve requirements.

Until the 1980s the level of political interference in real estate had been low, with the exception of control on residential rents. Recently, however, planning controls on office development and occupation permits (agréments) as well as fiscal measures to control land speculation have been introduced. On the whole, however, these measures are aimed at controlling the over-development of urban areas, particularly Paris.

Successive French governments have promoted policies of decentralisation aiming to reduce the importance of Paris, but the private sector is as reluctant to decentralise today as it has ever been and Paris and the surrounding area remain the lynchpin of French industry and commerce. Until the last decade most French institutional investment was made in the residential sector as a result of the encouragement provided by the government following the Second World War. Institutional development in commercial schemes was limited to the provision of development finance, and most property was immediately sold off to occupiers. It was only with the development of the letting market in the late 1960s and the arrival of foreign investment funds (including the British and the Dutch) that local institutions became conscious of the investment potential of commercial property. In the early 1970s medium- to long-term finance became more readily available and this further assisted the development of the fledgling rented sector.

There is a very clear division between Paris and the provinces in the French real estate market. Statistically, Paris accounts for more than 50 per cent of the total office stock for the whole of France, and it is estimated that the total office accommodation in the Paris area is in excess of 30 million square metres. In the twelve largest cities after Paris, by contrast, the total office stock is only approximately 10 million square metres. Ninety-six per cent of banks and 70 per cent of insurance companies have their headquarters in Paris. Approximately 65 per cent of people employed in the Paris region are in white-collar jobs.

Forms of tenure

In common with other Continental European countries, there has, historically, been a predominance of owner-occupation of property in France. The system of *co-propriété* (condominium or co-ownership) has existed since 1938 and this, together with *toute propriété* (absolute ownership), are the most common forms of real estate ownership in France. Effectively, both forms equate to a UK freehold except that, in the case of *co-propriété*, the rights are subject to various obligations and controls.

Long leasehold exists in two basic forms, *bail à construction* and *bail emphythéotique*: both are forms of building leases generally granted for terms of sixty-six or ninety-nine years. These long leaseholds have come into increasing use in recent years in relation to the disposal of land owned by government or quasi-public bodies, but, as in the UK, there is some resistance from institutional investors to such forms of tenure.

Additionally, new property is commonly sold 'off plan' before construction has been completed under a procedure known as purchase '*dans l'état futur d'achèvement*'. In such a case, legally, the purchaser becomes the immediate freehold owner of the site and of the construction as it progresses, while the developer remains in control of the development until delivery. Stage payments are made by the purchaser from the date of making a firm commitment.

It is also possible to acquire rights to air space and this has been of particular relevance in the La Défense area to the west of Paris, where much of the new construction is on a podium level. The air-space rights will usually furnish the right to construct a specified volume of space; unlike a building lease, which will ultimately revert to the grantor, these air-space rights are in perpetuity.

All land ownerships are registered in the Land Register (the *Cadastre*), together with any charges, restrictions, mortgages etc. Occupational leases, however, are not generally entered on the Land Register unless they are notarial leases.

Leases

The terms of French leases are dictated by a decree made in 1953 and there are two main principles worthy of note:

Propriété commercial

- The tenant's right to a lease renewal and to his entitlement to compensation if the landlord fails to renew. This right is known as the *propriété commercial*.

The 1953 decree

- The 1953 decree provides for the 3/6/9 lease, which is essentially a nine-year lease with a tenant's option to break every three years. At the end of the nine years' period, the tenant has a right to renewal of the lease for a further nine years and so on. However, at renewal, the rent will be reviewed to a market rental and should the parties not agree, the matter will be referred to a *tribunal de commerce*.

Assignment is generally restricted by landlords and leases are not granted for terms of less than nine years, unless they are shorter than twenty-three months, in which case they are deemed to be short leases which fall outside the scope of the 1953 decree. Under the provisions of the *propriété commercial*, compensation is payable to a tenant if a landlord does not wish to renew the lease, and compensation will be fixed by the *tribunal de commerce* having regard to the actual circumstances of the matter. Therefore, if an office tenant is evicted and there is a plentiful supply of similar suites in the vicinity, the damages payable will be limited to removal costs and a relatively small amount for general upheaval. However, in the case of retail tenants, where a tenant's entire livelihood and business may be prejudiced by his eviction, the damages can be very substantial – tens of millions of francs.

Retail leases

With retail leases, while the general provisions of the 1953 decree apply and 3/6/9 leases will be granted, on renewal of the lease the rent is not reviewed in comparison with an open market rental, but the indexation of the rent in accordance with the construction cost index continues. The construction cost index is the government's published index and it generally runs at a slightly lower level than the CPI (consumer price index). The rent is usually reviewed on a three-yearly basis, though it can be reviewed annually and this is becoming increasingly common.

The only way in which a landlord can retain some control of the rent and hope for an increase at some point is to grant the original lease with a highly restrictive user clause. Then, if the tenant wishes to change the nature of his trade or if he wishes to make an assignment, the landlord can seek to negotiate a surrender of the lease and grant a new lease at a new rent. Shop leases can be assigned but, if they are assigned during the last three years of a nine-year lease, they do not carry with them the benefits of the *propriété commercial* and the new tenant must seek to renegotiate a new lease with the landlord at the end of the original nine-year term. The user clause point is interesting in that even where the lease gives the tenant a wide-open user clause, if there is a dispute over the matter, the courts may deem that the user clause is restricted to that use to which the tenant put the shop in the preceding period. If a shop lease is granted for an original term of more than nine years, the 1953 decree does not apply at all, but the tenant still has protection at the end of the lease, although the rent must be negotiated to a market level.

The investment market

The total volume of space acquired for investment, or forward funded, in 1988 was between 1.2 million and 1.5 million square metres with a value of Fr 25 billion. Of these investments 80 per cent were bought by French investors, principally by insurance companies, pension funds and *sociétés civiles de placement immobilier* (SCPIs). The remaining five billion francs' worth was sold to overseas investors, with the Japanese acquiring 80 per cent and the remainder picked up by UK investors and to a lesser extent by the Dutch.

Japanese investors spent Fr 200 billion worldwide in 1988 and of this only Fr 20 billion were spent in Europe. Half of that Fr 20 billion was spent in London and only Fr 4 billion in Paris (including the ZAC Pasteur Montparnasse project in the 14th *arrondissement*, a 60,000 square metres building for Fr 2.6 billion and, in conjunction with PosTel, Les Trois Quartiers at the Madeleine for Fr 1.6 billion). Japanese investors are enthusiastic about the opportunities in Paris because they can see potential growth over the next five years, but they are uncomfortable with the registration tax on second-hand buildings and the exchange-rate risk.

Prime buildings such as one in the Avenue Foch, next to the Champs-Elysées, have shown 223 per cent growth in capital value over five years. Over the same period La Défense has shown 100–150 per cent growth, while prime rentals have increased by 150 per cent.

Yields (1988–9)	%
Paris	4.0–7.5
La Défense	6.0–8.0
Boulogne/Levallois-Perret	7.5–8.5
New towns	8.7–9.2

Financial

The principal methods of financing the acquisition of a commercial building – other than an outright purchase for cash – are by way of a long-term mortgage loan or by *crédit-bail immobilier*.

Long-term mortgage loan

French banks and other financial institutions provide long-term loans for the acquisition of property generally for terms of ten or twelve years on the basis of 70–80 per cent of the capital value of the property acquired. The loan will be secured by way of a first charge on the property, and the balance of the purchase price must be provided by the purchaser.

Crédit-bail immobilier

Crédit-bail immobilier was first introduced in 1967, following the creation of specific lending institutions known as SICOMIs. These *sociétés immobiliers pour le commerce et l'industrie* are companies created by legislation and financed by the French banks. Their sole function is to deal with the financial leasing operations and the construction and ownership of commercial property investments. They have privileged fiscal status but must operate within the scope of the legislation, which includes the distribution of at least 85 per cent of their net profits.

Other leasing companies provide finance on a similar basis, but are not bound by the same regulations. These operators are known as non-SICOMI companies.

Approximately 140 banks and leasing companies provide *crédit-bail immobilier*. Ninety are SICOMIs and fifty are non-SICOMI. The only advantage for a non-SICOMI company is that it is not bound to amortise the loan over fifteen years and can be more flexible in structuring the loan.

Crédit-bail loans can be on one of three bases: variable, decreasing or fixed term. Although the loan cannot be redeemed within the first seven years, the building can be sold subject to, and with the benefit of, the *crédit-bail* arrangement and subject to the approval of the institution. The occupier will usually take responsibility for outgoings on a property held by *crédit-bail* as if he were the outright owner.

Taxation

Local taxes

There are three forms of local tax:

- *Taxe professionelle*
- *Taxe foncière*
- *Taxe d'habitation*

Taxe professionelle

The *taxe professionelle* (business licence tax) is due from almost all individuals and legal entities carrying on a business on their own account. It is based on:

- The rent value of the tangible fixed assets leased for a period over six months or owned by the tax payer during the year prior to the tax year in question
- 18 per cent of the salaries paid

The rental value includes:

- The theoretical rent value of both improved and unimproved real estate used
- 16 per cent of the cost of other tangible fixed assets or of their value when they are rented, less a lump sum deduction of Fr 25,000.

The business licence tax is equal to this taxable basis multiplied by the tax rates voted annually by the city, the department, the region and the Chamber of Commerce in the jurisdiction of which the company is located. Business licence is a tax-deductible business expense. The calculated amount of the business licence tax is subject to the following limitations:

- Only 50 per cent of the investment that led to the fixed assets increase are taken into account in the fixed assets basis

- Only 50 per cent of the salaries of newly hired employees are taken into account in the salary basis

- A 16 per cent reduction of the business licence tax basis has been applied across the board since 1987

- The tax cannot exceed 5 per cent of the value added by the business

Taxe foncière

This is based upon a different rental valuation, which is also well below market rates. The level of this taxation is very low and will probably amount to less than 0.5 per cent of the value.

Taxe d'habitation

A similar tax to *taxe foncière* but applied to residential property rather than commercial.

Property transfer taxes

The purchase of land and buildings in France is subject to either Value Added Tax (TVA) or registration duties.

TVA

TVA is a recoverable tax, levied at 18.6 per cent on the purchase of new buildings, providing this is the first sale within five years of completion. A subsequent transaction within a five-year period and any sale outside this period renders the building subject to registration duty rather than TVA.

Registration duties

Registration duties are levied on all commercial property acquisitions at a total rate of 16.6 per cent plus *taxe régionale* (recently increased) and *taxe de publicité foncière*. The latter, which is levied at the rate of 0.6 per cent, also applies to TVA transactions. These duties are not recoverable, but may be amortised over a five-year period.

These transfer taxes can be subject to slight regional variance, notably in the Paris area. For a transaction falling within the TVA regime, the costs may be estimated as follows;

Taxe de publicité foncière	0.6%
Notary's fees	1.0%
	1.6%

In addition, non-resident purchasers sometimes take into account the incidence of financing TVA in the short term, prior to recovery.

For a building in the registration regime, the calculation for the Paris region is as follows:

Registration duty	16.6%
Taxe de publicité foncière	0.6%
Taxe régionale	0.8%
Notary's fees (approx.)	1.0%
	19.0%

Grant aid and investment incentives

There is a wide range of financial and fiscal incentives designed to encourage industrial development. DATAR (Délégation à l'Aménagement du Territoire et à l'Action Régionale) – the government agency responsible for assisting foreign investors considering France as a base for their overseas operations – will provide companies with advice on site selection, the availability of incentives and compliance with EC rules. DATAR provides cash grants that can finance up to 25 per cent of the investment in land, buildings and equipment purchased during the first three years of operation.

Investments eligible for this aid include greenfield projects which create at least twenty jobs within the first three years, and major expansions creating more than ten new jobs when this represents a 50 per cent increase in the workforce over a three-year period.

These grants apply in most areas of west, south-west and central France, as well as in traditional heavy industry sites in the north and the east which are facing redevelopment problems. The amount of the grant varies from 12 per cent to a maximum of 25 per cent according to the location. Grants are also available for research and development projects. For further information, contact DATAR (21–4 Grosvenor Place, London SW1X 7HU).

Local subsidies on land and plant

In France, the majority of business parks and industrial zones are owned and operated by municipalities or Chambers of Commerce. The owners usually sell or lease the land and may provide financing for existing buildings or buildings to be constructed. One of the most common financing procedures is *crédit-bail* (leasing), which provides an option to buy the property after a ten- to fifteen-year period and is arranged through a property development bank (SICOMI). Transfer and registration duties are paid only on the transfer price.

Eager to attract new businesses, most French municipalities will also subsidise up to 25 per cent of the cost of the new building or guarantee loans granted by a SICOMI, in order to provide a more attractive rate on such leases. By way of illustration, the municipality lease in Illkirch in Alsace is calculated on the following basis: 40–50 per cent of the cost of the building is financed through an interest-free loan with a three-year deferral period. The balance is financed with a 9 per cent interest loan. In Saint-Nazaire on the Atlantic coast, 20–25 per cent of the cost of the building is subsidised, and the remainder is financed with a loan bearing a 10.5 per cent interest charge.

Tax exemptions

Corporate tax

The corporate income tax rate in France is 42 per cent, but in three specific areas (Dunkerque on the English Channel, and La Ciotat and La Seyne on the Mediterranean coast) the government has established three enterprise zones of approximately 750 acres each.

Newly created companies located in these zones will be exempted from corporate tax for the first ten years of operation, provided they are incorporated, have operating facilities in the zone and employ at least ten persons after two years of operation.

Business licence tax

In certain areas of France, including those covered by the government grant programme, local authorities are entitled to provide newly established industrial or service companies with a partial or total exemption from the business licence tax for up to five years. To be eligible for this benefit, a company must meet certain minimum conditions regarding the amount of investment and the number of jobs to be created. In urban communities of over 15,000 inhabitants, for example, thirty jobs must be created and Fr 800,000 must be invested. Details of this exemption are available from DATAR.

Other aids, incentives and exemptions, which are not directly related to property, are available. Any individual or company seriously considering investment in France should, again, make direct contact with DATAR (21–4 Grosvenor Place, London SW1X 7HU).

Planning regulations

Although the French planning system is extremely complex, its basic structure is not unfamiliar. *Schémas Directeurs d'Aménagement et d'Urbanisme* (SDAU) equate to the UK structure plans, and outline long-term intentions at macro level. They cover matters such as building volumes and population, and are mandatory for all areas with a population in excess of 10,000 inhabitants.

Within the SDAU, there is a facility to prepare a *plan d'occupation des sols*. This will deal with a smaller urban area and delineate the proposed land use, identify major public projects proposed, and set out guidelines for such matters as plot ratio. These documents are available for inspection by the public, and the planners' official attitude to the development of a particular site can be obtained by seeking the issue of a *certificat d'urbanisme*, setting out the authority's attitude towards a particular site. When granted, planning consents are valid for one year.

The planning system is further modified by a number of other pieces of legislation.

Agrément

Specifically linked to the decentralisation policies of central government, this authorisation, provided by DATAR, is required when a company wishes to occupy more than 2,000 square metres of offices or 3,000 square metres of industrial premises or 5,000 square metres of warehousing. An *agrément* must be obtained prior to seeking a building permit.

Redevance

A tax levied on new office and industrial space in the Paris and Lyon areas, the *redevance* acts as a financial disincentive to development in these over-subscribed areas. The current rate of charge is Fr 400 per square metre for offices and Fr 150 per square metre for industrial space. The new towns around Paris are exempted from this tax.

Loi Galley

Introduced in 1978, the *Loi Galley* provides the local authorities with certain powers:

- A pre-emption right on all freehold transactions affecting properties more than ten years old, whereby the local authority can acquire the property at the price agreed. Although this power is used only rarely, it does give local authorities the opportunity to put together major development sites.

- The power to specify plot ratios on development in urban areas, presently fixed at 1.0 in the provinces and 3.0 in Paris. There is also provision for payment of a betterment levy, where exceptional consents are given which exceed this plot ratio. Although well intended, as is the case in other countries, this law has tended to put a brake on the development market and vendors are reluctant to dispose of sites. This law may be modified in the foreseeable future as part of the endeavour to promote new development.

Loi Royer

Introduced at the end of 1973, the *Loi Royer* required any new retail development with a sales area of more than 1,500 square metres to be approved by a commercial urban committee, the members of which were to consist of local traders, civil servants and politicians. The law has retarded hypermarket and shopping centre development in France and there has recently been a movement towards relaxation of the measures.

Brokerage

Brokerage services are regulated by the French law of 2 January 1970 (*Loi Hoguet*), which restricts the provision of services to holders of a professional card and requires the broker to have a written mandate.

To obtain a professional card, a broker must have studied for two years or have four to five years in approved employment or experience in the business. The rules can, however, be circumvented, since a member of staff in the employment of a registered broker is entitled to carry a card showing the registration of his employer.

French brokers do not perceive their role as being to act for one party or the other in a transaction, but rather to stand in the middle and broke a transaction between two independent parties. Traditionally, the broker's fees will be paid by the purchaser, although this is a matter for negotiation. Quite often the fees are shared by the purchaser and the vendor. Fees are negotiable downwards from a rate of 5 per cent for acquisition and sale or 30 per cent of the first year's rent on letting.

Conveyancing

Historically, the transfer of property was a straightforward operation carried out before a notary, who would prepare a single deed. As transactions have become more complex and generally dependent on the raising of finance or some other condition, it is normal now to proceed by way of an interim stage: either a *promesse unilatérale de vente* or a *compromis de vente*.

Promesse de vente A *promesse de vente* is effectively an option whereby the vendor agrees to sell the property to the purchaser provided that he satisfies himself about specific matters within a specified period. Generally, a deposit of 10 per cent of the purchase price will be paid, returnable if the option is not exercised. A *promesse de vente* must be registered within ten days if signed privately between the parties, and within one month if signed before a notary.

Compromis de vente A *compromis de vente* is a conditional contract, binding on both parties, subject to the conditions being satisfied. The formalities will then be concluded by a notary in a notarial deed, which will be registered at the Land Register following completion (*acte authentique*).

It is important to note that the concept of an agreement being 'subject to contract' is unknown in France and that, therefore, an exchange of correspondence could, in certain cases, be construed as a binding contract.

The fees of a notary vary but will generally not be in excess of 1 per cent of the value of the transaction.

The construction industry

The French construction industry includes major construction companies capable of handling the largest international projects. In terms of turnover, the leading companies are:

Bouygues	Fr 44,507,000
SGE	Fr 20,619,000
SAE	Fr 18,726,000
Spie Batignolles	Fr 17,876,000
Dumez	Fr 16,174,000

The regimented classification of goods and services in France applies just as much to contractors as it does to vegetables, and it is possible to consult the directory published by the Organisme professionel de qualification et de classification du bâtiment (OPQCB) on a regional basis to identify, for example, who are the 'four-star' plasterers in Toulon.

The industry has a broad expertise with no serious weaknesses and a particular strength in reinforced concrete structures and nuclear power installations.

State of the industry

The industry is buoyant and there is a good workload. The Paris region is currently the most active, and it has avoided the overheating experienced in London. It is still possible to secure an adequate list of tenderers for competitive bids on even the most complex of projects.

There is no serious shortage of skilled labour or materials. Costs, despite the increased volume, have not accelerated in the way they have in the UK. The annual increase in tender levels in the Paris region is running at 6 per cent and official cost indices, to which major contracts are revised, are running at 4.5 per cent. There is no difficulty in achieving competitive firm-price bids for schemes of up to eighteen months' duration. The current good workload will continue for the next two years; thereafter a downturn is expected, particularly in the private sector, which has been experiencing considerable growth in speculative property development over the last two years.

With the working population seeking greater environmental amenities and leisure facilities, there has been a strong growth of the new high technology industries in the provinces, especially in the southern conurbations such as Toulouse, Montpellier, Nice and Grenoble; this trend is likely to continue.

Structure

The contractors are members of the Fédération des Bâtiments; classified directories are available on a regional basis. All contractors have to be officially licensed and registered for the sector of work they execute, and under the Civil Code they have a legal liability for defects appearing within two years in respect of secondary trades, finishings and so on, and within ten years in respect of the structure and envelope.

Because of the legal status of the client in building contracts, the client usually takes a far more active role in the administration of projects than would be the case in the UK. Often the client appoints a client's agent. On small and medium-sized projects, the client usually appoints a lead consultant, rather than making individual direct appointments for architecture, structure, services and so on. The lead consultant is usually an architect for building projects and an engineer for civil engineering projects; the appointments carry a legal liability for ten years. On-site supervision of works is not always the responsibility of the design architect: quite often it is a separate architectural appointment or is included in the duties of the co-ordinator/pilot.

Cost control was, traditionally, the responsibility of the *vérificateur* in the architect's office, but there is a current trend to make an independent cost control appointment or to incorporate these responsibilities too in the duties of the project's co-ordinator/pilot.

Most projects in France are carried out by way of separate trades contracts, with the architect (or more often a co-ordinator/pilot) employed to manage the construction work. The employer contracts directly with the various trades contractors. This method has prevailed in France for many years, and has only recently been introduced in the UK under the title of 'construction management'. Unlike the UK counterpart, the French co-ordinator is generally not affiliated to any contracting organisation. Conventional general contracting is becoming more common on small projects and when turn-key projects are involved.

The design undertaken by the architect in France does not extend to detailed construction drawings. Accordingly, the contractors undertake considerable design work. Turn-key design-and-build contracts are not unusual, and the contractors readily accept unqualified responsibility for the design and construction. The group contractors or the main contractor warrant before entering into a contract that they have sufficient information from the client and the design team to carry out the project. The contract sum is, therefore, a true lump sum, which is only revised by means of a fluctuations formula in accordance with extensive officially published indices.

The client normally appoints a *bureau de contrôle* (quality control office). This consultant is responsible for overseeing the quality of design and the execution of the structure, façades, weatherproofing and technical services; the contractor is obliged at no cost to the client to comply with the requirements of the control office. On most projects – and certainly on all major projects – the client insures the decennial liability of the contractor. To effect the insurance, an unqualified certificate from the quality control office must be received as a pre-requisite of *réception* (practical completion of the works). The *réception* of the work is of legal significance as regards the rights and obligations of the contracting parties, and is concluded by an official document signed by both parties and by the consultants.

Design considerations

- The general codes operating are the French *normes*, DTU and CSTB, which are similar to British Standards but less extensive.

- Specified systems, products and materials are obliged to carry an agreement certificate.

- Though defined in the Civil Code, fire regulations are subject to the interpretation of the local Fire Officer.

Approvals

Prior to commencement of the works, the building project must receive a *permis de construire* (planning permission). This also embraces building regulation approval in the general sense. The particulars of the planning permission must be displayed at the site and any qualifications on the approval must be discharged in agreement with the local authority. Confirmation that the project has been constructed in accordance with the *permis de construire* and that all qualifications have been discharged is given by way of a certificate of conformity. This follows an official inspection which usually takes place several months after the project has been completed.

Adjoining owners must be consulted and their agreement obtained to any boundary party-wall issues prior to the execution of works.

Programme considerations

The pre-construction programme is usually determined by the period required for obtaining the construction permit. As in the UK, this varies according to the importance of the project. The shortest period in which a construction permit can be obtained is two months. The dossier to be submitted has to be signed by the client and by the architect. Because it embraces aspects of building regulation and planning, it is more extensive than a UK submission. The programme time for completion of the technical project and issue for tender can be as little as a few weeks because the construction permit dossier is so detailed. Compliance with the construction permit is usually an obligation imposed on the contractor.

Construction programmes are usually shorter than in the UK, and the contractor's approach is generally positive: having accepted the responsibilities by signing the contract, he has nobody to turn to.

Placing the building contract

The bidding of a construction project is based on specification and drawings, with the contractor's build-up of pricing only of relevance for the valuation of variations. Even though the project is on a separate-trades basis, it is common for the bidding of all trades to be done at one time. On major projects, the bidding is phased in accordance with the pilot's programme. The bidding and awarding of contracts tends to be less rigid than in the UK, and it is not unusual to receive bids from contractors who have not been invited. Invariably, a degree of negotiation takes place following receipt of bids; once finalised the contract is entered into on a lump-sum basis. On major projects, the building contract is usually drafted specifically for the project, there being no prevailing standard document. Minor projects tend to adopt a standard document (AFNOR PO3. 001). Variations to the contract generally arise only following a client's request; the variation is documented in price and programme and signed by both parties, the architect and pilot.

Properly managed, the client's financial commitment is accurately controlled throughout the project. On a separate-trades contract, the contractor enters into a *pro rata* account agreement. The *pro rata* account deals with the sundry site expenses which are charged to the contractors *pro rata* to the value of the works. Since all contractors are responsible for the account, the system encourages efficiency because contractors seek to minimise their liability. The account is normally managed by a small committee representing the contractors.

Cost comparison

Professional fees are significantly lower than in the UK. For a new build project of Fr 30 million (about £2.8 million) excluding VAT, the fees would be around 8 per cent for the architect and engineer and 3.5 per cent for the pilot (if it's a separate-trades contract).

Construction costs are also less than in the UK. For example, an air-conditioned speculative office building on the outskirts of Paris will cost in the region of only Fr 6,500 per square metre (about £56 per square foot) excluding VAT.

The retail market

Estimated value of retail sales	
1986 (Conseil National du Commerce)	Fr 1,335bn (£134.8bn equivalent)

Estimated volume of retail sales (1980 = 100)		
	1983	96.4
	1984	92.0
	1985	90.5
	1986	91.5
	1987	90.9

Estimated number of retail outlets	
1985 (Census)	547,170 total outlets
	193,030 food outlets
	353,140 non-food outlets
1986 (CNC)	209,400 total outlets
1987 (CNC)	686 hypermarkets
	6,316 supermarkets
	135 department stores
	10,000 non-food stores (DIY etc.)
	12,000 co-operative outlets
	700 franchisers
	30,000 franchisee outlets
	200 mail order firms

Shop hours	
	Mon. to Sat. – 08.30 to 12.30
	14.00 to 18.00
	Thur. to Sat. – late opening till
	19.30/21.00
	Many shops are closed
	Monday morning/all day.
	Many non-food superstores
	are open on Sundays.

VAT rates		
	Basic	2.1%
	Super reduced	5.5%
	Reduced	7%
	Standard	18.6%
	Higher rate	25%
	Luxury	25%

The French high street used to be dominated by small private traders who leased their units, and by large department stores which were, on the whole, developed and occupied by the operator. Shopping developed organically with little thought given to retailing in its own right. It was simply a peripheral activity of the central business district.

It used to be the case that retail use on the ground floor would not be included when calculating the plot ratio limits for a development site. Thus the majority of traditional office development would have shopping at ground-floor level, irrespective of the suitability of the position or the needs and demands of the consumers.

In the 1960s, the first shopping centres were developed. They consisted principally of a major supermarket with a limited amount of other shopping tacked on. By the late 1960s, plans were becoming increasingly ambitious, and in 1969, with the opening of Cap 3000 near Nice and Parly II near Versailles, France had its first multi-level controlled environment centres. The passing of the *Loi Royer* in 1973 slowed up new development, and the major developments since then have been in the new towns. The largest is Quatre Temps at La Défense, with over 100,000 square metres of shopping. Institutional interest in shopping centre development is now high following the Supreme Court's endorsement of turnover rents, effectively taking them outside the 1953 decree which pegs retail rents at very low levels.

Paris

Rue du faubourg St-Honoré

A very famous and very long street much favoured by *haute couture* fashion shops and jewellers, it runs from the junction of Avenue Friedland and Boulevard Haussmann through to the Rue Royale. Shop units vary in size from 50 to 200 square metres and some have retail space at first-floor level.

Traders represented in this street include Pierre Cardin, Yves Saint Laurent, Pierre Balmain, Ted Lapidus, Cartier, Guy Laroche, Hermès, Lanvin, Jaeger, Charles Jourdan and many other lesser known traders. The present full rental value of Fr 12,000 per square metres results in high premiums being paid. The current record premium of Fr 15 million was paid for a unit with 100 square metres at ground-floor level and 100 square metres at first floor, let at a rental of Fr 600,000 per annum. This was, however, somewhat exceptional and an average premium in Rue du faubourg St-Honoré would be between Fr 6 million and Fr 8 million.

Rue François Ier Recent retail development in this street (1988) has answered the exceptional demand from the market and has been endorsed by Société Cartier taking major representation there. This street now rivals Rue du faubourg St-Honoré and Avenue Montaigne, which it crosses. Rental values are similar to those in Rue du faubourg St-Honoré.

Avenue Montaigne One of the main shopping streets in the capital, the Avenue Montaigne combines top quality retailing with hotels and office blocks. A street designed for browsing, it includes Ungaro, Valentino, Cartier, Guy Laroche and Christian Dior.

Rue de la Paix/ The northern continuation of Place Vendôme, Rue de la Paix is a
Avenue de l'Opéra location favoured by jewellers and specialists in *objets d'art*. Avenue de l'Opéra is the established district for travel agents, airline companies and all travel-related retail organisations, and provides an interesting comparison with Piccadilly/Old Bond Street in London. Average rentals are between Fr 6,000 and 10,000 per square metre per annum.

Rue de Passy Out of the main thrust of downtown retailing, but rapidly growing in popularity, particularly among caterers and fast-food operators, Rue de Passy is also up-market in residential terms, with BC-BG (*bon chic – bon genre*) developments, especially near Muette. Rental values are between Fr 10,000 and Fr 13,000 per square metre.

Rue Tronchet Situated in the heart of Les Grands Magasins, behind the world-famous Fauchon, the Rue Tronchet is currently seeing the re-development of Aux Trois Quartiers to revive its retail fortunes. The interchanges of Boulevard Malesherbes (home of Burberrys), Place de la Madeleine, Rue Tronchet and Boulevard Haussmann provide a mecca of specialist and established retail names, rather like an up-market Oxford Street. Rental values of between Fr 8,000 and Fr 10,000 per square metre per annum reflect its market prominence.

The Left Bank The Left Bank provides a cornucopia of one-off retail businesses, with a predominantly specialist orientation. Costume jewellery, the arts, books, records, fashion from one extreme to the other, all abound in a district anchored additionally by its active night-time street life.

Specialisation is paramount, as evidenced by Boulevard St-Michel and its domination by the book trade. At its southern extremity La Tour Montparnasse, with its shopping and entertainment facilities, anchors the Rue du Rennes, home of FNAC and its head office.

The myriad of tiny streets surrounding the Beaux Arts is the stronghold of one-off retail specialists, who take advantage of both the local market and the tourist influx. Rue du Bac stands out as a growth area and as the western feeder route into the district.

Shopping centres

Parly II, Versailles   Parly II is located in one of the more attractive residential areas with a high-spend consumer profile, its extensive surface car-parking covers three sides of the centre, while visually the design is deferent to its surroundings. It is a two-level scheme, of which the 60,000 square metres first phase (early 1970s) is now being extended into a second phase. Ground level is the prime position, but the orientation of the escalators at the main entrances to the scheme re-inforces the twin level aspect by promoting ease of access to level two.

Parly II dedicates a major area to food to satisfy consumer demands for fresh food on a daily basis. An interesting aspect is the secondary use to which the main malls are put: it is not unusual to find an antiques market in full flow during weekly shopping hours. Of special note is the design feature of a bookshop running along the length of what would otherwise be a boring supermarket frontage. The accommodation in question takes up a space approximately twenty-two metres long but only a third of a metre wide!

As with most of the suburban schemes, there is no central theme to the design although further upgrading or refurbishment may address this in future. The mix of tenants ranges from established food (Auchan, Hediard) to new style service (express film processing) to quality fashion (Naf-Naf, Lynx, Cacharel and Celio).

Forum des Halles   The government of President Pompidou was marked by a number of events, not the least of which was the construction of the arts centre at Beaubourg. Still a major talking point in Paris, the area which once contained the food markets of Paris was razed to the ground. Out of it has grown a new public space and a three-level shopping centre, predominantly below ground. Beaubourg is a major tourist attraction and, as with Covent Garden in London, the spin-off in the surrounding streets has been remarkable. The forum development was constructed in the early 1980s, in three phases, and after a number of false starts is now a successful operation.

It is however a confusing scheme: it operates on a number of different levels, with poor directional signage. The mix includes all aspects of retail, with an emphasis on fashion, but with cinemas, exhibition space and numerous restaurants as well, there is always some new section to discover. The scheme houses both specialist and established retailers. It is also a focal point that attracted the likes of Habitat in the mid-1980s. Fashion names such as New Man, Daniel Hechter, Cacharel, Naf-Naf and Celio abound, and the scheme has found a vibrant and active market with the Parisian population.

Trends

Present legislation governing the fixing of retail rents even on renewal is resulting in a very imperfect market, in which the benefits of growth in the retail property market are being syphoned off in the form of large premiums to lessees rather than rental growth for investors. This will inevitably result in the continuation of inefficient retail trades in prime locations and a lack of new investment in French high streets. By contrast, a situation has now evolved whereby realistic variable rents can be charged in shopping centres and there will, therefore, be continuing investment in these at the expense of the high street.

The office market

The total stock of office space in Paris and the surrounding area is between 30 and 35 million square metres, of which central Paris accounts for 15 million square metres. About 7 million square metres of this are in the traditional central business district, the 8th *arrondissement*. La Défense currently has 2.5 million square metres, and a further 2.5 million square metres are due to come on the market between 1989 and 1991. The majority of these new developments have been forward funded by institutions, and the bulk of the major construction is to the west of Paris, where the major areas of activity are La Défense, Boulogne, Levallois-Perret, Courbevoie, Suresnes and Issy-les-Moulineaux.

Over the past few years the institutions have been quite happy to forward fund without pre-letting, and there are now plenty of buildings constructed and available to let. Even so, many companies would prefer to purchase their space by way of *crédit-bail* in view of the relatively low interest rates.

Tenants are principally service companies and financial companies. Until three years ago, a regulation prohibiting construction led to heavy demand and insufficient supply. This resulted in a doubling of rental levels over the past three years. Following a flood of new construction, there is now a good supply of new buildings coming to the market providing considerable choice for prospective tenants and purchasers; rents, too, have settled.

The trend is for major industrial and manufacturing companies to move to the outskirts of Paris, with only finance companies and service companies remaining in the central area.

Rental values

	Per square metre
Central Paris	Fr 3,000–4,500
La Défense	Fr 2,000–2,500
Levallois/Périphérique	Fr 1,500–2,200
New towns	Fr 750–900

Paris

The traditional prestige areas are still important for finance and service industries, but not for industrial companies. The best part of the traditional central business district is the golden triangle made up of the Avenue Montaigne, Avenue George V and the Champs-Elysées. In the middle of this triangle is the Rue François Ier which is currently considered to be the prime office location. All these streets are in the 8th *arrondissement* which contains most of the central business district apart from a small part which strays into the 16th *arrondissement* around Etoile. Rue François Ier has also become popular for upmarket shopping. Cartier have moved in from Place Vendôme to combine their head office activities with a Rue François Ier shop front.

The central business district has moved steadily westward from its traditional location in the Madeleine quarter. Many large French companies, particularly those in the manufacturing sector, have moved their headquarters to edge-of-town locations such as La Défense, and the space vacated in the central business district has been taken up by foreign companies seeking to expand. There is currently a stable supply-and-demand situation, with static rental levels both in the centre and at La Défense.

There has been a large increase in the supply of small office suites. Currently 200,000 square metres of space are available overall, against an annual absorption rate of 130,000 to 150,000 square metres. Stock will increase, but the market for top quality prestigious space with all modern facilities (such as raised floors) continues strongly and prices are continuing to rise. There is, therefore, to some extent, a two-tier market with top space commanding ever-increasing rents. Fr 4,000 per square metre has been achieved recently, although the average top prime rental is Fr 3,500 per square metre, while average quality space in the central business district is still available at Fr 2,500 per square metre.

La Défense

The vast office redevelopment at La Défense now amounts to 2.5 million square metres of office accommodation. La Défense is also the largest shopping centre in France. The complex was a government sponsored scheme started in the late 1960s to provide overspill space in response to the very limited supply of modern buildings in central Paris. In recent years it has become more successful than could have been envisaged, perhaps as a result of its excellent communication with central Paris by way of the Réseau Express Régional (RER).

Rentals in La Défense range from Fr 2,800 per square metre (the Grande Arche) to Fr 2,200 per square metre.

The rest of France

France's second city, Lyon, is the traditional heart of the textile industry and is now also a major centre for the chemical and phar-maceutical industries. France's third city is Marseille, where the port and docks activity plays an important role in distribution.

In terms of rental and capital values, there is very little variation throughout provincial France, with the exception of Nice or the very centre of Lyon, which are certainly more expensive. Elsewhere, office space is let, in general, at between Fr 600 and Fr 700 per square metre, with a variation of no more than Fr 100 between the central and peripheral locations.

New office development in the provinces will be forward funded by domestic institutions, even without a pre-let, but institutions will tend to look for a developer's guarantee and an initial yield of between 8.5 and 9.5 per cent.

Trends

While the market is at present quite strong, enjoying rental levels high by European standards, three factors are impacting upon the market:

- The penal registration tax on the transfer of second-hand property which, together with brokerage and notary fees, results in total transaction costs of more than 20 per cent. The use of trading companies (*marchands de biens*) and other devices to avoid or defer registration tax is now widespread and some reform in this area must be expected.

- There is presently an imbalance in the market – a significant supply of property to let and a significant volume of demand for buildings and condominiums for purchase. This is a result of the relatively low interest rates coupled with a doubling of rents over the past year, such that there is now rough parity between the cost of renting and the cost of a *crédit-bail* arrangement.

- The current lack of international institutional interest in investments outside the Paris area.

The industrial market

There is no heavy industry in the Paris area. Twenty or twenty-five years ago, the government decided to encourage heavy industry to relocate outside Paris. The traditional areas for heavy industry were to the north and east of Paris, where the aeroplane and car industries were located, and also to the south-east along the route of the Seine. Most of this industry moved either to the north of France or towards Lyon and Marseille, while the car industry moved to Brittany and the Seine valley to the west of Paris towards Rouen.

Between 1975 and 1982, these old industrial areas were in a state of major decline. Now they are being redeveloped with light industry and some limited high-tech property, together with social housing. Other new light industry centres have been created in the area around Paris, linked by the new ring road (the A86), which is presently under construction and now encircles almost 75 per cent of Paris. This new ring road is some 5 kilometres north of the Boulevard Périphérique on the north side, 8 kilometres from the Périphérique on the east side, and 12 kilometres from the Périphérique on the south side. It has not yet been completed as a result of resistance from the high quality residential areas to the west side of Paris.

Beyond this ring, another new motorway, 'La Francillienne', is under construction. This is due to be completed by 1998 and is designed to link the new towns of Marne-la-Vallée, Melun-Senart, Evry, Saint-Quentin-en-Yvelines, Cergy-Pontoise, as well as Charles de Gaulle airport at Roissy on the north-east side.

These new towns are playing an increasingly important role, because the new light industrial areas created around the A86 road have now been developed to a point where there is little or no land available for light industrial use. New businesses now need to expand in the new towns where land is owned by the local authorities and is designated (on a phased basis so that it is affordable) for particular uses including light industrial development. Transport links with the capital are excellent.

Most of these centres have been developed at the junction of the new circular motorway with the main arterial motorway serving the regions of France. Light industrial zones on the A86 are being redeveloped and replaced with high-tech developments and offices, particularly to the south-west of Paris in the Orsay region and in the north-east around Roissy and Paris-Nord.

Between 1970 and 1976 warehousing and distribution were developed within the light industrial zone around the new motorway. The lack of room for further expansion is a major problem as there is no more space for development of new warehousing or distribution centres between Paris and La Francillienne. The high cost of land makes it more valuable for other purposes. The two prime locations for warehousing and distribution have traditionally been in the A1 corridor to the north of Paris and the A6 corridor to the south and this is likely to remain so in the future, although the east site may be improved to some extent by the completion of La Francillienne and access to towns such as Marne-la-Vallée.

The shortage of space is likely to continue and industrial companies which require accommodation for their own occupation are left with little choice but to build for themselves as there is no significant speculative building of industrial units.

High-tech and office space is, however, built speculatively, sometimes with institutional forward funding. There is now substantial pressure on light industrial space, since developers have all followed the fashion of building high-tech space in order to command the higher rental levels. Some developers are now recognising that light industrial may be a less volatile market. The standard institutional specification for light industrial space provides for clear heights of between 6 metres and 7 metres.

In 1988 industrial rents in the Paris area rose around 10 per cent to between Fr 400 and Fr 500 per square metre. In contrast, high-tech premises currently rent for around Fr 600–800 per square metre, almost as much as offices in the outer suburbs. Modern industrial schemes in the new towns are let for around Fr 200–250 per square metre.

Greece

Geography

Land area	131,990 sq. km.
Population	9,980,000
Density	75 per sq. km.
Main cities	Population
Athens/Piraeus	3,010,000
Thessalonika (Salonica)	800,000
Patras	200,000
Larissa	140,000
Heraklion	120,000

Administratively, Greece is divided into fifty-one districts and ten geographical departments. The metropolitan region – including Athens, Piraeus, eastern and western Attica (the area surrounding Athens) – contains one third of the country's total population and is its administrative, financial and cultural centre. Much of Athens was redeveloped after the Second World War by private enterprise, with scant regard for town planning or the need for open space. As a result, the centre of the city is now choked – its infrastructure totally inadequate for a population three or four times the immediate post-war level. The lack of controls over land use, other than in respect of heavy industry, is unusual by northern European standards.

Historically, the town centre has been occupied by the professions, such as law and medicine. Now that the hospitals have moved out of the centre and the Law Courts are being relocated to the north of Leoforos Alexandras Street, there is a gradual shift of emphasis away from the city centre – a trend further encouraged by traffic and transportation difficulties and the level of pollution in central Athens. Much of the new development is taking place along Kifissias Avenue, in the north-east of the city, or along the road to Glifida, which runs south-east from Athens along the coast.

Although Piraeus, to the west of Athens, is also an important

GREECE

commercial centre, its principal activities are shipping and ship-building. Once again, the lack of planning controls, the volume of traffic and the effect of the tourist industry have a considerable impact on access and communications.

Transport and communications

Given Greece's historical association with the sea and the fact that, taking the islands into account, Greece's coastline is more than 15,000 kilometres long, it is no surprise to find so many large ports and harbours, including Piraeus, Thessalonika, Patras, Volos and Igoumenitsa (to the west of Yannina).

Shipbuilding and shipping (to Europe, the Middle East and the rest of the world) have long made an important contribution to the Greek economy and, in 1986, the Greek merchant marine comprised 2,138 vessels of over 100 gross tons, approximately 60 per cent of which were freighters, 37 per cent tankers and 2 per cent passenger ships and other vessels.

There is a comprehensive internal air network, with thirty-two airports, each of them linked to Athens. Fifty-four international airlines operate into Greece, with flying times to other European centres between two and four hours (London is three-and-a-half hours), New York eight hours away and Tokyo seventeen hours.

Greece has a road network of 40,000 kilometres, and had two million registered vehicles in 1986, including 1.35 million passenger cars. Almost half of the national total of vehicles are located in Greater Athens, where traffic congestion is so bad that, in 1982, legislation was introduced which decreed that only cars with odd number registrations could enter the city centre on half the days of the week, and only those with even numbers could enter on the other days. Just over a year ago, the law was extended to include taxis and despite a long strike by the drivers, the restriction still applies. Visitors wishing to reach the centre must now find a taxi with the appropriate registration plate, and a favourite joke among Athenians is to tell visitors that the government will next extend the law to cover buses!

The 2,577-kilometre-long national rail network links all the major urban centres and also connects with western and eastern Europe by way of Yugoslavia and Bulgaria.

General economic

The 1979 oil crisis revealed the fragile nature of the country's economic infrastructure and forced it to cope simultaneously with inflation, current account deficits, internal deficits in the public sector and the accumulated deficits of many large industrial units.

The Socialist (Centre Left) government sought, during the 1980s, to resolve these problems within the context of a political decision not to create social injustice, to extend the social services and not to disturb the country's defence capability. Its dual strategy consisted of a two-year 'Stabilisation Programme', which set specific targets for the price index, current account deficit and borrowing requirements as a percentage of GNP, together with five-year plans designed to ensure economic development in ways that would avoid the distortions and disproportions of the past. Throughout the 1980s, the government attempted to overcome structural and circumstantial problems, in addition to the specific difficulties created by the conditions arising from the country's full membership of the EC as of January 1981.

The General Election of 1989 did not produce a clear victory for either the New Democracy Party (Centre Right) or the Left Coalition. After lengthy negotiations, a three-month interim government was installed, under the leadership of Mr Tzannetakis, which combined the New Democracy Party and the Left Coalition, and declared itself committed to 'upgrading political life, taming public morals and consolidating democracy'.

Industry

Agriculture accounts for 17 per cent of the country's GNP and employs 29 per cent of the working population, with exported foodstuffs accounting for 25 per cent of the total value of Greek exports. In the manufacturing sector, textiles, clothing and footwear are among the most important items, supported by beverages, oil derivatives, chemicals, carpets, cement, glass and plastic products, yarns, socks and stockings.

With the number of foreign visitors reaching 7.2 million in 1986, tourism continues to be an important part of the Greek economy, accounting for almost 30 per cent of its invisible earnings. The government helps to promote tourism by providing investment incentives for hotel development and construction.

The international shipping industry's recovery from the recession of recent years will be of substantial benefit to Greece since shipping is a major source of foreign currency, contributing approximately 15 per cent of all invisible earnings. The government continues to provide special incentives for the development of shipping activities.

Forms of tenure

Property is held in fee simple and a large proportion of commercial property, including individual shop units and small office suites, is purchased outright. Conveyance of property is by way of a sale contract, which must be notarised. The notary will require a certificate from the municipality confirming that no local taxes are outstanding in relation to the property, as well as confirmation from the revenue department that no inheritance or donation duty is outstanding. If the selling price exceeds Dr 5 million, there must be a member of the Athens' Bar Association present, whose charge will be 1 per cent of the value up to Dr 5 million and 0.5 per cent beyond that level. Transfer tax is set at 11 per cent of the value up to Dr 4 million and 13 per cent beyond that.

A building, including the land, may be owned in its entirety by one organisation or it may be split up and owned by a number of individuals or organisations. The responsibilities, liabilities and costs in respect of the owner of each part are clearly identified in a 'constitution agreement' – a public document available for inspection at any one of a number of registers to be found in various locations (usually one or more in each city or town). The agreement will state clearly the percentage interest that each individual owner has in the overall value of the land upon which the property stands and in any adjoining land included in the overall ownership. This interest in the overall *value* does not indicate outright ownership of a particular percentage of the site itself. When ownership of part of a building changes, the new owner may not make any alteration to the terms of the agreement, except with the support of a percentage of the other owners – the actual percentage figure (usually between 75 per cent and 100 per cent) being specified in the agreement itself.

A similar constitution agreement exists when the property is owned solely by one party, but in this case when that party's interest in the property is sold, the new owner may change any terms in the agreement.

The Ministry of Finance provides lists indicating the objective value for any building, floor or part of a floor of any commercial building in Greece. Though similar to the gross value concept of the rating system in the UK, the lists should only be taken as a guide, since the actual prices achieved in private treaty sales are usually far higher than those contained in the lists. Updated at the end of 1988, the system had been introduced a few years earlier to minimise tax evasion – the transfer tax would be due at the government's discretion on the assessed value, rather than on the contract price.

Leases

Under Greek law, the minimum period for a residential or commercial lease is one year, although most leases are granted for three or five years. Rental levels are generally linked to the cost-of-living index established by the Ministry of Finance.

Leases are rarely assigned, since the landlord's consent is required for such assignment and he or she is free to seek, for such approval, a sum equal to the premium value. Consequently, the tenant will usually surrender interest to the landlord, leaving the landlord free to negotiate the best price possible for a new letting in the open market on the rack rental basis.

Retail leases

The retail lease provides security of tenure and the tenant cannot be evicted except under very particular circumstances, most commonly where the owner can demonstrate that the space is required for his or her own occupation.

In the absence of any other agreement, rents are reviewed every two years. If the landlord and tenant fail to agree, they may apply to the courts, although rental assessments made by the courts tend to be lower than the true market value.

Not surprisingly, leasing is unpopular with Greek investors and developers, and most shop units and office suites are offered for outright sale.

Financial

There are approximately fifty banks and financial institutions operating in the country, nineteen of them Greek.

The Bank of Greece is at the centre of the banking system, controlling the issue of bank notes, foreign exchange and credit policy and giving approval to other banks to lend money on particular projects. Until the Spring of 1989, the Bank of Greece did not permit loans to be granted for the development of residential, office and retail property. However, the political and practical expediency of this restraint was weakening, and dollar borrowing with drachma repayment is now permitted.

A number of state-controlled investment banks have been established to provide long-term funding for particular projects, either through straight lending or through equity participation:

- ETBA (the Hellenic industrial development bank), founded in 1964 by a merger of the Industrial Development Agency (responsible for financing economic development) and the agency of tourist credit. Its main objective is to assist with industrial, shipping and tourist-related projects.

- ETEBA, the national investment bank for industrial development, founded in 1963, has as its primary task to promote industrial and industry-related operations.

- The investment bank, SA, was founded in 1962 with a number of aims: the granting of long-term loans for productive investments, equity participation in existing companies and the underwriting of new issues.

Among other financial institutions, the most notable are the Agricultural Bank of Greece, the National Mortgage Bank of Greece and the Personal Savings Bank.

Taxation

Under Greek law, every individual or body, irrespective of nationality, domicile or the location of its registered office, is liable to pay tax on 1 January each year on the value of property held in Greece. After making deductions for any approved loan, as well as an allowance of Dr 40 million for legal entities, the balance of the value of the property is taxed at the rate of 1.5 per cent for legal entities and on a sliding scale between 0.5 per cent and 2 per cent for individuals.

Stamp duty

An indirect tax levied on transactions made in writing, stamp duty is charged in two ways:

- Variable duties computed as a percentage of the value stated in the document

- Fixed duties irrespective of the value stated in the document

Following the application of VAT in Greece in January 1987, the provisions concerning the levying of stamp duty on all transactions subject to VAT were repealed. However, stamp duty is still payable in respect of the exchange of real estate at the rate of 11 per cent for the first Dr 4 million and 13 per cent thereafter.

Grant aid and investment incentives

Investment incentives are available in respect of what is termed 'productive investment'. This includes the construction, extension and modernisation of industrial premises, tourist apartments and hotel facilities; the purchase or use by their owner for productive purposes of manufacturing, small industrial, hotel or auxiliary premises which have not been used during at least the two preceding years; and most construction related to tourism. The purchase of land or agricultural plots is not classified as a productive investment.

The details of the provisions are complex and interested parties would be advised to seek further information from the Greek Consulate, but, briefly, there are five types of aid for productive investments: investment grants, reduced tax-rates on profit, interest subsidies, tax allowances and increased depreciation rates. The prospective investor may select either of two mutually exclusive combinations: grant, reduced tax-rate, subsidy and increased depreciation rates; or tax allowances and increased depreciation rates. The ideal combination will depend on the nature and size of the investment, the area in which it is located and so on.

Grants are available up to a limit of Dr 1,600 million; beyond that, the government will require equity participation in the project equal to the value of any additional aid. The government has also designated development zones, where additional aid is available.

Planning

With no coherent legislation governing land use in Greece, the consequences – especially in Athens – are clear to see. Although industrial development is prohibited in certain areas, it is generally the case that a landowner may develop a site for whatever purpose he chooses and construct a building to any design, subject only to satisfying the requirements of the Ministry of Public Works.

In theory, consent may be refused on technical grounds (e.g. inadequate or inefficient drainage, unsafe electrical installations, lack of structural safety), for aesthetic reasons (e.g. where a building design is grossly inappropriate to the surrounding area) or (to a limited extent) on environmental grounds: environmental grounds would, for instance, prevent the building of a slaughterhouse in a residential area but *not* the construction of commercial premises or workshops.

The only significant form of control is plot ratio. Athens, for instance, is divided into sectors each of which is allocated its own ratio. In central areas this may be as high as 4:1, while at the city boundaries it may be as low as 1:0.8.

There are, however, very strict regulations throughout Greece and all the islands under its control regarding the preservation of antiquities. Any object of antiquity found during the course of excavation or construction must be reported to the Ministry of Culture. Following notification, all work on the site must cease indefinitely until it has been inspected by the national architectural service. If it is decided that no further development should be allowed, then compensation is paid. The state has no obligation to purchase the site, although the owner is permitted to donate it to the state free of charge! Failure to report any discovery can result in a fine or prison sentence and, irrespective of the stage of development, demolition of the building at the owner's or developer's expense in order that the site can be properly assessed. In view of the strictness of these regulations, it is hardly surprising that large areas of the country remain undeveloped.

Building regulations are very much concerned with the risk of earthquake and all new developments are required to anticipate the need to withstand such an event.

Brokerage

Of the very large number of real estate brokers in Greece, the majority are private individuals undertaking a limited amount of business within a very small area. Though highly negotiable, fees are generally between 3 and 5 per cent of the value of the transaction.

Conveyancing

The system of conveyancing in Greece is relatively straightforward: for a larger transaction, both sides are represented by a lawyer and the sale contract, when prepared and agreed, is executed before a notary and entered in the Land Register. The lawyer's fees are between 1 and 1.5 per cent of the value of the transaction.

Capital projects

The government has announced five major capital projects, each of which is likely to proceed irrespective of a change in the political climate following the general election.

- The Metro – Two new lines are proposed to add to the one which currently runs from Piraeus to Kifissia, north of Athens. Implementation of a further phase running to the airport will depend on whether or not Athens is chosen for the 1996 Olympic Games.

- Spata Airport – If Athens is selected for the Olympic Games, work will proceed rapidly on the development of this new airport as a replacement for the urban airport to the south-east of the centre of Athens. The site was selected many years ago, but work on the project was frozen in 1985, despite the dangerous proximity of the present international airport to the city centre.

- The Rio-Anterio project – Most of the seaborne goods brought to and from Greece pass through Patras, the principal commercial port on the Peloponisos Island. But from here they have to be taken some distance to the east by road to the Corinth Bridge before passing into the main part of Greece itself. A new bridge is proposed, just north of Patras.

- The Acheloos River diversion – It is proposed to divert this river in the north-west of Greece, bringing it through a mountain range in order to service the interior – a major agricultural plain currently subject to occasional drought conditions. Though being funded largely by the EC, political opinion in Brussels is against the project as it will significantly enhance Greek agricultural output in competition with Italy, Spain, Portugal and France.

- Transportation projects – the main road from the north to the south of Greece is to be upgraded to full motorway standard and 90 per cent of the present railway system is to be electrified.

The construction industry

Industry capacity

A limited domestic market means that, by comparison with other European countries, building contractors are small to medium-sized. No national classification exists, although there is a general qualification procedure applying to public works.

General state of the industry

The problems of the Middle East and a downturn in domestic demand led to a serious recession in the early 1980s. There has, however, been an increase in construction turnover during 1988–9 and the market is expected to maintain a good level of activity in the near future.

Considerable investment in the country's infrastructure is planned, although how it will be financed is still uncertain. If Athens is selected as the venue for the 1996 Olympic Games, the industry will clearly see a major increase in activity.

Structure of the industry

The design of private-sector projects is under the control of a lead consultant, while public projects must be supervised by a licensed engineer. The supervising engineer's role is equivalent to that of a Director of Works, with responsibility for the accountancy as well as for quality control. There are no independent quality control offices. Main contractors only face a qualification procedure in the case of public works.

Design considerations

The only mandatory legislation is that requiring a building permit to be obtained before construction work begins.

Programme considerations

There is no fixed timescale for obtaining the necessary building licence. The construction programme can be equally unpredictable.

Placing the building contract

In the private sector, there are no nationally adopted procedures for the placing of the building contract. Projects are usually bid as a lump sum on the basis of specification and drawings.

In the public sector, certain set rules apply nationally. Building projects are usually bid on the basis of drawings, specification and schedules of quantities. Civil engineering tenders are often expressed as percentage adjustments to rates proposed by the client authority. Fluctuations are calculated in accordance with nationally published indices.

Foundation and siteworks are usually remeasured by the supervising engineer and valued on the basis of the contract rates.

Cost comparison

The level of professional fees in Greece is lower than in the UK. For a new build project of Dr 800 million excluding VAT (about £3 million), the fees for architects and engineers would be around 5 per cent.

Construction costs are also lower than in the UK. An air-conditioned speculative office building on the outskirts of Athens, for example, will only cost around Dr 100,000 per square metre (about £35 per square foot).

The retail market

Estimated value of retail sales		
1984	Dr 1,383bn	(£6.9bn equivalent)
1986	Dr 1,470bn	(£7.9bn equivalent)

Estimated volume of retail sales (1980 = 100)		
	1983	92.2
	1984	96.2
	1985	93.8
	1986	91.3
	1987	96.2

Estimated number of retail outlets	
1984 (Census)	56,800 total outlets
	29,650 food outlets
	27,750 non-food outlets
1987 (Trofima)	370,000 total outlets
	87,000 food outlets
	283,000 non-food outlets
	1,200 super/hypermarkets

Shop hours		
	Mon., Wed., Sat.	– 8.00 to 15.00
	Tue., Thu., Fri.	– 8.00 to 14.00
		and 17.30 to 20.30
		No Sunday trading

VAT rates		
	Lower	6%
	Standard	18%
	Higher	36%

Source: Corporate Intelligence Research Publications Ltd

A number of factors contribute to the lack of sophistication in the Greek retail market. The government's anti-inflationary policy since the late 1970s has produced a highly restricted credit policy. Until the beginning of 1989, trading companies were not allowed to borrow in order to purchase stock.

Although the method of calculating net taxable income is extraordinarily complex, in simple terms the tax rates rise to a ceiling of 63 per cent. Import taxes on goods vary widely: from 200 per cent on electrical goods and the average foreign car to 400 per cent on a luxury car such as a Jaguar. The effect on retail prices is dramatic, with a small Ferguson portable television, for instance, retailing at Dr 314,700 (£1,200).

To this background of high taxation and credit squeeze must be added the lack of planning control and the poorly defined shopping areas. As a result of the appalling traffic congestion, the paucity of parking facilities and the prohibition on half the potential customers against bringing their cars into the central area on any one day, the traditional shopping areas in the centre of Athens have declined in importance and have been replaced by facilities situated in the upmarket suburbs, particularly Kifissia and Glifada. Unfortunately, the lack of effective planning control has led to a larger number of small shopping developments being constructed on the fringes of the city, generally with very little success.

Central Athens

Kolonaki

To the north of Kolonaki Square, a network of small streets is filled with small boutiques and shops, typically with frontages up to 4 metres and depths no more than 10 metres. The narrow streets rising up the hill are very busy with traffic and parked cars; only one – the Voukourestiou – has been pedestrianised. Among the jewellers, fashion shops and patisseries, very few international traders can be found, although Sanderson (the British interior design and wallpaper group), Bang & Olufsen, Pierre Cardin and Benetton have taken units.

Ermou

Central Athens' other principal shopping area is Ermou, a street running towards Syntagma Square, to the west of Kolonaki, close to the Plaka – the city's ancient centre – and almost in the shadow of the Parthenon. It is a rather claustrophobic two-lane, one-way street, with buildings rising to six or seven storeys on both sides, and contains a considerable variety of unit size, although the average single unit has a 6 metre frontage and a depth of between 20 and 30 metres. The traders are mostly Greek, although there is quite a large Mothercare unit and – unusually for Greece – a small department store (Diamanth) with some 5,000–6,000 square metres of retail space on four or five floors. Stefanel, Bambino and Rosenthal Studiohaus are also to be found at the Syntagma Square end of the street.

Suburban Athens

Kifissia

The most prestigious of Athens' suburbs, Kifissia is built on a hill, some fifteen kilometres to the north-east of the city centre. The small shopping centre built here about twenty years ago, and now providing approximately sixty shop units, was the first of its kind in Athens. The three two-storey blocks set in a square are linked by walkways at first-floor level.

Although it has no international traders, this centre trades well because of its location in the very heart of the best Athenian suburb – one where residential property prices rival those almost anywhere in

Europe, with apartments selling at Dr 26,225,000 (£100,000) and 1,000 square metre building plots for villas fetching Dr 26,225,000–31,470,000 (£100,000–120,000).

Kifissia's success has prompted several imitations along the main arterial road linking the suburb with the city centre (Kifissia Avenue). Three such centres have been built, each offering between twenty and thirty units and, despite their poor trading results, two more are under construction. The most obvious reasons for their failure are the absence of car parking facilities within or near the centres themselves, the lack of local catchment and possibly problems with deliveries. To succeed in such a location, a shopping centre probably needs to be on a larger scale.

One centre currently under construction – the Cosmos Centre – is providing underground parking on six levels and 10,500 square metres of retail space arranged on eight floors. As in all the other schemes, the units are offered for sale, not for lease; prices in the Cosmos range from Dr 262,250–1,049,000 (£1,000–£4,000) per square metre.

Glifada

Overlooking the Aegean, Glifada is Athens' second most favoured residential area. It has a pleasant high street a little way inland with a variety of shop units and three small shopping centres. (A fourth – the Eurocentre – is currently under construction.)

The largest of the three small centres, the Galleria, contains thirty-seven shop units, most of them occupied by Greek traders but with some franchised Italian fashion shops, including Benetton, Valentino and Uomo. It consists of three levels, built on galleries around a cramped central atrium, linked by the seemingly obligatory panoramic wall-climber lift; the upper levels, however, trade poorly. Servicing provision is inadequate and the lift doubles as a service lift from the small basement car park, even though there is insufficient headroom on the ramp for even a large van.

Edge of town

There has been some piecemeal development on the periphery of Athens, including hypermarkets, car showrooms, furniture showrooms and so on. Prisunic Marinopolous, a joint venture between the French group and the Greek supermarket chain, has a number of units in and around Athens, including two new outlets: one on the road serving the airport's east terminal and close to the American Air Force base, the other overlooking the leisure harbour at Piraeus, which is set apart from the port's commercial and ferry harbour.

The office market

With the hospitals and law courts moving out of congested central Athens, its historical association with the medical and legal professions is drawing to a close. The future for the principal central streets such as Venizelou looks bleak, particularly as the custom of selling office space on a condominium basis could make any wholesale redevelopment or refurbishment very difficult.

Meanwhile, in the area to which the courts are relocating – to the north of Leoforos Alexandros on the north side of the city, immediately to the east of Pedion Areos Park – demand for offices is increasing.

New office development along the main arterial routes (Kifissia Avenue to the north-east and Glifada Road to the south-east and out towards the airport) is almost invariably developed by owner-occupiers.

Taxation and the financial structure discourages the speculative development of office space.

The industrial market

As part of its emphasis on the decentralisation of industry, the Greek government has established industrial estates with facilities specially designed to suit the needs of modern industrial units and also with substantial financial incentives. Each industrial estate offers a complete road network, water and power supply, sewerage, telephone lines and a waste water treatment unit. Units operating on these estate are also served by banks, while first-aid stations and other facilities are provided on site.

Companies involved in manufacturing, craft industries, ship-building and activities ancillary to agriculture are eligible to establish within these industrial estates, and various incentives are provided, including discount on the land value, permission for 60 per cent site coverage and grant aid. Already some 500 manufacturing and small craft industrial operations have moved into these estates.

The following nineteen sites are now operating in the investment areas under Development Law 1262/82:

Area A: Thessaloniki
Area B: Patras, Heraklion, Volos, Larisa
Area C: Kavala, Drama, Serres, Ioannina, Preveza, Lamia, Tripolis
Area D: Komotini, Xanthi, Kilkis, Florina, Alexandroupolis,
           Kalamata, Edessa

Italy

Geography

Land area	301,230 sq. km.
Population	57,450,000
Density	191 per sq. km.
Main cities	Population
Rome	2,826,000
Milan	1,515,000
Naples	1,206,000
Turin	1,035,000
Genoa	736,000
Palermo	720,000

Italy is a long and, for the most part, mountainous peninsula which extends south-east for about 700 kilometres from the Alps to the Mediterranean and includes the islands of Sicily and Sardinia. Within mainland Italy, there are two independent states: the Vatican City, in Rome, and the Republic of San Marino, the oldest state in Europe, situated about 24 kilometres inland from Rimini on the Adriatic coast. The country is made up of twenty regions and is divided for purposes of local government into ninety-five provinces. Certain powers are further delegated to the authorities of each municipality within each province.

Transport and communications

The country has some 30,000 kilometres of roads and its motorway system is recognised as being one of the best in the world. It carries some 70 per cent of the country's total freight traffic and 66 per cent of its passenger traffic. At the end of 1986, 5,337 kilometres of the toll motorway system were in use with a further 800 kilometres under construction.

ITALY

SWITZERLAND

AUSTRIA

Trento

Udine

Varese
Como
Bergamo
Biella
Treviso
Vicenza
Trieste
Novara
Milan
Brescia
Verona
Padua
Turin
Cremona
Mantua
Venice
Piacenza
Alessandria
Parma
Ferrara
FRANCE
Reggio
Modena
Bologna
Genoa
Ravenna
Savona
La Spezia
Forli
Rimini
YUGOSLAVIA
Pistoia
Prato
Pesaro
Ligurian Sea
Lucca
Pisa
Florence
Livorno
Ancona
Sienna
Arezzo
Adriatic Sea
Perugia
Elba
CORSICA
(to France)
Terni
L'Aquila
Pescara
ALBANIA
ROME
Pomezia
Frosinone
Aprilia
Latina
Campobasso
Foggia
Barletta
Caserta
Bari
Naples
SARDINIA
(to Italy)
Olbia
Sassari
Tyrrhenian Sea
Salerno
Potenza
Brindisi
Taranto
Lecce
Oristano
Arbatax
Porto Veseme
CAGLIARI
Corfu
Cosenza
Ionian Sea
Catanzaro
Messina
Trapani
PALERMO
Reggio Calabria
Marsala
Catania
SICILY
Agrigento
Caltanissetta
Caltagirone
Syracuse
Ragusa

International boundary ....
Road ....
Railway ....
International Airport ....

0 20 40 60 80 100 120 miles
0 40 80 120 160 200 kms

Department of Trade and Industry CDO 6928, 1988

There is also an extensive rail network (19,726 kilometres at the end of 1985), 80 per cent of which is owned by the state, while the remainder is privately owned.

The Italian merchant marine totals more than 8 million gross tons and its principal routes are in the Mediterranean, to North America and to Australia. The main sea ports are Genoa, Naples, Venice and Trieste. There are car and passenger ferry services to Corsica and Sardinia as well as to Yugoslavia and Greece.

The state airline, Alitalia, operates a wide network of domestic and international services. From the airports at Rome and Milan both Alitalia and foreign airlines provide excellent services to all parts of the world.

General economic

Apart from the UK, Italy suffered more seriously from inflation after the oil crisis of 1973–4 than any other member of the Community. The crisis had a major impact on the country's balance of payments and severely restricted exports.

The mid-1970s saw a turbulent period of rapid expansion in the country's industrial base, together with a constant round of economic crises and problems with the balance of payments, but the first half of the 1980s brought greater confidence and a considerable recovery in the private sector. Small and medium-sized companies were notable for their ability to adapt and survive in difficult circumstances, and by the end of the 1970s such companies in northern and central Italy were recognised as an important part of the economy, having made as significant a contribution as their larger counterparts.

During the 1980s, the government has attempted to tackle its economic problems, fighting against devaluation and adopting a monetary policy which included a programme of wage indexation, intervention in wage negotiations with the trade unions and a strong attack on the black economy.

In 1988, the Italian economy grew at a very satisfactory rate: GDP is 3.6 per cent up on 1987. Private consumption (up by 4 per cent) and investment (up by 8 per cent) have been the driving forces of domestic demand. Inflation is stable at around 5 per cent. A major cause of concern, however, is the huge public deficit, which has reached over 80 per cent GDP.

Although Italy still suffers from political instability, substantial public debt and rather cumbersome public industries, there is a new air of confidence based on a general acceptance of the market economy and of capitalism. The industrial giants, such as Pirelli, Fiat and Olivetti, have become much leaner and more efficient, and the contribution made by small and medium-sized companies has been recognised by the government. (Almost 60 per cent of all employment in Italy is provided by companies with fewer than 100 staff; such firms now account for 26 per cent of total manufacturing sector exports.)

Industry

Historically, around a third of all labour in Italy was engaged in agriculture. Although, as in the rest of Europe, the numbers have declined rapidly to an estimated 10 per cent of the total employed population, there is still some way to go before Italy is in line with the European average. Both manufacturing and construction industries have also decreased significantly in terms of employment and output.

In January 1988, unemployment had reached 12.4 per cent, having increased at the rate of 1 per cent per annum in the three years previous. Of more than 3 million uncmployed, 71 per cent are between the ages of 14 and 29. However, small firms in the northern and central parts of Italy have gone against the general trend and maintained or even increased employment. A powerful lobby of small business associations and small local banks has promoted their interests and been instrumental in the passage of a law, in 1987, designed to provide easier access to finance for small firms, as well as extra aid to industry in certain geographical areas.

Apart from Fiat (the largest), Olivetti, Pirelli, Montedison and Ferruzzi, there are relatively few large private companies in Italy. The other major indigenous organisations are the state holding companies ENI (Ente Nazionale Idrocarburi), IRI (Istituto per la Ricostruzione Industriale) and EFIM (Ente Finanziamento Industria Manifatturiera).

The level of direct investment by foreign private firms has, until recently, been lower than in most of western Europe, although it is now increasing rapidly. One of the most important foreign multinationals manufacturing in Italy is ITT, which is controlled by GEC.

Forms of tenure

Under Italian law, real property can be transferred by the execution of a notarial deed before a public notary or by the execution of a sale/

purchase contract, the signatures of which must be certified by a public authority. In order for a sale/purchase contract to be fully effective in relation to third parties, it must be registered with the relevant land register and a registration tax equal to 8 per cent of the property's market value, plus 2 per cent tax, must be paid.

Leases

The minimum period for a commercial lease is six years and, even if the parties seek to agree a shorter duration or do not stipulate any specific duration, the lease contract will still be valid for six years. (In the case of hotel buildings, the commercial lease may not be for less than nine years.) The only exemption covers temporary commercial activities.

In all cases, the lease contract has to be registered within twenty days of execution, and a registration tax is payable equal to 2 per cent of the value of the property. The parties can agree that the lessee will be able to terminate the contract by giving the lessor six months' notice. At the expiration of the first six-year period, the commercial lease is automatically extended for a further six years at the same rental level, unless either of the parties has notified the other of its intention to terminate the contract. The lessor may, however, terminate the contract at the end of the first six-year period if:

- He or she wishes to use the property for their own commercial activity.

- He or she intends to demolish the property in order to rebuild or restore it. (In this case, the lessor must possess a valid licence to undertake the work as issued by the competent authority.)

- He or she is obliged to restore the property in compliance with orders issued by the town authority.

Whenever the lease contract is terminated for any reason other than the default of the lessee or by the lessee giving notice to quit, the lessee normally has the right to compensation based on the rent payable and varying according to the type of activity carried out in the property.

Rent reviews

Rent reviews are not permitted within the first three years of the lease, but may occur every two years thereafter. However, the rent increase may not exceed 75 per cent of the annual increase in the retail price index (ISTAT Index).

Taxation

Corporate income tax

Rental income		46% (combined national and local)
Realised gains	Rate	36%
	Basis	Proceeds over cost
	Indexation relief	No
Relief for rentals		Yes
Relief for capital expenditure	Land	3% p.a.
	Factories	3% p.a.
	Warehouses	3% p.a.
	Offices	3% p.a.
	Special rates	Light buildings, sheds	10% p.a.

VAT

Land	19% (exempt for land which may be used for buildings)
New buildings	19%
Old buildings	19%
Construction services	19%
Professional fees	18%

Transfer taxes

Transfer tax	8%

Other national/federal taxes

Transcription and cadastral tax	2%

Local taxes

Taxes on the increase in value of land located in Italy levied every 10 years (if not directly used for business purposes) or when sold	Vary from 3% to 30%

Grant aid and investment incentives

Since 1950, the government has been attempting to use tax and other investment incentives to attract new industrial enterprises to the southern part of Italy (the *mezzogiorno*). This area consists of the provinces to the south of Rome, Sicily, Sardinia and certain small islands, as well as designated zones in the northern and central parts of the country. Non-tax incentives include loans at low rates of interest, outright grants towards capital investment and rebates on social contributions. These benefits are available to all who qualify, whether Italian or foreign.

In the highly developed northern regions, incentives for new investments consist of low interest loans to small and medium-sized firms.

Planning regulations

Italy has a multi-tiered and highly bureaucratic planning system. The *regioni* (regional governments) have the power to lay down planning laws. According to the constitution, these laws must remain within the fundamental principles established by central government, but in practice the central government has failed to enact any legislation aimed at defining these principles. As a result, the *regioni* have considerable discretion.

The basis of the planning system remains the Act of 1942, which provides for the preparation of general urban development schemes (*piani regolatori generali*). Each of these schemes covers an entire commune, defining the infrastructure, land use, development areas, public areas and areas of historic, environmental or scenic importance.

A general urban development scheme is implemented through a detailed planning scheme (*piano regolatore particolareggiato*), which deals with land use on a plot-by-plot basis. Previously, all planning applications were dealt with under the same procedure and every development required a building licence (*licenza edilizia*). The building licence has now been replaced by a *concessione*, and any activity causing an alteration to the agreed urban development or land use of the commune's territory requires a *concessione* provided by the Mayor. Certain minor works have been excluded from this provision, such as the maintenance, restoration and preservation of buildings for which authorisation (*autorizzazione*) is already required.

The *concessione* deals not only with land use but also with regulations on hygiene and sanitary features. Any application which conforms to the general planning scheme and to the development by-laws cannot be refused. However, the granting of the *concessione* is subject to payment to the commune of a tax in proportion to the cost of construction and of infrastructure works. The *autorizzazione*, by contrast, is free. The other significant difference between the two types of consent is that the *autorizzazione* benefits from the rule of *silenzio-assenso*, whereby the commune's failure to respond within ninety days of the application is deemed to signify assent. With the *concessione*, the commune's failure to respond within the same ninety-day period is taken as a refusal.

An appeal may be brought against either form of consent by the owners of other land in the area or by anyone who considers that they will be injuriously affected by the proposed development. In the first instance, the appeal is brought before the Tribunale Amministrativo Regionale (regional tribunal), whose judgement may subsequently be challenged on further appeal to the Consiglio di Stato (national court).

Both forms of consent are valid for a limited period.

Brokerage

Real-estate brokers must obtain an annually renewable licence from the local Chamber of Commerce. Apart from this, no other regulation exists, although the Federazione Italiana Mediatori e Agenti d'Affari (FIMAA) is considering the introduction of a compulsory examination. Although fees are not regulated, they are usually between 3 and 5 per cent for sales and one month's rent for letting.

The construction industry

Capacity

The Italian construction industry has a broad experience of the international market and, in terms of capacity, its domestic market ranks third in Europe (behind West Germany and France). The industry has the highest proportion of government-sponsored projects in Europe.

In terms of turnover, the leading companies are:

Fiatimpresit	L 950,000 million
Cogefar	L 770,000 million
Impreglio	L 653,000 million
Astaldi	L 506,000 million
Condotte	L 504,000 million

Italian construction companies are registered nationally; the register gives the type and financial size of project which the company is capable of handling. The status provided in the register is also used as a qualification for public works.

General state of the industry

The industry has seen slow growth in recent years and, although the market varies from region to region, there has been no significant rise in tender levels (as has happened in the UK). With major public investment programmes now committed, the indications are, however, that growth will continue. Private investment is highest in the north of Italy, where the majority of Italian manufacturing and commercial industry is located. The availability of labour, materials and general resources is not a problem.

Structure of the industry

The lead consultant on a building project is usually the architect; in civil works, the engineer has a similar responsibility. The scope of the design duties of the consultants is very similar to that in most other European countries – the working design details being the responsibility of the contractor.

Cost control is traditionally carried out by a member of the architect's team. A general contractor is appointed to carry out the majority of projects but, where projects are let on a trade-by-trade basis, it is usual for the architect to be responsible for their co-ordination. An independent quality control office is not usually employed, because the control of on-site works is seen to be the responsibility of the architect, acting on behalf of the client.

Design considerations

Mandatory building regulations and standards apply at local authority level and vary between authorities. Additional discretionary guidance codes are also published. Systems and materials may be subject to approval, although this is not compulsory. The government is making a considerable effort to introduce tighter quality control regulations in line with the more established European control procedures.

Approvals

Prior to construction, a building licence must be obtained and displayed publicly at the site. This approval is broadly in accordance with a UK planning approval. On completion, the local authority makes an inspection to confirm conformity with the licence.

Programme considerations

The process of obtaining the building licence dictates the programme. The time this will take will vary significantly according to the scale and political importance of the project, but a minimum of six months should be allowed for securing the licence. Consultants in Italy do not readily accept client discipline, so the preparation of the construction scheme and the bidding of the project will take a further six months. This total of twelve months for the pre-construction programme must be considered an optimum for a thoroughly researched and designed project. Timescales for the construction itself are comparable to those in the UK.

Placing the building contract

Bidding is usually by way of specification and drawings. On a public project, it is usual for the contractor to be required to pay a deposit in order to receive the bid documents; the deposit is refunded to unsuccessful tenderers. On public projects, it is also not uncommon for the tendering contractors to use the client's estimated cost for the project and to bid on the basis of a percentage adjustment to the estimate.

It is important that the client ensure that the bid documentation is sufficiently comprehensive to avoid the possibility of claims by the contractor during execution. Variations are normally valued in accordance with the contractor's build-up of the contract sum. There is no standard form of building contract.

Cost comparison

The level of professional fees is significantly lower than in the UK. For a new build project of L 6,000 million, the total professional fees will be around 8 per cent for the architect, the engineer and the other project organisers.

Construction costs are lower than in the UK: an air-conditioned speculative office building on the periphery of one of the northern commercial cities, for example, will cost only around L 1,400,000 per square metre (around £55 per square foot).

The retail market

Estimated value of retail sales	
1986 (Commerce Ministry)	L 255,027bn (£123.2bn equivalent)

Estimated number of retail outlets	
1986	849,513 total outlets
	316,060 food outlets
	533,453 non-food outlets
1986	2,352 supermarkets
(Commerce Ministry	43 hypermarkets
estimates)	792 department/variety stores

Shop hours
Tue. to Sat. −09.00 to 12.30
15.00 to 19.00
Sun. − many super/hypermarkets open
Mon. morning − all shops frequently closed
Wide regional variations

VAT rates		
	Lowest	2%
	Lower	9%
	Standard	18%
	Higher luxury	38%

Source: Corporate Intelligence Research Publications Ltd

The most significant feature of Italian retailing has always been the extraordinarily high number of shops – many of them small, family-owned, single units – per head of population. The 1984 Census showed one retail outlet for every 65 people; that is around twice the average elsewhere in Europe. Such a high volume of traditional retailing has limited the development of supermarkets and hypermarkets along the lines of other European countries. In 1986, the Ministry of Commerce estimated that large selling units, including department stores, had only 9.2 per cent of the total retail market value of sales.

However, although the volume of small units has not fallen, there has been a substantial increase in the number of proposed town-centre and out-of-town shopping developments: in 1987 there were only twenty-two hypermarkets in operation, but there were no less than twenty-seven proposals for new developments. In 1988, major new shopping centres were opened outside Milan and close to Turin.

Retail market in Milan

Unlike Rome, Milan remains a popular location for the retail industry, although the number of shops coming on the market each year is small, with the result that both rents and capital values have been driven up accordingly. In 1988, it is estimated that capital values rose by 30 per cent to break the L 20 million per square metre barrier, with one unit on the Via Monte Napoleone changing hands at L 27 million per square metre.

Although suburban shopping complexes and hypermarkets have been resisted both by the planners and by local retailers, in 1988 a new 4,000 square metre complex, the Centro Bonola, was opened just to the north-west of the city.

Corso Buenos Aires Just to the north-east of the city centre, the Corso Buenos Aires is one of the main arterial roads in and out of Milan. A busy road with three lanes in each direction, it is also the route of an underground line. The buildings are a mixture of 19th and 20th century development, mostly offices but with some residential property built to six or eight floors.

At the southern end, there are several multiple stores, including Stefanel, Benetton, Bata and Upim. As elsewhere in Europe, the mixture of office, retail and residential property means that fashion shops rub shoulders with butchers and patisseries in what is a prime retail location.

At the top of this street, with its unpleasantly high volume of traffic, the Piazzale Loreto once again contains a mixture of large stores (Coin and Upim) and a number of office buildings.

Corso Vercelli   A wide and busy street with parking on both sides, two-way traffic and trams, the Corso Vercelli also contains both 19th and 20th century buildings and a mixture of retail and office property, including a very large branch of Coin (four sales floors and a 70-metre frontage).

Via Monte Napoleone   A relatively narrow one-way street with many period buildings and small, often arched, shop frontages, the Via Monte Napoleone carries a number of high quality fashion shops as well as international traders, including Gucci, Valentino, Gianni Versace, Benetton, Daniel Hechter, Louis Vuitton, Cartier, Ungaro and Ferragamo.

Corso Vittorio Emanuele II   The retail outlets on this, the main pedestrianised shopping street, include Bruno Magli, Maxmara, Cacharel, Benetton, Stefanel and Fiorucci. The shops are set back in covered arcades.

The office market

The Italian office market is booming: prices paid for vacant buildings for occupation and refurbishment are breaking records. The boom is being fuelled by strong demand and by the very limited supply of quality office buildings in the urban centres. The supply is simply unable to meet the demands of Italian financial and industrial companies, as well as of foreign investors who have recently been attracted to Italy. There is particular demand for prestigious buildings in the historic centres of the major cities, especially Rome and Milan, and Italian and foreign investors compete for what opportunities arise.

Unfortunately, the realities of the market are that relatively few really attractive properties become available and that complex, inadequate and restrictive city planning legislation, together with unattractive tax regulations, are discouraging investment and development in this sector of the property market. Luigi Arborio Mella, the managing director of AEDES, one of Italy's most highly respected real estate companies – it is publicly quoted – described the problems in a recent

125

interview: 'In Milan, we are still not able to guarantee the serious development of the property market. It is true that we have millions of cubic metres that are unused and reconvertable, and that there are a great many sites available that were once occupied by industry, but political and legal problems stymie the vast majority of entrepreneurial initiatives. Our company bought part of a disused site at Bovisa. We still don't know what we will be permitted to do with it.' (*Lombard Magazine*, February 1989.)

Many buildings in the historic centres of Italy's greatest cities are in the same situation, with buildings continuing to decay while bureaucracy and politics delay the process of development.

The office market in Milan

The very centre of Milan, including the area around the stock exchange, is closed to general traffic and accessible only with a special permit. Coupled with narrow streets, a complex one-way system and the Italians' continuing enthusiasm for driving, the restrictions have a depressing effect on the quality of the centre as an office location. Perhaps it is for this reason that the Corso Venezia, with its large, converted *palazzi* built around quiet courtyards and garden squares, rivals the financial district for popularity.

Office rents in Milan can be as high as L 600,000 per square metre per annum, with capital values as high as L 12 million to L 14 million per square metre in exceptional locations such as the Via Monte Napoleone.

Edge-of-town Milan

Milano Fiori

The largest office and commercial development outside the city, Milano Fiori is about 31 kilometres to the south along the Autostrada Fiori. There is a substantial volume of residential development and local authority housing as well as a Euromercato supermarket of around 30,000 square metres with extensive car parking, filling stations, tyre service and so on. Immediately adjacent is a very large office development.

Via Ripamonti

In view of the near-impossibility of development in the centre of Milan, together with the acute problems of access, a location such as the Via Ripamonti will assume increasing importance. Just inside the city boundaries, it provides sufficient space for extensive and flexible development and is within easy distance of the city centre. In addition to the existing office, hotel and residential complexes, there are plans for a substantial volume of additional development.

The industrial market

The major centres of Italian manufacturing are Milan, Genoa and Turin, although there are further areas of activity south of the Appenines, in the Arno valley, immediately south of Rome and in the Marches region. The problem with southern Italy is its distance from the rest of the Community. The government is attempting to minimise disadvantages by offering financial incentives to companies setting up in the region but this has resulted in a belt of industry in the most northerly tier of the qualifying area for aid. Consequently the northern limit of the area has been moved from just south of Rome to just north of Naples.

Between 1983 and 1988, the Italian industrial property market suffered from a substantial excess of supply over demand and from depressed prices. When the market turned in 1988, rents in Milan rose from L 46,000 to L 65,000 per square metre per annum and yields tightened to 8 per cent, with a consequent stimulus to new construction for the first time in five years. In the best locations around Milan, close to the ring road, rental prices have now reached L 90,000 per square metre.

With the approach of 1992, a large number of Italian companies are already expanding into other member states and trading links are being actively pursued. As elsewhere in Europe, there has been a major change in emphasis from heavy to light industry and to the service sector, with new activities taking up the old industrial space on the periphery of cities such as Milan and Rome. Many such sites have been redeveloped with small industrial and office units and residential and leisure facilities.

The most impressive inner-city redevelopment project is on the northern edge of Milan, where Pirelli and its partners are redeveloping the Pirelli factory site in the Biococca district. When complete, the scheme will not only accommodate Pirelli's headquarters and laboratories (on 312,000 square metres) but will also provide a further 130,000 square metres of industrial space, 65,000 square metres of residential space and 151,000 square metres of office space. A further 176,000 square metres will be transformed into a public park.

Although this is the largest scheme currently under way, there are others: in Turin, the Agnelli group is developing the Lingotto district, while a similar undertaking is planned in the Novoli area of Florence. In Genoa, Italsider, Piaggio, Marconi and Fincantieri are planning to reconvert their own sites.

Luxembourg*

Geography

Land area	2,586 sq. km.
Population (1987)	372,100
Density	141 per sq. km.
Main cities	Population
City of Luxembourg	80,000
Esch-sur-Alzette	25,000
Dudelange	14,100

Luxembourg is divided into two clearly defined regions: the Oesling – a plateau 450 metres high which forms part of the Ardennes – and the Gutland, which rises to an average height of 250 metres. Approximately one-third of the country is covered by forest. In both regions, the everyday language is Letzebuergesch, although French and German are used for administrative purposes.

Transport and communications

The road network (some 5,200 kilometres of it) is extremely dense. It includes motorway links to France and Belgium, while the link to West Germany is soon to be completed. With 270 kilometres of rail network and an international airport at Findel, just outside the City of Luxembourg, this small country is well served in terms of communications. The national airline, Luxair, offers regular flights to most European destinations.

* For map, see p. 40.

General economic

Luxembourg's geographical position and economic structure have necessarily led to co-operation with other countries. There has been particularly close co-operation with Belgium since 1921 and, since the Second World War, with both Belgium and the Netherlands, through the creation of Benelux, an economic union which became the first step towards the present European Community.

Tax rebates, help in obtaining credits, and a number of other incentives are offered to companies which set up industrial plant in Luxembourg. Despite these efforts, however, the country's industrial activity is decreasing, and there is a parallel rise in service sector activity.

As a result, Luxembourg now plays a major role as a financial centre. Because of fiscal legislation dating back to 1929 in favour of holding companies, a considerable number of banks and major investment trusts have settled in the capital. Indeed, with more than 6,000 domiciled holding companies and 123 banks, this small country is not only a major international centre but also contains the greatest concentration of banking activities anywhere in the Community. Large insurance and re-insurance companies are setting up subsidiaries in Luxembourg, and it seems that Luxembourg will soon be one of the major centres for this sector of business too.

The 1988 rate of inflation was 1.4 per cent, but by the middle of 1989 it had been reduced to 0.7 per cent. The average rise in prices in recent years has been 7.1 per cent, which compares favourably with the 1980–85 Community average of 9 per cent. Consumer prices tend to be lower in Luxembourg than in neighbouring countries, and its rates of VAT – 3 per cent, 6 per cent and 12 per cent – are the lowest in the Community.

Industry

Since the end of the Second World War, great efforts have been made to bring diversity to an industrial sector previously dominated by steel. Although the steel industry still contributes 48 per cent of the value of the country's export trade (foreign trade represents some 75 per cent of the country's GNP), many other sectors – including aluminium, glass, cement, tyres and computer manufacturing – are now well established.

Of the total land area 49 per cent is used for agriculture, and (in

1984) agriculture, forestry and fisheries represented 3.2 per cent of GDP, while industry contributed 35.4 per cent.

The country depended on imports for 99 per cent of its energy supply in 1985, although Vianden, to the north-east of the country at the border with Germany, now houses Europe's largest hydro-electric pumping station.

Forms of tenure

In general terms, the law in relation to property ownership in Luxembourg follows Belgian law, which is based on the Napoleonic Code.

Leases

As a rule, the terms of a lease are entirely a matter of commercial negotiation between the landlord and the tenant, and both parties are free to negotiate such terms as they wish. Rents may or may not be indexed and they may or may not have a fixed rate of augmentation. In practice, most leases are granted for terms of either nine or twelve years, either with a provision for indexation or an agreed augmentation rate of between 2 per cent and 5 per cent. Upon expiry of the lease, the tenant's rights are limited, although he or she may be entitled to three further periods of six months' occupation as well as to compensation related to any improvements undertaken during the tenancy.

On commercial leases, the landlord retains responsibility for the fabric of the building, for insurance of the fabric, as well as any property owner's tax. All other liabilities are the responsibility of the tenant.

Any clause in a commercial lease which prohibits the sub-letting or disposal of the lease will be regarded as void if such sub-letting or disposal coincides with the disposal of the business, provided the successor is in an identical line of business to the outgoing tenant.

It is important to ensure that any lease or transfer is formally registered as the Civil Code provides for the new landlord of a property to be bound by any lease in existence which has been drawn up by a notary or by a registered informal lease (i.e. a lease signed by the two parties without the intervention of a notary but registered with the state and legally valid). When a commercial lease is agreed informally, it is clearly in the interest of the tenant to ensure that it is registered.

Taxation

Corporate income tax

Rental income	34% (different rates apply if total income is below Luxfr 1,312,000) plus 2% surcharge on total tax payable	
Realised gains	Rate	36%
	Basis	Proceeds over cost less depreciation (as indexed)
	Indexation relief	Yes (if at arm's length)
Relief for rentals		Yes
Relief for capital expenditure (rates most commonly applied)	Land	Nil
	Factories	2–3% p.a.
	Warehouses	2–3% p.a.
	Offices	2–2.5% p.a.

VAT

Land*	Exempt
New buildings*	Exempt (unless all or part of the building has been built under a sale or construction agreement in which case the rate is 12%)
Old buildings*	Exempt
Construction services	12%
Professional fees	6%

* Purchaser and vendor may opt for sale to be subject to VAT

Transfer taxes

Transfer tax	6% (3% surtax on certain property located in Luxembourg City) plus 1% mortgage duty

Other national/federal taxes

Net worth tax (levied on value of net assets)	0.5%

Local taxes

Ground tax	Rates vary but in practice will be up to 1% of the market value of the property
Municipal business tax on income (Luxembourg City)	10%
Municipal business tax on capital (Luxembourg City)	0.5%

Grant aid and investment incentives

Public aid for investment projects is available in a number of different forms, including unconditional capital subsidies, loans at reduced interest rates and tax reliefs. Various local authorities and government agencies may also make land available for industrial purposes, factory sites and premises.

The recent law on economic development renews and extends the opportunities for the government to acquire, develop and make available industrial land to manufacturing companies, including land within the national industrial parks which have been developed across the country during the past few years. Fully equipped with public services such as roads, water, sewerage, electrical power and natural gas, they are located on or close to major international road transportation links. Some are even provided with railway tracks which feed into the international rail network. The location and size of the land made available (under a 30-year renewable superficial right deed) is determined by mutual agreement between the government and the company.

Outside these national industrial parks, further land may be available in a variety of regional or municipal industrial estates managed either by the local authorities or privately. The government may be helpful in identifying suitable land or buildings.

The government and local authorities may undertake the construction of industrial buildings for subsequent sale or letting. They may also contribute in whole or in part to the financing of the construction of industrial or business premises.

Further information, advice and assistance are obtainable from the Chambre de Commerce du Grand Duché de Luxembourg, 7 rue Alcide de Gasperi, L-2981 Luxembourg.

Planning

Planning is the responsibility of the municipality and the commune, subject to the right of appeal to various government ministers. Each commune prepares its *plan d'aménagement*, which specifies in broad terms the land use. All material development (including change of use) requires planning permission, and planning controls are particularly strict in Luxembourg City.

On average, a period of two to three months is needed to obtain provisional approval and a further eight to twelve months for the definitive consent.

Brokerage

Although Luxembourg has no surveying profession as such, no property qualifications and no equivalent to the RICS, *géomètres-experts* (similar to those in Belgium) provide a basic agency service. Their work is by no means professionally orientated, and most firms are very small, although there is a handful of larger practices covering most areas.

Nor is there any sophisticated commercial agency service; the agents are not involved either before or after the letting stage. Often a company prefers not to use an agent but to handle its own advertising. The standard agency fee is 3 per cent for a sale and one month's rent for a letting.

The construction industry

(See under the Netherlands, pp. 147–9).

The retail market

Estimated volume of retail sales (1980 = 100)		
	1983	103.3
	1984	101.1
	1985	100.8
	1986	103.6
	1987	108.6

Shop hours
Similar to Belgium (see p. 45), although many retail outlets close all day Monday.

VAT rates		
	Lower rate	3%
	Standard rate	12%
	Higher rate	12%

Source: Corporate Intelligence Research Publications Ltd

As befits such an international community, the retailing market in Luxembourg City includes a pleasing mixture of European traders and caters not only for its own rather small population but also for visitors from Belgium, France and West Germany. Intent on taking advantage of lower prices on items such as cigarettes, alcohol, coffee and petrol, this cross-border trade is mostly captured by a number of larger hypermarket developments near the frontiers. Around the city itself, there are four shopping centres, the largest of which is the Belle Etoile at Strassen. Further centres are to be found on the roads to Longwy, Hawald and on the Route d'Echternach.

Luxembourg City

La Grande-Rue

The main shopping street of Luxembourg City, La Grande-Rue begins at the junction of Rue du Fosse and Côte d'Eich. Attractively cobbled and planted with small trees, this pedestrianised street runs east–west with a slight incline. A catholic mix of retailers includes Etam and Le Must de Cartier (both at the east end), Benetton, Van Cleef, Arpels, Newman and Bata (which has a double unit). The majority of traders are local, and provide a good mix of generally upmarket food and fashion, jewellery, white and brown goods. Most outlets are single or double width, based on a unit of some 5 or 6 metres and a depth of between 15 and 20 metres. The buildings are in good repair and the trading areas tend to be busy. As the street reaches the Avenue de la Porte-Neuve, the pedestrianised section comes to an end. Although the retail area continues for a little way, the quality of shopping falls considerably. Close to the eastern end, at the junction of Rue du Fosse and Place Guillaume II, stands C&A.

It should be noted that, although it suffers now from considerable pressure of traffic, this small and very restricted city is currently investing heavily in car-parking facilities.

The largest speculative scheme within the central area is between La Grande-Rue and Rue Beaumont. These two streets will be linked by a mall with eighteen ground floor retail units, supported by 8,000 square metres of offices and apartments in four blocks and by underground car parking. 80 per cent of the offices have been sold and only three of the retail units remain available for sale at betweeen Luxfr 260,000 and Luxfr 290,000 per square metre. (The Luxembourg Franc is at par with the Belgian Franc.)

The office market

Unlike many other European centres, Luxembourg has had no problems of over-supply of office space in the past twenty-five years. Together with relatively low interest rates and low inflation, this has helped to create a climate of conservative confidence. Currently there are more than 150 foreign banks located in the city – particularly around the Boulevard Royal – and there are many more looking to establish a base here. Certainly, supply seems set to trail gently behind demand for the foreseeable future.

Some of the buildings on the Boulevard – a four-lane, one-way, inner ring road – are less than pleasing concrete structures. The downside of the City's international character is also evident in the Place d'Armes, a beautiful square in which the bandstand and plane trees have now been joined by Pizza Hut, McDonalds and Quick – albeit in the best possible taste, with tables and chairs arranged beneath the trees.

Office space lets at between Luxfr 850 and Luxfr 1,200 per square metre and sells for between Luxfr 30,000 and Luxfr 40,000 per square metre. Construction costs are in the region of Luxfr 110–130 per square metre.

Edge-of-town

Route de Trèves A number of companies in Luxembourg City have established their headquarters on the road to the airport, where office buildings rub shoulders with large warehousing and distribution centres. Privett Bank and Arthur Anderson share one three-floor office building. Close to the airport and next to the Aerogolf-Sheraton Hotel stands the new 33,000 square metre European Bank and Business Centre.

The Grund At the bottom of a deep ravine, the Grund has traditionally been a poor quality area where immigrants have, over the centuries, made their homes. Although the scope for development is limited, this old part of the city is very beautiful and already contains one bank and another recently converted headquarters building (a former brewery).

Kirchberg Plateau

Although the campus of the Community already contains a large number of important buildings, a considerable volume of new development is under way. The first building to be erected on the Plateau was the 22-storey tower block – a multi-purpose administrative complex containing offices and conference rooms. The Robert Schuman hemicycle houses the departments of the Secretariat General of the European Parliament in Luxembourg, while the Jean Monnet building contains various departments of the European Commission.

One of the major landmarks, the Court of Justice – significantly redeveloped in 1985 – has been on this site since 1972. Other buildings include the European School, the Data Processing Centre and the Court of Auditors (since 1988).

A new administrative building, containing 400 offices and with underground tunnels linking it to other buildings, was opened in 1988. The development programme could lead to a final capacity of more than 1,500 offices. There is also a large conference centre, designed to create both horizontal and vertical communication lines to all the key areas of this administrative building.

A number of additional buildings are under construction: the Deutsche Bank should be fully operational in early 1991 and an administration building for Luxembourg Television will be completed by the end of 1990. Future plans include the construction of self-contained living quarters, which will provide the inhabitants with all the facilities of a modern town as well as cycle routes linking all the major buildings.

Although, in the political arena, the government is fighting hard to retain the European Parliament, the local business community would have no real objection if the Parliament left for Brussels. The space thus vacated would, they believe, be taken up rapidly by other Community operations, such as the Court of Justice and the Investment Bank. The personnel of these operations would, by virtue of their presence throughout the year, make a greater contribution to the wealth and economy of Luxembourg than do the Members of the European Parliament who tend to be on site for little more than forty days a year.

The industrial market

The traditional view in Luxembourg is that any company unable to afford to own its premises must be in financial difficulties. Although this perception will, no doubt, alter over time, more than 80 per cent of the industrial property is owner-occupied, so it is difficult to obtain current market information on industrial lettings.

In addition to the foreign companies working in the steel sector, a number of other foreign companies are based in Luxembourg and make a major contribution to employment and the economy. They include Dupont and Goodyear, whose plant at Ettelbrück is their largest outside North America and the USA. The more recent arrival of a number of pharmaceutical manufacturers in the south of Luxembourg may well signal a new trend.

THE NETHERLANDS

International Boundary.... — · — · —

Principal Roads and
Motorways...................... ————

Railway........................... ┼┼┼┼┼

International Airport........ ✈

0   5   10   15   20   25 Miles

0 5 10 15 20 25 30 35 40 Kms

North Sea

Terschelling

Ameland

Texel

Ijsselmeer

Markerwaard

Dokkum

Delfzijl

Leeuwarden

Groningen

Drachten

Sneek

Assen

Stadskanaal

Heerenveen

Emmen

Meppel

Hoogeveen

Den Helder

Alkmaar

Hoorn

Lelystad

Zwolle

GERMANY

Beverwijk

Velsen

Zaandan

Almelo

Haarlem

AMSTERDAM

Almere

Hengelo

Enschede

Hilversum

Amersfoort

Apeldoorn

Leiden

Zutphen

The Hague

Utrecht

Hook of Holland

Europoort

Gouda

Arnhem

Doetinchem

Winterswijk

Rotterdam

Nijmegen

Dordrecht

s – Hertogenbosch

Roermond

Breda

Sittard

Middelburg

Roosendaal

Tilburg

Geleen

Vlissingen
(Flushing)

Heerlen

Eindhoven

Maastricht

BELGIUM

Continuation

Roermond
Continued on inset

Department of Trade and Industry CDO No.6558,1988

The Netherlands

Geography

Land area	41,200 sq. km.
Population	14,715,000
Density	355 per sq. km.
Main cities	Population
Amsterdam	1,020,000
Rotterdam	1,030,000
The Hague	680,000
Arnhem	360,000
Utrecht	229,000
Eindhoven	191,000
Groningen	168,000

The Netherlands is a densely populated and highly developed country. Much of its land area has been reclaimed from the sea, some of it from as much as 6 metres below sea-level. Most new development, including – in some locations – railway lines, requires extensive piling.

For administrative purposes, the Netherlands is divided into twelve provinces, each of which is administered by a representative council (*provinciale staten*) in which the number of elected members varies according to the province's population. Elected for four years, the members appoint a sub-committee of six who, under the chairmanship of a senior civil servant, are charged with executive power, including supervision of the financial aspect of municipal administration.

The most important commercial area, with almost half the country's population and approximately 65 per cent of its total office stock, is The Randstad, which includes part of the provinces of North Holland, South Holland and Utrecht, and is bordered by the towns of Amsterdam, Rotterdam, Utrecht and The Hague.

The other major cities tend to concentrate on one particular activity or industry, even at times on one particular company: Eindhoven in the south is, some would say, owned by Philips; Arnhem, on the German border, is the headquarters of Azko; the famous university town of Groningen, in the north, is the location to which PTT, the state telecommunications company, has decentralised from The Randstad; at the opposite end of the country, close to the Belgian border, Maastricht is heavily occupied by the paper and cement industries.

Transport and communications

The Netherlands has an extensive road network of 97,000 kilometres, including 2,000 kilometres of motorway, and a comprehensive, 2,800-kilometre rail system, which links the major towns and Schiphol Airport and handles 200 million passenger journeys and 20 million tonnes of goods traffic per annum.

The principal seaports are Amsterdam, Velsen, Scheveningen and Vlaardingen (near The Hague), Hoek van Holland, Vlissingen (on Zealand) and, of course, Rotterdam, which alone handled 255 million tonnes of goods in 1987.

With so much of the land area having been reclaimed from the sea, the country has an extensive inland waterway system and its inland fleet of more than 6,000 barges, with a total carrying capacity of over 5 million tonnes, now handles around 100 million tonnes of freight per annum, approximately half of which is international traffic.

General economic

Historically a prosperous nation with a mature economy and high *per capita* income, the Netherlands – in common with the rest of Europe – suffered economically during the 1970s but has seen a recovery in exports and profitability in the 1980s.

One of the costs of this recovery has been unemployment (presently static at around 12 per cent of the working population) and, although public spending is high, strenuous efforts are now being made by the government to control and reduce it, and various initiatives have been set in place to stimulate the private sector.

Prime interest rates are low by comparison with most other European economies and inflation is below 3 per cent per annum.

Industry

There are three principal industrial sectors: manufacturing, mineral extraction and agriculture. As well as the traditional iron and steel activities, the Netherlands is heavily involved in the manufacture or processing of food, drink, tobacco, textiles, paper, chemicals, leather, footwear and electrical products. The agricultural sector includes dairy and arable farming, market gardening and fishing.

Forms of tenure

Lease terms

Property may be owned freehold or, where the land is held by the municipal authorities, it may be subject to a ground lease.

Occupational leases are traditionally granted for a term of five years or a multiple thereof, with a rent review every five years, as well as annual indexation against the cost of living. The landlord retains the obligation to repair and insure the property, while local taxes are apportioned between the landlord and the tenant.

Retail leases

There are significant differences between leases applied to retail premises and all other types of lease. Tenants in retail property are afforded considerable protection by Article 1624 of the Civil Law: effectively, any lease granted is renewable every five years and the landlord can only recover possession by proving that the premises are required for the landlord's personal use.

Rents may be indexed against the cost of living and will be renegotiated at the five-year renewal date. If the tenant believes that the new rent proposed by the landlord is too high, he or she may apply to the courts. The courts are advised by a committee of lay members, who will consider evidence of comparable rents submitted by both sides before fixing the rent and making an award.

Office and industrial leases

Rental contracts in the office and industrial sectors – generally granted for a term of five years, with an option of renewal for a further five –

may contain a provision for indexation or for rent review. There is no legislation overriding the terms of the lease and the tenant has only limited security of tenure at the end of the lease term. The tenant can apply to the courts and plead for an extension of up to three years, but there must be good grounds for failing to surrender possession and it is most unusual for the court to take the tenant's side. Full repairing and insuring leases are unknown in these sectors, and all leases are given on an internal repairing basis.

Taxation

All registerable transactions, including sales and lettings, are subject to stamp duty at the rate of 6 per cent and, although these taxes are normally payable by the purchaser, this is by agreement between the parties.

Corporate income tax

Rental income		35% (40% on first Fl 250,000 of profits)
Realised gains	Rate	35% (or 40% as above)
	Basis	Proceeds over cost
	Indexation relief	Yes
Relief for rentals		Yes
Relief for capital expenditure (rates are not prescribed and differ according to useful life of asset)	Land	Nil
	Factories	1½–3% p.a.
	Warehouses	1½–3% p.a.
	Offices	1½–3% p.a.

VAT

Land*	Exempt. (Taxable at 18.5% if newly cultivated land is sold which has not been used or is sold within two years from date of first use.)
New buildings*	Exempt. (Taxable at 18.5% if sold within two years from date of first use.)
Old buildings*	Exempt. (Taxable at 18.5% if substantial rebuilding has created a new building which is sold within two years from date of first use.)
Construction services	18.5%
Professional fees	18.5%

*Purchaser and vendor may opt for sale to be subject to VAT

Transfer taxes

Transfer tax	6%

Other national/federal taxes

None.

Local taxes

Real estate tax	Various

Planning

In the three-tier planning system, applications are made first to the city or local authority. Any approval or refusal may be referred by either party to the province administration, and their decision may be referred to the government. A planning application will normally take between two and six months, except in specific areas, such as the south-east district of Amsterdam, where the process has been accelerated by having planning briefs defined for all available sites.

Brokerage

Although the professional body representing real estate brokers (the Nederlandse Vereniging van Makelaars) lays down a sliding scale of charges, the average is 2 per cent of the value of the transaction. A high percentage of transactions is undertaken by brokers.

Conveyancing

Straightforward property transactions do not generally involve a lawyer but are handled entirely by a notary, whose charges are based on a sliding scale beginning at 1 per cent for the smaller transactions and averaging 0.25 per cent. A 6 per cent duty on all registered transactions including sales and lettings is normally paid by the purchaser, although it is by agreement between the parties.

The Benelux construction industry

Capacity of the industry

The industries of Belgium, the Netherlands and Luxembourg have a limited domestic market, and the major contractors earn a significant proportion of their income overseas. Dutch contractors offer particular expertise in coastal civil engineering, harbours and land reclamation.

In terms of turnover, the leading companies are:

Hollandse Beton Groep (N)	Fl 2,797 million
Koninklijke Volker Stevin (N)	Fl 1,706 million
Ballast Nedam Groep (N)	Fl 1,030 million
SBBM (B)	BFr 14,716 million
Nerenigde Bedryven NBM (N)	Fl 674 million
CFE (B)	BFr 10,493 million

There is no specific classification of contractors, although they have their own federation representing their interests in government, local authorities and trade unions.

General state of the industry

After several difficult years caused by the lack of investment in both the public and private sectors, the construction industry is now recovering. Brussels, in particular, is attracting considerable private investment in anticipation of 1992. The annual rate of inflation is running at just under 3 per cent, and tender prices run slightly ahead of inflation. There are no shortages of labour or materials, and no problems are anticipated in servicing the increased demand.

Structure of the industry

The client normally appoints an architect as the lead consultant for a building project, and the architect is responsible for all aspects of design although he or she will invariably sub-contract the production of engineering designs. Although cost control has traditionally been within the remit of the architect, it is not unusual for the client to appoint an independent cost-control organisation. Quality control, although it is the architect's responsibility, is also often the subject of an independent appointment. Building guarantee insurance is not a standard requirement.

The client usually appoints a main contractor, but retains control over the mechanical, electrical and other specialist works. The client obtains direct bids, makes a selection and imposes it on the main contractor. Both architect and contractor have a ten-year responsibility for their services.

The use of external contractors or consultants meets no significant obstacle, although with a limited market there is little incentive for foreign companies.

Design considerations

Apart from the requirement to conform to the building licence laws, there are no mandatory national regulations. Various guidance notes are not binding unless specifically incorporated. In the low-lying Netherlands, particular consideration must be given to groundworks and foundations.

Approvals

It is a pre-requisite of construction to obtain a building licence within the zoning of the particular site. (The regulations vary from town to town.) It is possible to obtain this licence in two stages: first, an outline approval to establish use and volume; and second, a detailed consent.

Programme considerations

As in most other countries, the critical stage is the securing of a building licence, after which it takes about four months to complete the tender enquiry documents, to obtain bids, and to start on site.

Construction itself takes about as long as in the UK, and as in other European countries, concrete structures predominate.

Placing the building contract

For general building projects, the tender enquiry document consists of specification and drawings. Bids are made on a lump sum basis.

In the Netherlands, a standard form of building contract is widely used (*uniforme administrative voorwaarden voor de uitoering van werken* – the UAV68). In Belgium, a form of contract is published by the Fédération Royale des Sociétés d'Architectes in agreement with the Contractors' Association, although the majority of private contracts are individually drafted.

The contractor's price build-up invariably forms the basis of a valuation of variations, and the contract usually provides for agreement on cost and programme prior to commitment. Fluctuations, where they apply, are geared to a national construction index.

Cost comparisons

The level of professional fees in all three Benelux countries is lower than in the UK. For a new build project of BFr 200 million (about Fl 11 million or £3 million excluding VAT), the total fees for the architect and engineers would be in the region of 9 per cent.

Construction costs are also lower than in the UK. For example, an air-conditioned speculative office building on the outskirts of the capital cities will cost in the region of only BFr 41,000 per square metre (say, Fl 2,200 per square metre or £58 per square foot excluding VAT).

The retail market

Estimated value of retail sales		
1985	Fl 90.7bn	(£26.7bn equivalent)
1986	Fl 92.0bn	(£27.1bn equivalent)

Estimated volume of retail sales (1980 = 100)	
1983	91.8
1984	89.3
1985	89.7
1986	91.9
1987	94.6

Estimated number of retail outlets	
1987 (KNOV trade association)	135,000 total outlets
1984 (Census)	49,000 food outlets
	103,000 non-food outlets

Shop hours
Mon. to Sat. – 9.00 to 17.30/18.00 Extensions to 21.00 permitted once a week or once a month in some areas. No Sunday trading. Early closing Tuesday or Wednesday afternoon. Shop hours determined by weekly maximum of 52 hours for all outlets.

VAT rates		
	Lower	6% (mainly food)
	Standard	20%

Source: Corporate Intelligence Research Publications Ltd

Dutch retailing follows very traditional patterns, with the old-established high streets still the prime shopping locations. Although most of the Netherlands' main shopping streets have been pedestrianised, many of the period buildings on them are subject to preservation orders and retailers are obliged to operate within the limitations imposed.

Resistance from the local business community, which has considerable influence over the planning authorities, has severely limited the number of edge-of-town and out-of-town developments. The principal exceptions to this – the so-called 'furniture boulevards' at Beverwijk (to the north-west of Amsterdam), Diemen (to the south-east of Amsterdam) and elsewhere – are the result of sustained pressure from retailers who argued, correctly, that their needs could not be met within existing centres. These edge-of-town developments have not, however, proved to be the Trojan horse feared by local shopkeepers and, despite considerable effort, other forms of retailing have had only limited success in obtaining planning consent.

Multiple retailers – both indigenous and international – play a significant role in Dutch retailing, including major store operators such as Peek & Cloppenburg, C&A and Hema, while traders such as Blokker, M&S Modes, Bata and Manfield are found on many of the country's high streets.

Amsterdam

Kalverstraat

A long, pedestrianised street running north–south from Dam Square to Munt Plein, Kalverstraat has one of the country's best known department stores at each end: Peek & Cloppenburg in the north, Vroom and Dreesmann in the south. The southern end is quite narrow and, with period buildings on four or five floors and an average unit size of around 4 to 5 metres frontage and 15 to 20 metres depth, seems dark and claustrophobic. In the middle section, where, although frontages remain the same length, depths are as much as 35 metres, traders include La Brioche Dorée, Manfield, Sacha and Body Shop. Towards the northern end, a greater number of buildings have been redeveloped and some frontages are up to 7 or 8 metres wide. There are also smaller units and a small department store (Kreymborg). Traders here include Stefanel, Yves Rocher, Fiorucci and McDonalds. Average rents in Kalverstraat are Fl 1,600–2,000 per square metre.

Of several smaller shopping streets running east and west from Kalverstraat, the most significant is Heiligeweg, where the choice of retail outlets includes Tie Rack, K-Shoes, Benetton 0–12 and Rosenthal Studio Haus.

Dam Square marks the end of Kalverstraat, and another shopping street (Nieuwen Dijk) runs out of the northern side of the square. In general, the standard of shop-fitting and presentation is noticeably lower here, although there is a large C&A unit about 75 metres from the square with 4,000 to 5,000 square metres of retail space on four floors. Despite the development of a small arcade adjacent to C&A which provides direct access from Nieuwen Dijk to Damrak, this unit is something of 'a rose among thorns'.

Pieter Cornelisz Hoofstraat

Located close to the Rijksmuseum, south of the centre of Amsterdam and near the Concert Hall and the increasingly popular Buitenveldert, Pieter Cornelisz Hoofstraat was no doubt once just a local shopping street for the fashionable residential area which surrounds it. Today it offers an appealing combination of international fashion and jewellery retailers, including Mulberry, Daniel Hechter, Maxmara and Bally, and delicatessens, patisseries and local traders.

Units at the northern end offer 4 to 5-metre frontage and 10 to 15 metres' depth, while towards the southern end, close to the junction with Van Baerlestraat, some units are significantly larger, with frontages up to 7 metres wide and depths as great as 18 metres. Rents in this street (at Fl 800–1,000 per square metre) are around half those on Kalverstraat.

Suburban centres

Known as the 'ABC of Shopping', three traders dominate the suburban centres: Ahold, a food retailer with 636 outlets; Blokker, with 300 branches selling household appliances, gifts and toys; and C&A, with 71 branches. Since forming a joint venture operation, ABC Stores has opened six new shopping developments providing space for each of the three retailers.

Retail warehousing

There are no general retail warehouses in the Netherlands, but there are extensive furniture retail developments ('furniture boulevards') in a number of locations, including Beverwijk and Diemen.

Rest of the Netherlands

Although the traditional high street, often pedestrianised, generally provides the prime retail locations throughout the country, there are shopping centres in Rotterdam, Utrecht, Arnhem and Haarlem. The great demand for prime units in some regional centres, such as Maastricht and Groningen, keeps rents almost equal to those in Amsterdam and is perhaps an indication of the even spread of population across the Netherlands and the incentives on offer to many national multiples.

The office market

Trends

One feature of the Dutch office market is that a substantial volume of good quality development is undertaken in spite of rentals being, by

European standards, depressed and there being no shortage of supply. Pension funds are accepting keen yields (as low as 6 per cent on investments with first class covenants). The relocation of banks, insurance companies and other major office users has created much of the activity of recent years, but this process is now drawing to a close.

The tendency of the planning authority to require a pre-let prior to granting permission for development inevitably creates a tenant's market. Although the rentals are seriously out of line with the rest of the Community, the poor performance of the Dutch economy, together with the fragmentation of the office market within The Randstad, makes it hard to envisage any significant growth in the near future.

Central Amsterdam

Although, historically, business and commerce were located in the heart of the town, the City Council's conservationist policies, together with the ever-increasing transport problems and the pressures of tourism, have produced a major shift out of town, leaving only the Stock Exchange and the major banks in the central area.

When, about thirty years ago, the textile companies moved out of the original commercial and industrial sector in the north-west of Amsterdam and into the western part of the city, the old buildings were converted into apartments. The majority of the former commercial occupiers of this area are now to be found to the south and south-east of Amsterdam.

Except for the old central area, most of the land within the boundaries of Amsterdam is owned, and leased, by the city. Until the mid-1970s, properties were traditionally leased for a term of seventy-five years, but then the law was changed to provide fifty-year leases with a provision for rent review at five-yearly intervals.

The rental is a ground rent, payable on the basis of the land value only, and is assessed by the local authority according to the volume of development permitted upon the site. Once the value has been assessed, the lessee has a choice of either making a once-for-all payment or premium for the fifty-year period (calculated on the basis of 12.8 times the assessed annual ground rent) or of paying the ground rent at five-yearly intervals, at which point the rent is increased according to a complex cost-of-living index operated by the local authority. Any tenant dissatisfied with the rent increase may appeal to the courts, although this occurs only very rarely. Not surprisingly, in the majority of cases, the lessee – perhaps a development company or pension fund – will elect to make the one-off payment.

Specification The low volume of speculative development and the encouragement to pre-let means that tenants have considerable choice and flexibility. Generally, however, although recessed lighting, false ceilings, double glazing and underfloor trunking will be standard, office specification is quite modest, with no requirement for air-conditioning or raised floors.

Service charges Average service charges, including heating, maintenance, insurance, window cleaning, lifts and water supply but excluding air-conditioning, are approximately Fl 25 per square metre per annum.

Edge-of-town centres

South-east

A substantial new development of commercial buildings on a greenfield site to the south-east of Amsterdam provides a huge variety of office, high-tech, industrial and retail warehousing premises. Some of the premises are still under construction, but they include low rise buildings, ten-storey blocks, buildings in steel and glass, as well as in brick. In order to simplify planning procedures, the local authorities have provided a planning brief for each plot in this area, prescribing a plot ratio of 1.25. Rents are in the region of Fl 230 per square metre per annum.

Hoofddorp

A new location close to the increasingly popular Schiphol Airport, Hoofddorp accommodates all the ancillary services associated with an airport as well as several new tenants, including Hertz and Canon. Averaging 3,000 to 5,000 square metres, the new office buildings are smaller than those in the south-east, although rents are similar at around Fl 230 per square metre per annum.

Buitenveldert

An area to the south of the Rijksmuseum, Buitenveldert is a pleasant residential and commercial environment in which office use, especially by professionals such as accountants and solicitors, is now tending to dominate. The period buildings provide, on average, around 500 square metres of space. Those seeking larger premises have moved further south, adjacent to the motorway ring, where a World Trade Centre and the city's main conference centre have been built. A development of three large office buildings let in small suites, the Trade Centre achieves rentals well in excess of any others in Amsterdam (Fl 400 per square metre).

Amstelveen

To the south of the motorway, close to the Trade Centre, Amstelveen is the site of one of Amsterdam's universities, a massive hospital complex and a fairly extensive development of office buildings, most of them purpose-built for specific tenants although some were speculative. Existing tenants include the advertising agency Result, Hewlett-Packard and Ricoh, while Rank Xerox are at present constructing a new headquarters. Very few sites or buildings are still available.

The rest of The Randstad

Rotterdam

Although there is a very high level of owner occupation of the larger office buildings, supply still exceeds demand by a considerable margin. The main users of office space are in businesses connected with Rotterdam's shipping and docks activities.

Utrecht

The most central city of The Randstad, and one well placed for road connections to West Germany and the Benelux countries, Utrecht is the location for some major headquarters, including those of ICL, IBM and a number of banks and mortgage companies. Utrecht has its own large conference centre.

The Hague

The Hague is dominated by the government and by parliament, and most of the remaining space is occupied by those providing related services.

The industrial market

The high level of owner occupation of factory and light industrial units throughout the Netherlands, and the absence of institutional investment in industrial property, have hindered the development of any significant letting market other than for warehousing.

Although the bulk of Dutch industry is spread throughout the country – from PTT at Groningen in the north and the pharmaceutical industry near Utrecht, to Philips at Eindhoven and the new chemical industries at Heerlen in the south – the majority of the warehousing distribution units tend to be centred in or around The Randstad.

The most important locations in the Amsterdam area are in the south-east and around Schiphol Airport, where there has been significant institutional investment in new high-tech buildings. Although these have been letting well at rents in excess of Fl 1,000 per square metre per annum, the institutions will look for a ten-year lease from a satisfactory covenant.

The IJ Zone

Along the banks of the River IJ ('IJ' is the Dutch transliteration of the letter 'Y'), the so-called IJ Zone is the site of a major initiative by the local authorities aimed at the redevelopment and regeneration of the former dockland area. Stretching from the newly completed railway station at Sloterdijk in west Amsterdam as far as the IJmeer, the country's largest lake, to the east of the city, the initiative includes three inter-connecting zones:

- West IJ – In the western zone, the Sloterdijk development includes the Teleport office park and is intended to provide a centre for telecommunications; the Alpha Triangle, bordered by the Coen Tunnel Highway, the old Haem railway tracks and the new Schiphol line, will provide sites for high-tech and ancillary activities; the old timber wharves at Houthavens are destined for housing development.

- Central IJ – Around Centraal Station, close to the inner city and across the water from some new residential accommodation now under construction on the north bank, this zone – centred upon a new five-star hotel and upmarket shopping precinct, with sites allocated for conference facilities, exhibitions, recreational space, hotel and residential areas – will provide the link between old Amsterdam and the new docklands development.

- Eastern IJ – The eastern zone is centred on the old Eastern Docks, IJ Island and Zeeburg, all of which will be redeveloped to provide between 10,000 and 22,000 dwellings.

- Communications – The IJ Boulevard running along the waterfront joins the three zones and will provide easy connection with the Amsterdam ringroad and thus with Schiphol airport. A new railway line will link Sloterdijk Station and Zeeburg with the inner city, the industrial estates, the south and south-eastern commercial areas and the new housing developments in Eastern IJ.

In this most ambitious project, the release of land and the pace of development will need to be carefully controlled if Amsterdam is to overcome the problem of unrealistic rents created by long-term over-supply.

PORTUGAL

0 20 40 60 80 Miles
0 20 40 60 80 100 120 Kms

Atlantic Ocean

Viana do Castelo
Braga
Chaves
Bragança
Matosinhos
Oporto
(Porto)
Vila Real
Lamego
Aveiro
Viseu
Guarda
Figueira da Foz
Coimbra
Covilhã
Leiria
Castelo Branco
Tomar
Abrantes
Santarém
Portalegre
SPAIN
Sintra
Estoril
LISBON
(LISBOA)
Elvas
Setúbal
Évora
Bay of Setubal
Sines
Beja
Castro Verde
Lagos
Portimão
Ⓐ
Vila Real de Santo Antonio
Tavira
Faro
Gulf of Cadiz

International boundary	━ ∙ ━
Road	━━━
Railway	┼┼┼┼
International airport	✈
Airport	Ⓐ

Department of Trade and Industry C.D.O. 7273. 1988

Portugal

Geography

Land area	92,100 sq. km.
Population	10,270,000
Density	111 per sq. km.
Main cities	Population
Lisbon	820,000
Oporto	330,000
Coimbra	142,000
Braga	135,000
Setúbal	114,000

Portugal is a small country, lying on the western side of the Iberian Peninsula. Extending for about 900 kilometres down the coast, it varies in width between 180 kilometres and 350 kilometres. There are eighteen administrative districts, as well as the autonomous regions of the Azores and Madeira. The coastal region to the north and immediately to the south of the capital, Lisbon, is the most important from a commercial point of view, and some 64 per cent of the country's population and 70 per cent of its purchasing power are located in the districts around the five major towns listed above. The Algarve, the southern coastal region, is a very popular tourist area and its population is nearly ten times larger than normal during the summer months.

Transport and communications

Portugal's national airline TAP (Air Portugal) operates out of Lisbon's international airport and also runs daily flights linking the capital to Oporto and Faro. Air connections with most other large towns (Vila Real, Bragança, Guarda, Coimbra and Portimão) are provided by LAR (Linhas Areas Regionais), a private airline in which TAP is a minority shareholder.

There are two major ports: Lisbon, at the mouth of the Tagus, handles international shipping, and Leixoes, in the north of the country, serves Oporto. The current annual capacity of Leixoes is approximately 12 million tonnes, including the throughput of a new container terminal, which became operational in 1981.

Construction of Lisbon's 1,013 metre toll bridge over the River Tagus (the Ponte 25 de Abril) began in 1962. Opened in August 1966, it is the longest bridge in Europe, and was designed to carry both road and rail traffic between Lisbon and the Setúbal Peninsula, and to link the capital with the industrial manufacturing areas on the far side of the estuary (although the double railway-line is not yet operational). The bridge is also the main route to the Algarve, the Alentejo and Spain. Tenders have recently been published for the addition of one more lane in each direction.

The country's total of 18,815 kilometres (1985) of roads includes 196 kilometres of motorway. The principal motorways provide a link between the major industrial and agricultural production region in the north (around Oporto) and the capital, Lisbon.

Approximately half of Portugal's railway network of 3,607 kilometres is owned by the State, and 458 kilometres are electrified.

Infrastructure projects

The motorway between Lisbon and Caxias is now being extended to Cascais, which is to the west of the capital on the north bank of the Tagus estuary. A new north–south link is being constructed on the western side of Lisbon, connecting the motorway to the northern ring road at Campolide.

Lisbon Airport is located immediately to the north of the city, within the conurbation itself, so planes approach the city – noisily and dangerously low – over the city centre. The formal decision to construct a new airport at Ota, some 40 kilometres to the north-east of Lisbon, is about to be taken: the outcome will depend on local mayoral elections, and the proposed development would not be completed before 2010.

The city's local authority (the *camera*) is currently considering proposals from various local architects for the redevelopment of the docks and shoreline of the River Tagus (approximately 26 kilometres of waterfront).

General economic

In recent years, Portugal's economy has been marked by three factors: little or no growth, high unemployment and high inflation. At the end of 1985, unemployment was approximately 13 per cent and inflation stood at around 20 per cent. Most of the country's large-scale industry has been established since the 1950s, prior to which Portugal relied on the basic metal, chemical and mining industries, as well as on the more traditional textile, cork and beverage sectors.

In the 1960s, contact with the rest of the world opened up, and domestic demand began to rise rapidly. The manufacturing sector expanded swiftly, and mining and manufacturing output increased at an annual average rate of approximately 15 per cent between 1963 and 1973. During the next decade, however, industrial production did not perform well, and growth rates dropped to 2.5 per cent and even fell as low as 1.3 per cent during the austerity years between 1982 and 1984. The principal cause of the slowdown was the general political uncertainty in the country and the erosion of business confidence. There was a strong recovery in 1985–6 and, although recovery has slowed again, various sectors continue to prosper, including footwear, textiles and electronics.

The property market

The overall majority won by the Centre Right party in the general election of 1987 ended a long period of uncertainty in Portuguese politics and brought a significant change to the property market. For the first time since the revolution of 1974, the old Portuguese families who took flight at that time are now reinvesting their money in the country. This factor – together with substantial foreign investment – has brought very large percentage price increases to all sectors of the property market. The economy is now benefiting from EC membership as well as from continuing political stability, and 1987 saw Portugal's GNP grow by approximately 4.7 per cent – one of the highest rates in Europe – and its inflation fall to 9.8 per cent from its 1984 peak of 29 per cent.

Industry

Portugal's principal industries are textiles, food processing, ship-building and ship repairing, wood and cork processing, fishing and fish processing, and wine production. The main agricultural area is around the Algarve.

Forms of tenure

The majority of property in Portugal is held in outright ownership, either by way of the Portuguese equivalent of freehold or by way of a condominium holding. All rented property, whether retail, office, industrial or residential, is subject to the same landlord and tenant legislation. The effect of this legislation is to confer absolute security of tenure on the tenant and to prevent any increase in rent, other than by indexation at a rate discounted from the rate of inflation. The annual rate in any calendar year – calculated in October and implemented around January – is generally equivalent to approximately 80 per cent of the actual inflation rate. In 1988, an increase of 7.3 per cent was permitted, although in previous years it had been much higher, and the projected rate for 1989 is 12 per cent.

A lease is open ended in that it is granted effectively for an indefinite period and it cannot be terminated by the landlord unless the tenant is in clear default. Even if the landlord requires the premises for his or her own occupation, this is not sufficient grounds for possession. Responsibility for repairs, maintenance and local taxes remains with the landlord and, as if this were not sufficient, the former dictator Salazar's long-term freeze on rents in Lisbon and Oporto (from the mid-1930s until 1984) means that much of the indexation is on a base rent fixed some thirty years ago. Although there is some relief for landlords because the rate of indexation is slightly higher for tenancies created prior to 1984, the difference is only a few per cent.

Residential tenants are not permitted to assign their tenancies, but commercial tenants may quite legitimately do so, provided it is to another trader in a similar trade. With rents as low as Esc 1,000–1,500 (a few pounds a week), very high premiums (*trespasse*) are asked and paid. The downside for tenants is, of course, that landlords either cannot afford or do not care to maintain their properties. As a result, Lisbon is littered with dilapidated buildings.

The absence of an open market rent review remains a problem; even at the new Torres Amoreiras shopping centre, where shops were first let in 1986, leases are now changing hands for substantial sums of *trespasse*. As a result of criticism from all political parties about the unsatisfactory impact of the current landlord and tenant legislation, the Minister of Finance has recently announced a government review of the whole rental system, although he indicated that he did not regard the matter as a high priority.

The redevelopment of property in Portugal is hindered by the traditional inheritance regulations, whereby a deceased person's estate, including property, is split between a multitude of beneficiaries. The consequent multiple ownership of the majority of sites – combined with the presence of protected tenants and the need to provide rehousing – makes it very difficult to put together a development site.

Taxation

Local taxes

Occupiers used to pay 18 per cent of the assessed rental value of their property as a local tax, but as of 1 January 1989 the system changed. The *contribuição autarquica* for urban buildings has been reassessed; the former assessed value (*rendimento colectavel*) is multiplied by a factor of fifteen and then increased by 4 per cent per annum since the date of the last assessment, subject to a maximum of 100 per cent. Local tax is then payable at a rate of between 1.1 per cent and 1.3 per cent of that value.

Capital Gains Tax

From 1 January 1989, Capital Gains Tax, which previously applied only to companies, has also been payable by individuals.

- *Individuals*: the rate of tax on the proceeds of property transactions is between 16 per cent and 40 per cent, with the 40 per cent ceiling reached for taxable profits in excess of 30 million escudos. (The Capital Gains Tax on the sale of shares and bonds, by comparison, is set at 10 per cent.) The tax on property transactions is payable on 50 per cent of the difference between the original purchase price and the sale price, after allowing for the rate of inflation since the original acquisition. There is, however, no Capital Gains Tax on the proceeds from the sale of a private home, provided that the proceeds are reinvested in a residential property within two years.

- *Companies*: the rate is 40.15 per cent, payable on 100 per cent of the net profit from the sale, although companies may avoid payment by reinvesting in either property or other assets within a two-year period.

Sisa *Tax*

Sisa is a property transfer tax payable by the purchaser to the tax authorities at the rate of 10 per cent of the purchase price on properties in excess of Esc 15 million. Property up to Esc 5 million is exempt from this tax, and for properties between Esc 5 and 15 million there is a progressive rate of between 0 per cent and 10 per cent. This excessively high tax tends to encourage the practice of understating the consideration in the transfer of the deeds (*escritura*).

Grant aid and investment incentives

Although the government is seeking to promote investment in a number of areas, including finance, electronics, machinery and transport, textiles and tourism, its efforts are currently directed towards promoting information technology, agricultural business, biochemical industries and sports goods manufacturers. Promotion is based on the country's natural resources, including the available labour force, and on the easy access it provides for trade with Portuguese-speaking Africa, especially Angola, and with Brazil. The government's means of promotion (the Foreign Investment Institute) has now been abolished. Its responsibilities are being shared by the Bank of Portugal and by ICEP (Instituto do Comercio Externo de Portugal).

Regional aid

To qualify for the SIBR Investment Grant a project must be viable, the promoters must provide a minimum 25% of the total investment, the investment must be for a minimum four-year period, and jobs created by the investment must continue for a further four years. The value of the project must be at least Esc 10 million, and the maximum grant aid is Esc 220 million or 65 per cent of the project value, whichever is lower.

Grant aid for tourism projects

Substantial aid is available for tourism projects, except in the Algarve. The parameters of the SIFIT scheme (a system of financial incentives for investment in tourism) are much the same as those for regional aid.

The maximum grant is Esc 220 million, with an upper limit of 60 per cent of the total project cost, whichever is lower.

Local grants

SIPE (a system of incentives for the development of local potential) grants are available for the development of local projects across a broad spectrum of sectors, including manufacturing, mining, tourism, restaurants and car hire. They seem to be designed for smaller businesses, with an upper limit of Esc 15 million or up to 70 per cent of the project's value. (In Lisbon and Oporto the maximum is 50 per cent.)

Planning regulations

For all material development, planning permission is required from the local authority. Lisbon is controlled by one single *camera* which, though it has not been accustomed to applying coherent land-use policies, has recently laid down policies concerning specific locations, including most of central Lisbon, where it is seeking to retain some residential content in any new development.

Planning procedures in Portugal are similar to those in the UK. The applicant first seeks outline planning permission based on an architect's submission, which is concerned primarily with the volume of the scheme both above and below ground-level and with the intended use of the building. Once outline consent has been granted, the applicant must submit detailed plans within six months. Development must commence within one year of the granting of full consent, failing which the consent will require renewal. The applicant must also obtain approvals for drainage, water, electricity and so on. Unfortunately, the planning system is very bureaucratic, and the fixed periods of time may vary.

Brokerage

Property brokerage in Portugal is undertaken by government-licensed *mediadoras immobiliarias*. In order for a company to obtain its licence, its directors must have no criminal record and must deposit with the government a cash bond to the value of 150,000 escudos. The only other impediment is the six months' time limit for dealing with the necessary paperwork.

It is customary for the vendor of a property to pay the broker's fees, at the rate of 5 per cent plus VAT. As a result of increased competition, however, the fees on larger transactions now tend to be negotiated downwards: for major commercial sales, they can be as low as 2.5 per cent. Brokerage fees on lettings are traditionally the equivalent of one month's rent.

Twenty-five of Portugal's leading firms are now working together to set up a training school for students wishing to enter professions related to land and property.

Conveyancing

The services of a notary (*notario*) are required for any conveyance of property in Portugal and, although not obligatory, it is unwise to proceed without employing a lawyer (*advogado*).

Title to all land in Portugal is registered at the relevant local land registry. The vendor must prove evidence of his ownership by producing a certificate issued by the registry (*certidão de registro*) which also shows whether there are any charges on the property. The vendor also has to produce his *caderneta predial*, a document issued by the local tax office indicating that all taxes raised on the property have been paid. In the case of a new property, he must also produce a certificate issued by the local town council (*licenca de habitacão* in the case of residential property, and *licenca de utilização* for commercial property) which indicates that planning permission was obtained and that the local authority has surveyed the building and approved of its use.

Once the necessary enquiries have been completed, both parties will enter into a promissory contract (*contrato promessa de compra e venda*) – a document which is legally binding on both parties and should be registered before the notary. The purchase will complete upon the signature of the *escritura publica de compra e venda*. The notary will require proof of compliance with all tax laws and appropriate exchange control regulations and will require sight of the receipt for Sisa (transfer tax).

The lawyers' fees – based on time and expenses – will generally be 1 per cent of the value of the purchase price, although on larger transactions they are more likely to be 0.5 per cent. The notaries' fees vary from 0.3 per cent to 1 per cent depending on the transaction, although they will most often be around 0.5 per cent. Registration fees are on a similar scale.

The construction industry

Capacity of industry

Severely depressed from the revolution of 1974 until the country's entry into the EC in 1986, Portugal's construction industry has, until recently, faced a very limited market.

In terms of turnover, the country's leading construction companies are:

Sociedade de Construcoes Soares de Costa S.A.	Esc 23,000 million
Teixeira Duarte Engenharia e Const. S.A.	Esc 11,000 million
Construcoes Tecnicas	Esc 10,200 million
Mota e Companhia	Esc 8,000 million
Engil	Esc 6,500 million

The only classification of contractors is that applying to the public works programme; classification is essential for tender qualification.

General state of the industry

Since 1987, there has been a considerable increase in activity, particularly in the tourist areas, and there is now a strong programme of work in the major conurbations of Lisbon and Oporto.

A serious doubt exists as to the industry's capacity to cope with this increasing workload, particularly in respect of skilled labour, much of which emigrated to France, West Germany and other countries during the period of Marxist government. The labour market is still protected by the labour laws introduced by that regime, with the result that productivity levels are low.

A considerable volume of external funding is entering Portugal to finance the regeneration of the commercial centres of the major cities. The badly neglected public works programme will be dependent on the availability of finance, and such funding is far from certain.

As a consequence of stricter credit control, the housing market is less buoyant than in 1988, with the number of planning approvals for housing projects only 1 per cent higher than the 1987 level.

Construction costs have suffered considerable inflation in the past eighteen months, with forecasts for 1989 indicating 15 per cent inflation in tenders, compared with the official cost inflation of 9 per cent.

Structure of the industry

Building contracts are executed either through a general contractor or through a separate trades contract, with the project under the control of a co-ordinator. Major building contracts are usually contracted on a separate trades basis.

The client normally appoints an architect, who is then responsible for all aspects of design, including structure and services, but who has only a limited role in the on-site supervision. It is customary to appoint a project manager to oversee the design and bidding stages on a major project, and to co-ordinate and supervise the work. International quality control organisations are beginning to have a role in major projects, for which they provide a supplementary service to the local design teams, who are usually quite small operations with limited resources and experience.

Design considerations

Legal regulations (*regulamentos*) cover the general fabric and services of a building, and are supplemented by official technical specifications (Normas Portuguesas) and by the standards of the National Civil Engineering Laboratory (LNEC), although these standards are only recommendations.

Approvals

Prior to construction, the building licence must first be obtained and the project must conform to the city's zoning plan and to the legal regulations. Secondly, construction permits must be obtained for the structure, drainage, fire regulations and service installations. The local authority will carry out inspections during the construction period and, on completion, will issue an occupation completion certificate.

Programme considerations

The pre-construction programme is dictated by the securing of the building licence. This is a lengthy process, with no fixed timescale, and the approval is both technical and political. Construction productivity varies from region to region, with project timescales in the centre of Lisbon significantly longer than in neighbouring Spain.

Placing the building contract

The bidding of a project is usually based on specification drawings and quantities. The contract may be entered into on a remeasurement basis or alternatively the contract sum may be a lump sum (*forfait*) without remeasurement.

No standard form of contract exists, and the terms and conditions of the building contract are the subject of individual negotiations.

Cost comparison

The level of professional fees in Portugal is lower than in the UK: for a new build project of Esc 800 million (£3 million) excluding VAT, for example, the fees would be in the region of 8 per cent for the architect or engineer and 3 per cent for the project manager or co-ordinator.

Construction costs are lower than in the UK: air-conditioned office buildings in central Lisbon are costing around Esc 110,000 per square metre (£39 per sq. ft).

The retail market

Estimated value of retail sales	
1983	Esc 950bn (£4.3bn equivalent)
1985	Esc 1,330bn (£5.8bn equivalent)

Estimated number of retail outlets	
1983 (Neilsen)	40,750 food outlets
1987 (Census)	68,500 total retail outlets

Shop hours
Weekdays — 9.00 to 13.00
15.00 to 19.00
Saturday   — 9.00 to 13.00
(No major shops open on Sunday)

VAT rates	
Lower	8%
Standard	16%
Higher	30%

Source: Corporate Intelligence Research Publications Ltd

The retail market in Portugal is relatively unsophisticated. Its development has been severely hindered by the protective landlord and tenant legislation, which effectively insulates inefficient traders from market forces and obstructs the entry of new retailers. The need to pay a very high premium (*trespasse*) to acquire a retail lease for life is disadvantageous to international traders. They would be reluctant to commit a substantial capital sum in return for rights which might disappear if new legislation were approved, and they would also face difficulties in deciding how to treat such a payment in their accounts.

None the less, the country's economy is now in a period of prosperity, and the Portuguese are themselves enthusiastic shoppers, as the success of the Amoreiras shopping centre in Lisbon has shown. Modernisation of the landlord and tenant legislation could well mark the beginning of a period of considerable beneficial change in Portuguese retailing.

Until the early 1980s, retailing had been dominated by the small shop sector; by 1987 there were some 450 supermarkets. Recently, a number of hypermarkets have been opened, and more are planned both by Portuguese operators and by foreign groups (including, it is believed, the French group Euromarche). French and German groups are expected to open DIY stores soon and provide the first major outlets in a sector which has, as yet, been hardly developed. It has also been suggested that a major foreign group, with solid international experience, is about to enter the cash-and-carry market in Portugal.

Lisbon

The Baixa

The historical centre of Lisbon, the Baixa was the original heart of the banking and trading area and viewed by many as the capital's principal retailing area. At its heart is the Rua Augusta, a pleasant pedestrianised street which runs from the waterfront of Lisbon north to Rossio. The shopping area extends to several other adjoining streets but the shopping there is generally of a poorer quality, particularly in the streets which are not traffic free. Unfortunately, a serious fire in August 1988 destroyed two department stores and sixteen other buildings, thereby severely reducing the quality of shopping in the area in the short term. The local authority has taken responsibility for the redevelopment and commissioned a leading Portuguese architect, Siza Vieira, to present design proposals which retain all the existing old façades. The project is complicated by the highly protective landlord and tenant legislation, under which the previous tenants must either return to their premises or receive compensation.

The Baixa suffers throughout from this very restrictive legislation, with most of the shops in the Rua Augusta held under old leases at very low rents and the *trespasse* required on assignment generally up to five times the annual profit rent.

A retail unit along one of the most popular roads, Avenida da Liberdade, now commands a rent of between Esc 5,000 and Esc 8,000 per square metre per month.

Amoreiras Shopping Centre
Part of the Torres Amoreiras development on the west side of central Lisbon, this development consists of four towers – three containing offices and the fourth residential – above a two-floor shopping centre of some 50,000 square metres. Level 2 contains 158 retail units together with 58 units in a food court, while Level 1 has 149 units as well as a supermarket operated by Pao de Acucar. Separate companies operate a ten-screen cinema complex, a health club, sporting and other facilities. As a condition of their occupancy, tenants have to undertake to trade seven days a week, from 10.00 to 23.00. As a result, the centre has rapidly become an integral part of Lisbon's social scene by day and by night.

Even though, initially, the shop units were offered to let on rack rental terms (in which no premium is payable), relatively few international traders are represented in the centre. Those present include Benetton, Body Shop and Lacoste – all of them probably franchise operations. Rents in the Torres Amoreiras complex are between Esc 5,000 and Esc 7,000 per square metre per month.

Out-of-town retailing

Following the success of the Torres Amoreiras development, the Portuguese company Sonae have proposals for a development at Benfica, but out-of-town retailing in this country is, on the whole, still in its infancy.

There are at present two hypermarkets at Alfragide, to the northwest of Lisbon. The Continente is a joint venture between a French group (Continente) and Sonae; it consists of a large hypermarket with twenty or so small shop units attached. A newer hypermarket (Jumbo) stands on the same road, about half a kilometre away. Owned by the largest Brazilian supermarket chain, it is similar in size to the Continente. Both are currently trading well.

The office market

The office market in Portugal has traditionally been dominated by owner-occupiers, although the rented sector is now growing. As a result of the chronic lack of supply, particularly of small suites, price and rentals of office space are currently rising very rapidly. The costs for residential construction – already in excess of Esc 100,000 per square metre – are also rising fast. Building costs for commercial property currently stand at between Esc 70,000 and Esc 80,000 per square metre.

Although a significant amount of speculative building is now under way, the lack of suitable opportunities in central Lisbon is bound to result in an increasing emphasis on edge-of-town development. In view of the proximity of the Carnaxide Industrial Area to the residential zones of Estoril and Cascais, it is likely that other companies will join international companies such as Atlas Copco, Tetra Pak, Miele and Philips in choosing the Carnaxide location. Siemens have recently completed the construction of an attractive new office headquarters in the Alfragide area next to the hypermarket schemes.

Central Lisbon

The traditional business centre of Lisbon – the Baixa – used to be the location for all the major Portuguese banks, as well as for the capital's major shopping outlets. The physical constraints of the old buildings in this area led some companies to move slightly to the north – to the Avenida da Liberdade, where attractive office buildings mingle with high quality residential accommodation.

The Avenida became the city's premier office location, but, more recently, there has been a shift even further north, to the Avenida Fontes Pereira de Melo, the Avenida da República and the streets on either side, with many of the major banks abandoning the Baixa for the rather more open spaces to the north of the city centre. The new Bank of Portugal headquarters is to be constructed on the west side of the Avenida da República, in the Praça d'Espanha at the end of the Avenida de Berna. On the east side, close to the Bull Ring, the new 225,000 square metre headquarters of the Caixa Geral de Depositos is under construction. In the Cinco de Outubro, the new headquarters of the Banco Nacional Ultramarino has just been completed, and the new headquarters of the Banco Pinto e Sotto Mayor is under construction close by. On the corner of the Avenida da República and the Avenida de Berna, the Credito Predial Portugues has its new headquarters, while in the Avenida de Berna itself stands the Monte Pio Bank. The trend set by so many banks seems destined to continue; increasing interest is now being shown in the Campogrande area even further north and closer to the airport.

In addition to the buildings being constructed by the major banks for owner-occupation, a number of speculative office development schemes are under construction, although not in sufficient quantity to meet the demand. At present, indeed, it is estimated that as much as 80 per cent of users of small office space in Lisbon's central area (including lawyers and other professionals) occupy residential premises which they use illegally for office purposes.

Torres Amoreiras

Immediately to the west of the central area, and almost within walking distance, stands the Torres Amoreiras development, with its 225,000 square metres of office and retail space. Two of the office blocks have been let, while the third has been sold by the floor or in smaller units. Small units of up to 100 square metres are now commanding rents as high as Esc 50,000 per square metre. Even so, the average office rent in the city is in the region of Esc 40,000 per square metre per annum.

Specification

New office construction is usually air conditioned and double glazed. In view of central Lisbon's parking problems, the provision of parking space is essential.

Although the average sales price for a small suite is in the region of Esc 350,000 per square metre, prices in the Torres Amoreiras for small suites of up to 100 square metres have now exceeded Esc 400,000. The letting price can be calculated on the basis of a yield of between 11 and 12 per cent, which provides a convenient rule-of-thumb that the monthly rental will be 1 per cent of the purchase price.

The industrial market

Until quite recently, the industrial market in Portugal presented a very sorry picture, with an over-supply of poor quality buildings and with publicly funded industrial parks failing to attract the necessary tenants. Lately, however, with the general rise in the level of optimism in the country as a whole, new developments have begun to appear. Local developers are now looking at the possibility of the speculative development of industrial and high-tech units, as well as at the sub-division of existing vacant units to provide smaller refurbished units.

Lisbon

Heavy industry was traditionally located to the south of the River Tagus and in the docklands area which, in Lisbon, is on the north bank, to the north-east of the city centre.

With the importance of heavy industry in Portugal now in decline, new light industrial and high-tech activities are being developed to the west of the capital, close to the two motorway links at Carnaxide and Alfragide. Much of this development has been to a high specification, with international companies increasingly combining office head-quarters with warehousing or manufacturing facilities. Tetra-Pak, the drinks packaging group, is one such example. Having substantially extended and modernised its existing factory premises, it has added good standard office accommodation on two floors and is now developing an extensive new plant on an adjoining site. Siemens, too, has built for its own occupation some very high standard high-tech units, while other sites are available in the area for similar development. When one of these large high specification units was offered for sale on the market recently, most interest came from developers proposing to sub-divide the unit into smaller spaces which could be let to show a very attractive return.

With considerable demand for the smaller units, rents are in the region of Esc 1,250 per square metre per month for warehousing and Esc 2,500 per square metre per month for the office element – an attractive rental by European standards. None the less, it must be stressed that these rentals are for small units in the best location with a very high specification. Elsewhere, light industrial rentals range from Esc 500 to Esc 1,000 per square metre per month, according to location and quality, for units of between 500 and 2,000 square metres.

Capital values are currently in the region of Esc 100,000 to Esc 150,000 per square metre, with industrial land in the Alfragide/Carnaxide area available at between Esc 20,000 and Esc 25,000 per square metre for plots of 3,000–10,000 square metres.

Edge-of-town

The Portuguese conglomerate, Sonae, is one of the country's largest companies. It has proposed a very large scheme on land opposite the Benfica Stadium on the northern ring road. A mixed retail, office and residential development of approximately 325,000 square metres, the scheme, when completed, will be larger even than the Torres Amoreiras.

The Republic of Ireland

Geography

Land area	68,890 sq. km.
Population	3,540,000
Density	50 per sq. km.
Main cities	Population (1986)
Dublin City Borough	520,000
Dun Laoghaire & Rathdrum	181,000
Cork	133,000
Limerick	56,000
Galway	47,000
Waterford	40,000

The Republic of Ireland has the smallest number of inhabitants of any member state apart from Luxembourg. Although more than twice the size of Belgium, for example, it has approximately one third of its population.

A lack of natural resources has restricted industrial development and led to a reliance upon agriculture and to a tradition of emigration. Over the past two decades, however, the industrial base has expanded, particularly in the electronics, food and pharmaceutical sectors.

Transport and communications

No part of the Republic is more than 112 kilometres from a harbour or airport which provides a direct link to the UK and Continental Europe. The main harbours are at Dublin, Foynes (west of Limerick) and Cork – with throughputs (in 1986) of 6 million, 3.3 million and 2.1 million tons respectively – although Limerick and Waterford are also active ports. The principal car ferry services to the UK and Europe operate out of Dun Laoghaire, Dublin and Rosslare.

THE REPUBLIC OF IRELAND

There are international airports at Dublin, Shannon, Cork and near Knock in County Mayo, although most passenger and freight traffic is handled by the first two. Provincial airports at Galway, Waterford, Sligo and Farranfore (County Kerry) are capable of handling commuter aircraft.

The total road network of 32,200 kilometres includes 2,600 kilometres of main roads. A rail network linking Dublin to the other major centres is operated by Ianroid Eirann, while the more extensive bus network is operated by Bus Eirann.

General economic

After a long period of overspending during the 1970s and early 1980s, the government has more recently made significant progress in reducing expenditure. Inflation has been as low as 2 per cent per annum (although it is currently at 3.3 per cent) and interest rates are currently around 9 per cent. During 1989, the government began to cut taxes, reducing the standard rate from 35 per cent to 32 per cent and the top rates from 58 per cent to 56 per cent.

The harmonisation of VAT under Community regulations will bring VAT down from its present rate of 25 per cent and lead to the abolition of the current high level of excise duty on certain goods, including cars. The confidence now returning to the business community is bolstered by the belief that the EC will provide substantial aid for infrastructure work, such as the proposed Dublin orbital motorway.

Industry

Manufacturing activity in the Republic falls into two main categories: new, export-orientated firms, usually in the more modern sectors and often foreign-owned; traditional and smaller Irish-owned firms in older sectors supplying the domestic market. Ireland is now recognised as a centre for the computer industry and, to a lesser degree, for the pharmaceutical business.

In the last twenty-five years, the emphasis of development policy has been on encouraging overseas companies to establish subsidiaries in the Republic. This has had little effect in terms of net employment growth in the manufacturing sector, largely because productive expansion has been met by increased productivity. Foreign firms have developed few linkages with the indigenous economy and a large share of profits has been repatriated. As a result, the proportion of added value retained by the Republic is low.

Principal industries: Nationality of ownership (1985)				
Industry	Employees in Irish-owned firms		Employees in foreign-owned firms	
Chemicals	4,327	(33.8%)	8,473	(66.2%)
Metals and engineering	25,435	(41.0%)	36,607	(59.0%)
Drink and tobacco	5,596	(60.2%)	3,696	(39.8%)
Textiles	6,566	(58.2%)	4,715	(41.8%)
Clothing, footwear and leather	10,875	(63.4%)	6,149	(36.1%)

Forms of tenure

All forms of tenure in the Republic are the same as or similar to those of the UK, as the UK statute powers operating in 1922 were enacted *en masse* by the Irish government. Its courts also operate under the same system as in the UK.

Freehold and rights of enfranchisement

Property is generally held by way of either a fee simple absolute or a fee farm grant (effectively a lease in perpetuity at a low fixed rent). When a property is held by way of a building lease (i.e. where the landlord is deemed to own the site only), the right of enfranchisement allows the tenant to acquire the fee simple absolute subject to certain conditions being satisfied. In broad terms, provided that the original lease was for more than fifteen years and the rent is less than the rateable value, the tenant of either commercial or residential property has an automatic right to the freehold. In the case of commercial property this will be at a price to be agreed, which is currently twenty-five to thirty times the value of the ground rent.

Commercial leases

Although twenty-one-year leases used to be the norm, commercial leases are now granted for terms of thirty-five years. Some landlords have introduced three- and four-year rent reviews, but a five-year period is more usual.

Security of tenure

As a result of the Republic's long history of absentee landlords, the rights of tenants have become a particularly important political issue, with protection first embodied in the Landlord and Tenant Act of 1931 and subsequently amended and extended.

The present state of the law is that, if a tenant has been in occupation of commercial property for more than three years under a lease other than one deemed to be of 'temporary convenience', that tenant has a statutory right to renew the lease for such period as he or she chooses, up to a maximum of thirty-five years. Irrespective of the length chosen, rent reviews will remain at five-yearly intervals. The rent is fixed by the courts at the open market rental value. Where landlord and tenant fail to agree and the lease has to be settled by the courts, subsequent rent reviews will be either upwards or downwards and any future dispute on review must again be settled by the courts. This is why landlords are keen to settle by negotiation: they can seek to agree terms on the basis of upwards review only and on the basis that any future dispute will be settled by an independent surveyor or arbitrator rather than by the courts.

Lease terms

Other lease terms are broadly similar to those operating in the UK. Leases, for instance, will be either full repairing and insuring or proportionally repairing and insuring. Provisions for assignment and sub-letting are also broadly similar to those in the UK although, under Irish law, there is no privity of contract. The assignor is, therefore, released from any obligation once an assignment is made for which the landlord's consent has been obtained.

It is worth noting that no arrangement exists (as it does in the UK) whereby the landlord and tenant can jointly apply to the court for exemption from the provisions of the landlord and tenant legislation, and any attempt to contract out is null and void. Any attempt to make the tenant responsible for the landlord's legal or surveying costs on a letting is also null and void.

Financial

Pension funds and insurance companies have always been inclined to invest premium income in its country of origin. Irish institutions, as well as UK and Canadian institutions, continue to make a substantial investment in the Republic – some 75 per cent of all premium income generated in Ireland is invested there. The size of the country, however, does not make it easy to find a home for lots of more than IR£4 million.

Now that exchange controls (from which UK property was exempted) have effectively been scrapped and the long period of recession is at an end, the banks are more favourably disposed towards property than formerly.

New types of financing, such as the unitisation of property assets, are being imported from the UK and all the four major banks (Bank of Ireland, Allied Irish, Ulster Bank and National Irish) are actively lending against property for acquisition and development.

Taxation

Local taxation (rates)

Each local authority levies rates on commercial and industrial property (excluding machinery) for its own jurisdiction based on valuations derived from an estimate of the net annual letting value of the property and adjusted downwards to match valuations of similar properties made or revised within a recent period. The rate is expressed as an amount in punts payable in respect of each IR£1 valuation.

In designated areas, the local rates on grant-aided industrial buildings may, at the discretion of the local authority, be reduced by two-thirds during the first ten years. Qualifying new companies should apply to the Irish Development Agency (IDA) for the necessary certificate. In designated urban development areas and in the Custom House Docks area, a full rates remission applies for ten years.

Capital Gains Tax

The rate ranges between 60 per cent and 30 per cent, depending on the period of ownership. The inflationary element in gains is not taxable. Companies reinvesting the proceeds on the disposal of assets are able to defer liability on the gain until such time as no further reinvestment takes place.

Residential Property Tax

A person owning and occupying residential property whose market value exceeds a market value exemption limit (adjusted annually by new house price inflation and currently set at IR£74,321) is liable to a residential property tax charged at the rate of 1.5 per cent on the excess value above the limit. Where the gross annual income of the household does not exceed IR£25,795 (also adjusted annually for inflation), no tax is payable.

Capital Acquisition Tax

Applied to gifts and inheritances, Capital Acquisition Tax is a tax on the donee or successor, for whom there is a level of tax-free exemption defined by the relationship between the donor/testator and the donee/successor.

Donee/successor	Exemption (IR£)
Spouse (inheritances)	150,000
Spouse (gifts)	150,000
Each child (no age-limit)	20,000
Grandparents and grandchildren	20,000
Brother, sister	20,000
Nephew, niece	20,000
Others	10,000

On inheritances, the tax is levied in successive slices on the basis of a single table at varying rates from 20 per cent to 55 per cent. The rates on gifts are 25 per cent less than those on inheritances.

Stamp duty on transfer of property

This duty does not apply to industrialists who build (or cause to be built) their own factory. Plant and machinery are not liable in any circumstances. The rates of stamp duty on transfers of property are as follows:

- Sale -- whether by transfer of ownership or assignment of lease on payment (not including stocks and shares):

Price/value	Rate of duty (%)
up to IR£10,000	2
IR£10,000–20,000	3
IR£20,000–50,000	4
IR£50,000–60,000	5
over 60,000	6

- Leases of property:

Length of term	Rate of duty
not exceeding 35 years	1% of annual rent
36–100 years	6% of annual rent
exceeding 100 years	12% of annual rent

Grant aid and investment incentives

The government has introduced a package of measures designed to revitalise the run down areas at the heart of the Republic's major cities by stimulating investment in new buildings, reconstruction and development. The tax incentives announced by the Taoiseach on 23 October 1985 and incorporated in the 1986 Finance Act fall under two main headings:

- Capital allowances on the construction costs of new commercial buildings and for the capital improvement of existing ones. Double tax allowances to tenants for business rents payable.

- Capital allowances – available both to owner-occupiers and landlords – for the construction costs of houses or flats.

The measures also provide full remission of rates on new buildings for ten years and on any increase in the valuation of enlarged or improved buildings. The incentives apply to certain designated areas only.

Dublin

Of the four areas designated in the capital, the largest (368,000 square metres) runs northwards from the Customs House through Gardiner Street and Mountjoy Square to Dorset Street. The second area covers 280,000 square metres to the north and south of the River Liffey between O'Connell Bridge and the Guinness factory and includes some of the worst urban decay in Dublin. The third area is Custom House Dock (109,000 square metres), and the fourth, and smallest, is the 8,100 square metres around Henrietta Street, including some of the finest Georgian architecture in the capital.

Cork

The main designated area in Cork (328,000 square metres) lies to the south and west of the commercial centre and includes South Parish, The Marsh and part of Shandon Street. A second area – of 72,600 square metres – has been designated at Blackpool.

Limerick

In Limerick the designated area extends from John's Gate through Charlotte Quay to Arthur's Quay, including land and premises between St Mary's Cathedral and the River Shannon.

Waterford   The 56,500 square metres designated area in Waterford extends from Meagher's Quay to Alexander Street, including land and premises between High Street and Lady Lane.

Galway   The designated area in Galway (of 56,500 square metres) runs from Eyre Square to the River Corrib and between Merchants Road, Middle Street and Quay Street.

Capital allowances

The existing capital allowances for industrial buildings have been extended to include all new commercial buildings and improvements to existing ones within the designated areas. An owner-occupier may claim up to 100 per cent write off of qualifying expenditure in the first year, while a lessor may claim 54 per cent write off in year one and 4 per cent annually thereafter. These percentages apply to all designated areas outside Dublin and to the Custom House Dock area in the capital. In Dublin's other three designated areas, the allowances are at 50 per cent of these figures. The new allowances apply to qualifying expenditure incurred between 23 October 1985 and 31 May 1989, although it is anticipated that the period will be extended.

Double rent allowance

In all the designated areas, business tenants will be allowed a deduction against taxable profits of double the amount of rent payable. A company paying corporation tax at 43 per cent will therefore gain a tax saving of IR£1 for each IR£1 of rent payable; an individual trader paying income tax at 58 per cent will have a tax saving of IR£1.16 for each IR£1 of rent payable. The relief will apply for a ten-year period where a new lease is entered into for a new *commercial* building which is eligible for a capital allowance in accordance with the 1986 Finance Act or for a new *industrial* building.

Existing industrial buildings may also qualify without any additional capital expenditure being incurred, but existing commercial buildings will qualify only if expenditure is incurred which brings entitlement to the new capital allowance on construction or improvement costs. Lessors of existing commercial buildings which fail to qualify will, therefore, be at a significant disadvantage both in attracting and retaining tenants.

179

Planning regulations

The Republic's means of planning control – based on the 1963 Planning and Development Act and subsequent amendments – is very similar to the system in the UK, under which local authorities prepare a development plan for approval and adoption. Planning permission is required for material development, but the timetable is rather different from the UK timetable. In the Republic, the local authority must make a decision with regard to a request for planning permission within two months. (Any failure to respond is deemed to signify consent.) The local authority's 'decision to grant' is publicised for a period of three weeks, during which time the applicant, the local authority or any third party can appeal against the decision. If there is such an appeal, the application is referred to the Appeals Board. The Board may take up to six months, although many appeals are heard quite rapidly.

Brokerage

The Auctioneer's Act of 1973 requires brokers to be licensed and to be bonded as a protection for their clients' money. The average fees for residential transactions are 2.5 per cent in Dublin and 3.5 per cent in country districts. As in the UK, fees for commercial transactions are by agreement and tend to be in the region of 1 per cent to 2.5 per cent, depending on the value of the transaction and whether the broker is working for the vendor or purchaser.

The recognised professional qualification is that awarded by the Society of Chartered Surveyors of the Republic of Ireland which is a constituent body of the RICS in the UK.

Conveyancing

As in the UK, conveyancing is undertaken by solicitors, although the costs are greater (at 1 per cent of the transaction value plus IR£100).

The construction industry

Capacity

The majority of building contractors in the Republic of Ireland are, by international standards, small and medium-sized firms. For major construction projects, there are probably only two or three contractors with the necessary resources and expertise. Only two companies operate nationally – John Sisk & Sons (turnover IR£100 million) and P. J. Hegarty (turnover IR£40 million). Except in the house-building sector, there is no national classification of contractors.

General state of the industry

The industry has experienced serious recession since the mid-1970s and is currently showing only marginal signs of recovery. As a result, there has been a continuous exporting of skilled labour, particularly to the UK, and there has also been increasing involvement by the major contractors in work in the UK. No major public or private investment is committed that will, in the immediate term, alter the current state of the construction market.

The general rate of inflation is running at approximately 6 per cent per annum; the tender market is experiencing around 4 per cent inflation.

Structure of the industry

Contractors are members of a national federation and, by and large, the industry is similar to that in the UK. The role and responsibilities of the consultants are much the same, too. Responsibility for quality control lies with the architect, and there is almost no involvement by independent quality control organisations.

Design considerations

The structure of the building regulations and other standards is similar to that in the UK and, in the absence of special codes in the Irish Standards, it is usual to comply with British Standards. The regulations are mandatory, while the standards arc advisory only.

Approvals

Prior to the commencement of works, planning approval must be obtained. The works must also be subject to building regulation approval.

Programme considerations

The first step in the pre-construction programme is to obtain the building permit. On a medium-sized project, around six months should be allowed after receipt of the approval to complete the construction project, prepare tender documents and obtain the tenders.

Placing the building contract

The bidding of a contract is generally similar to the process in the UK, and standard forms of contract are issued by the Architects' Institution and widely used. The majority of contracts are based on drawings, specifications and bills of quantities. They are administered exactly as in the UK.

Cost comparisons

The level of professional fees is similar to that in the UK. For a new build project of around IR£3 million excluding VAT (about £3.2 million), the total fees for architect, engineer and quantity surveyor would be around 12 per cent.

Construction costs are lower than in the UK. For example, an air-conditioned speculative office building on the outskirts of Dublin will cost only around IR£700 per square metre (£590 per square metre) excluding VAT.

The retail market

Estimated value of retail sales	
1987	£5.7bn

Estimated volume of retail sales (1980 = 100)	
1984	89.4
1985	91
1986	90.5
1987	89.3

Shop hours
Mon. to Sat. — 09.00/09.30 to 17.00
Thur. or Fri. — late closing at 19.00/20.00
Some unofficial Sunday opening

VAT rates		
	Nil (zero)	0%
	Lower	1.7%
	Standard	25%
	Higher	25%

Source: Corporate Intelligence Research Publications Ltd

The second half of 1988 saw a significant upturn in the retail market and the forecast for growth in 1989 is 3 per cent in volume terms.

Trends

In the past twelve to eighteen months, international multiples have shown increasing interest; traders such as Body Shop, Benetton, Laura Ashley, Ratners, Tie Rack, Sock Shop, Virgin, Next and Burtons have all entered the market. However, a shortage of units in the 140 to 190 square metre category has come to light and this has made entry difficult for some multiples.

The removal of cross-border barriers in 1992 may benefit the Irish retail market in two ways. Firstly, international traders who previously considered the Republic too small a market to support a separate management structure will be able to administer the North and South of Ireland as one. Secondly, the removal of import quotas on cheap goods (particularly clothes from the Far East), previously eaten up by existing Irish chains, will create a more competitive market and allow access to new traders. These two factors, together with the general economic improvement and the prospect of further tax cuts, add up to a healthy outlook for the retail market.

The retail market in Dublin

Of Dublin's two distinct retail centres, Henry Street/Mary Street in the north has traditionally been the preferred location for the larger multiples, especially the fashion stores. Grafton Street, on the more prosperous south bank of the River Liffey, has provided smaller units for speciality shops and boutiques.

Although from the mid-1960s to the late 1980s the centre of Dublin suffered from competition with suburban shopping facilities, the current recovery – the result of the pedestrianisation and upgrading of the two main streets, improved parking facilities and the electrified commuter rail service (the DART) – is evidenced by the volume of refurbishment work, the number of new traders in the marketplace and the new shopping schemes proposed or under construction.

Rents in Henry Street are slightly higher than those in Grafton Street, although by a differential of less than 10 per cent.

Henry Street

The Ilac Centre, developed by Irish Life in the early 1980s, provided some 23,000 square metres of enclosed retail space and was the first such scheme within the city centre. Though very successful, it is, by today's standards, rather outdated. The first rent reviews fell due in October 1986 and are now being settled at rents showing a 100 per cent increase in the principal trading malls. Rents of around IR£540 per square metre overall are being agreed on review for the most common size of unit (75 to 80 square metres), although new tenants are prepared to pay premiums of between IR£100,000 and IR£150,000 in view of the scarcity of open market lettings which has resulted from the landlord and tenant legislation. This suggests that a full rental value may be between IR£700 and IR£1,000 per square metre overall.

In Henry Street itself, a standard unit (5.5 metres, frontage and 18.25 metres depth) providing approximately 90 square metres on the ground floor, with a basement and (perhaps) three floors above is letting at IR£115,000 per annum. Some larger units of approximately 140 square metres are letting at between IR£150,000 and IR£185,000 per annum.

A major new scheme is proposed on the corner of Mary Street and Jervis Street, next to Marks & Spencer.

Grafton Street

The pleasant Georgian architecture of this semi-pedestrianised street combines with a gentle gradient towards St Stephen's Green to create an attractive shopping environment. Containing smaller units with three floors over, the street offers rents of about IR£900–970 per square metre Zone A (see p. 225) and rental values for a typical building of between IR£75,000 and IR£100,000 per annum. Once again the infrequency with which vacant units are offered to let at a rack rent on the open market has led to prospective tenants paying premiums of between IR£100,000 and IR£200,000 for possession.

New retail developments

British Land has recently completed a new scheme providing some 23,000 square metres (14,000 square metres net) retail space on the corner of St Stephen's Green at the south end of Grafton Street. Dunnes Stores are the anchor tenant and the scheme has let well. There is provision for expansion in a second phase on land to the south of the site.

Trafalgar House is seeking planning permission for a new shopping scheme providing 14,000 square metres' retail space next to Marks & Spencer on the corner of Jervis Street and Mary Street. Subject to approval, the scheme will open before 1992.

Further south, on the banks of the Liffey between Bachelors Walk and Abbey Street and outside the existing retail area, Arlington has a scheme for a mixed development of 60,500 square metres gross, including 23,200 square metres' retail space. Although the developers have yet to assemble the whole site, and planning permission has not yet been sought, the site lies within one of the designated areas, which attract considerable tax advantages.

Suburban shopping

Between 1966 and 1980, some thirty or forty suburban shopping centres were built in greater Dublin. Typically containing a super-market and between twenty and fifty units, they attracted convenience shopping away from the city centre. Since 1980, suburban rents have been static at around IR£160–215 per square metre overall although the better centres, such as Stillorgan, Northside and Nutgrove, have seen rents rise to IR£325 per square metre. More recently, there has been a considerable recovery in inner city retail.

Multiple traders

Of the relatively small number of multiple traders in the Republic of Ireland, Dunnes Stores – a food and clothes retailer – is the largest. Since the withdrawal of Tesco and the demise of H. Williams, the only supermarket multiples are Dunnes Quinnsworth (part of Associated British Foods) and Super Quinn.

Out-of-town retailing

Though nothing more than a group of retail warehouses on the Naas Road running south from Dublin, the first out-of-town retail park was given planning consent in 1989. The first occupants include Atlantic House Care, Powercity (franchise) and Payless (franchise).

The retail market in the rest of Ireland

Cork

On Patrick Street, Cork's principal retailing street, the present rental level is IR£380 to IR£430 per square metre overall. A major new scheme (Merchants Quay) being developed by an Anglo-Irish joint venture between O'Callaghan (Properties) Ltd and Heron Property Corporation, has arranged pre-lets to Marks & Spencer and Dunnes Stores. There are also forty or so small units of 45 to 55 square metres letting at IR£540 per square metre overall. This scheme is now open and most of the units are let.

Limerick

In the principal shopping streets (O'Connell Street and William Street), prime rents are approximately IR£270 to IR£380 per square metre overall.

| Galway | A university town with a prosperous catchment from the local farming community, Galway's shopping rents have always been at a slight premium. Prime rents on the main retail street (Shop Street) are between IR£325 and IR£380 per square metre. |

| Waterford | Prime rents in Broad Street are in the region of IR£270 per square metre. |

The office market

Trends

Following an over-supply since the early 1980s, the shortage of prime space is now driving rents upwards. The prospect of an increase in supply following the completion of Custom House Docks in Dublin and the government's own decentralisation scheme is likely to cater for some of the future demand, although some further development is under way.

Dublin

In the 1960s, there was a serious under-supply of good modern space. Increased demand in the 1970s led to a substantial amount of speculative building, but the market crash in the early 1980s left a considerable volume of empty space. Until the latter part of 1988, prime office rents were still IR£90 per square metre, although pre-let new space was achieving IR£108 per square metre. Space in the city centre could be had for as little as IR£70 per square metre. The recent change in the situation is due in part to the absorption of this surplus, but rather more to the two-tier market created by occupiers' changed requirements.

Older speculatively built space remains unlet at low rentals, while well specified new space is pre-letting at substantially higher rents. In 1989, rents of IR£150 or IR£160 were being achieved, and office development sites are now fetching very high prices.

A structural problem remains, however, in terms of the length of leases available. During the recession, tenants asked for and obtained break options from their landlords, but now that the market has recovered a little the tendency is for landlords to refuse. Because the landlord and tenant legislation provides that any lease granted for more than three years entitles the tenant to seek a new lease of anything up to the traditional thirty-five-year period, landlords are now offering leases of either two years and nine months or of thirty-five years. Neither term meets the requirements of most international companies.

The government recently introduced legislation enabling leases to be granted for more than three years to tenants in the Custom House Docks without those tenants gaining rights under the Landlord and Tenant Act. It is likely that this legislation will, in due course, be extended to all new lettings.

Dublin 2: The central business district

A number of pre-lettings of new space at around IR£110 per square metre demonstrate a significant increase in the past twelve months in the central business district, where the average take-up of space in recent years has been in the region of 28,000 square metres per annum. In the summer of 1987, 2,300 square metres at 50 Dawson Street were let at IR£95 per square metre; in the autumn of 1988, the adjoining space in a sister block achieved IR£108 per square metre and the remaining space in this block is now on offer at IR£160 per square metre. The developers of The Plantation, a 1,200 square metre self-contained office building now under construction, have negotiated with a tenant a letting at IR£150 to IR£160 per square metre. (The Plantation is one of only four new buildings in Dublin with raised floors, even though raised floors are now regarded as essential for any new office development.)

Custom House Docks

An ambitious scheme for the wholesale redevelopment of between 121,500 and 162,000 square metres of riverside space within a designated zone offering substantial tax reliefs, the Custom House Docks project will provide 70,000 square metres of office space, a 300-bed hotel, 200 flats, a 1,500-seat conference centre and 27,900 square metres of leisure/community space. On the north bank of the River Liffey and away from the traditional office centre, its impact is not easy to assess. The developers claim that the scheme is aimed at the international financial services industry rather than at tenants of the central business district, although several large Irish banks and institutions have already indicated a wish to take space for new departments.

In order to obtain the licence necessary to qualify for the tax breaks, prospective occupiers must be involved in export and/or international services. The consortium of developers is seeking rents of IR£290 per square metre. Clearly the tenants are unlikely to resist such high rents during the period of tax breaks, but there must be some concern about the long-term effect of this distortion of the market. Phase II buildings, which have a lower specification, are on offer, at IR£195 per square metre.

Out-of-town office centres

Both out-of-town office locations – Ballsbridge and Blackrock, to the south-east of Dublin – are served by the rapid rail link, the DART, bringing them within approximately ten minutes of the city centre.

Although the local authority will grant no further planning consents for development in Ballsbridge, a number of sites are currently available at Blackrock. A pleasant, affluent residential area providing a good catchment for office workers, Blackrock has good shopping and car-parking facilities and little in the way of traffic congestion. Most of the offices are speculatively built, and although a sharp rise in rental values in line with Dublin 2 is expected, they have let at between IR£75 and IR£80 per square metre – approximately IR£10 per square metre less than in Dublin 2. However, a recent transaction in the Maritime Court development is being let at IR£110 per square metre.

High-tech

Apart from the computer industry, the high-tech market in the Republic is not very well developed at present. One office park built by McInerneys in the early 1980s was successful because of its proximity to the Sandyford Industrial Estate, and Clonskea Court and Clanwilliam are further examples of successful office park development situated around Dublin. Other schemes have been less successful: the Harold's Cross development, of four 930 square metre buildings, was in mid-construction when the developer went into receivership. Small office buildings of 90 to 185 square metres are, however, in great demand and will fetch betweeen IR£1,100 and IR£1,300 per square metre in the town centre and in excess of IR£1,100 per square metre in the suburbs.

Major space users

Although committed to decentralisation, the government is, predictably, the largest single user of space, occupying 242,000 square metres. It will be shedding space in the centre of town, but this property is unlikely to come on the market before the end of 1990.

In the private sector, 362,500 square metres is leased and 223,000 square metres is owner-occupied. The largest users in the private sector are the four main Irish banks, the insurance companies and computer companies. A number of substantial tenants, including one large accountancy firm, are currently seeking space, although they are said to be waiting to see how the Custom House Docks scheme progresses before committing themselves.

Planning

Town centre redevelopment is limited to 600 square metres, except in the designated areas of Dublin 1 and 2 close to the River Liffey, where large-scale redevelopment is actively encouraged by the tax incentives.

The industrial market

Background

The industrial market was the hardest hit by the recession of the early 1980s, with rental and capital values halved on average and, in the worst hit locations, falling to one third of previous levels except on the prime estates of Sandyford, Airways and Airton Road (all in the Dublin area).

1989 was the first year since 1981 in which any new industrial building work was undertaken. It also saw a significant increase in demand and, with the slack taken up over the last three years, the market is now unable to meet the requirements for good quality space. Most of the empty space in and around Dublin consists of sheds built speculatively in the early to mid-1970s, which no longer meet current requirements. There are shortages of prime space in good locations in all size categories.

Dublin

Stillorgan/Sandyford is the best of Dublin's four good industrial estates. A well designed, low density estate situated in a pleasant residential suburb to the south of Dublin, it has experienced a very low turnover of property and rents have held up well despite the recession. Of the other three estates, the Tallaght Estate and the Western Industrial Estate are to the south of Dublin, while Airways Industrial Estate is to the north.

Future prospects

Now that the market is reviving, developers are taking an interest in acquiring industrial land. Whereas the average price is IR£148,000 to IR£222,300 per hectare, land at Sandyford and Tallaght is reaching between IR£247,000 and IR£296,000 per hectare, which indicates the scarcity of space in these much favoured locations.

Although there is plenty of land zoned for industrial use around the Naas Road (the main route south from Dublin), Irish developers are reluctant to speculate with large units until they are confident that a rental value of IR£43 per square metre or a capital value of IR£430 per square metre can be sustained. Small-scale speculative units (550 to 750 square metres) are achieving rentals of IR£43 per square metre against a previous average of IR£21.50 per square metre.

Rest of Ireland

The Irish Development Authority has built a series of small industrial estates in many parts of the country, including Waterford, Cork, Limerick and Galway, which provide high quality sheds for manufacturing use only. Although the rents payable often exceed the true rental value, they must be seen in the context of the aid and incentives package provided by the Authority.

Future developments

By cutting through large areas of land already zoned for industrial use, the proposed Dublin orbital motorway will provide a number of important industrial opportunities. Although there may be a shortage of prime space in the immediate future, once developers are confident that rentals will remain above IR£43 per square metre new development will begin in order to meet the demand.

Spain

Geography

Land area	504,750 sq. km.
Population	38,990,000
Density	76 per sq. km.
Main cities	Population
Madrid	3,200,000
Barcelona	1,750,000
Valencia	750,000
Seville	650,000
Malaga/Marbella	620,000

Mainland Spain occupies part of the Iberian Peninsula; it is very mountainous, with an extensive central plateau. Madrid, the capital, is the administrative, banking and transportation centre. The most active industrial and commercial region is Catalonia, with Barcelona as its focal point.

Transport and communications

There are 317,000 kilometres of road in Spain, but this includes only 2,142 kilometres of motorway, of which 1,700 kilometres are toll roads. Under the current building programme (1988–91), the construction of new roads will form the largest area of public expenditure, with a total investment of £5 billion. Within this programme, however, there is no provision for any new motorways. This means that Madrid and Lisbon (in Portugal) will be the only capitals *not* linked to the European motorway network. Currently, almost 75 per cent of all freight traffic is carried by road.

Spain has international airports at, *inter alia*, Madrid (12 kilometres from the city at Barajas) and at Barcelona (15 kilometres from the city).

SPAIN

International boundary	
Road	
Railway	
International Airport	
Airport	

The 1992 Olympic Games are to be held at Barcelona and a major road-building programme is planned in time for this and for the Seville Expo in 1992.

Over the next decade, the government also plans a major overhaul of the national railway (RENFE) to bring it up to the most advanced European standard. A contract has been awarded to Alsthom SA of France and Siemens AG of West Germany to build a high-speed train line by 1992 which would cut travel time between Madrid and Seville from seven hours to three.

General economic

After a particularly difficult period during the 1970s and a very slow return to growth, recent years have seen a dramatic surge in foreign industrial and financial investment, with the 1987 GDP (at 5.2 per cent) well above that of its European partners and with a projected growth for 1989 of 4.5 per cent. The economy is continuing to perform well despite signs of overheating and the government's use of monetary steps to raise the cost of borrowing and soak up liquidity in order to stave off the threat of inflation and higher unemployment (the current unemployment rate is around 17 per cent).

The construction sector is outstripping the general economic growth rate and is estimated to have created 115,000 new jobs in 1988 as well as recovering over 60 per cent of the jobs lost since 1974.

The private sector – both domestic and foreign – is heavily engaged in real estate development, with many new buildings being constructed and older ones being restored. Although some commentators have suggested that the construction boom might end by 1993, there is a considerable growth in property acquisition by the services sector.

Industry

The main locations for Spain's industries are as follows:

Barcelona
- Barcelona, the focal point of Spain's principal industrial region, contains a free port zone. Its local industries include textiles, paints, chemicals, plastics, fertilisers, electrical engineering products and appliances, machinery and tanning.

| Bilbao | • Bilbao, too, is a major port with large-scale handling facilities, extensive shipbuilding yards, engineering, steelworks, iron ore mines, chemical works, two power stations and an oil refinery. |

Bilbao • Bilbao, too, is a major port with large-scale handling facilities, extensive shipbuilding yards, engineering, steelworks, iron ore mines, chemical works, two power stations and an oil refinery.

Madrid • Industries in the capital, Madrid, include engineering, metal working, vehicle manufacture, electrical appliances, clothing, printing and publishing, cosmetics and other light industries.

Vitoria • Vitoria is the seat of the Basque government and its industrial activities include steel making, ferrous and non-ferrous casting production, motor vehicles, light metal industries and confectionery.

Valencia • An important centre for the furniture and ceramic manufacturing industries, Valencia is being developed as an automobile and steel manufacturing area and is also rich in agriculture, producing mainly citrus fruits, onions, rice and potatoes.

Alicante • Alicante province is a centre for the shoe and carpet industries and exports large quantities of agricultural produce, including tomatoes.

Seville • Seville is a river port located within a very fertile region which also contains lead and copper mines. The region exports olives, olive oil, cork, fruit, wine and essential oils; its local industry includes shipbuilding and aircraft engine manufacturing.

Vigo • With its free port zone, Vigo is Spain's most important centre for the fishing and fish canning industries as well as for cattle raising. Its other activities include ceramics, food processing, glassware, motor car manufacturing, plastics and rubber, shipbuilding, engineering, container port handling equipment, pharmaceutical goods and fertilisers.

Other areas • Zaragosa, Tarragona, Pamplona, San Sebastián and Huelva are major centres for industries such as automobile, mining and petrochemicals. Algeciras is an important harbour, trading with North Africa, and the centre of a growing industrial area. Oviedo, Gijón and Aviles form an important industrial triangle close to the country's largest steelworks and most important coal-mining area.

Forms of tenure

Article 348 of the Civil Code defines property ownership as: 'The right to enjoy and dispose of a thing without any further limitations than those provided for in the law. The owner has the right of action against the person holding and possessing the thing in order to claim it.' This definition effectively accords with the UK concept of fee simple, in that the owner has the right to charge or dispose of property and the right to exclusive possession. The Civil Code also contains, for the mutual benefit of adjoining owners, rights and obligations in relation to boundaries and party walls, as well as to construction and planning.

Real estate in Spain is normally acquired through a purchase-sale contract, for which both parties appear before a notary to make a declaration for the sale and purchase. A public document is then granted, and the contract inscribed in the Propety Register. Except where the parties agree to the contrary, notary charges are paid by the seller, while fees for additional copies of the contract are charged to the buyer. The inscription in the Property Register is very important, since the first person to register the title is deemed to be the legal owner.

The Civil Code also provides for co-ownership or condominium-type ownership, in which the owners' rights are similar to those of a sole owner except that they are subject to restrictions and limitations designed to be for the benefit of all the co-owners.

Real estate acquisition by foreigners

The acquisition of real estate is generally regarded as a business activity which requires prior government authorisation and, although there are exceptions for private individuals (including the acquisition of residential property), verification by the Spanish authorities is required in all cases where the investor is a foreign company.

For the purpose of verification, details of the proposed acquisition must be submitted in advance to the foreign investments authority. Provided the acquisition falls within the current regulations, the authority may not generally withhold approval unless the proposal is deemed to be harmful to the national economy.

Thirty days is the period allowed for approval, although it generally takes no more than seven to fifteen. Once the necessary approval has been obtained, the company is entitled to repatriate the proceeds from any subsequent sale, provided all legal and tax obligations have been met. The company may also remit any rental income abroad again, subject to the fulfilment of any tax obligations.

Leases

Until 1985, crippling landlord and tenant legislation not only gave security of tenure to tenants but fixed their rents too. The result, as elsewhere in Europe, was ludicrously low rents with large sums of key money changing hands and generally dilapidated buildings. The Boyer Law introduced in 1985 effectively reversed the situation: for any leases subsequent to that date, there is no security of tenure at all. Provided a landlord gives notice between sixty and forty-five days of the expiry of the lease, the tenant must quit. Combined with the current severe shortage of space, particularly in the office sector, the present law has resulted in spiralling rental levels.

In the past, the majority of speculatively built office blocks have been sold off on a condominium basis to investors who have then sub-let the suites. These private investors have yet to see the benefits of a long lease to a good quality tenant, and the majority of suites are let on terms of three years or less, with rental increases linked to a cost-of-living index (IPC).

Recently, however, a Spanish development company (Fabriga) has built 10,000 square metres of office space to the west of Madrid's airport and let it to Colgate on a ten-year lease, with annual indexation and open market rent review at the end of the fifth year. This may herald a new era for Spain, in view of the fact that the recent surge in the economy is attracting considerable institutional interest in the property market. Northern European institutions bring with them the idea of leasing a whole building to a good quality tenant on full repairing terms with open market reviews.

In Spain, floor areas are measured gross and include a proportion of the common areas, as well as lavatories and utilities serving the space. With the common area somewhere in the region of 10 to 12 per cent, the overall net lettable space will be around 20 per cent lower than the gross area quoted. All rents and service charges are quoted and payable monthly. In general, service charges are quite low (around 10 to 12 per cent of the rent); like the rent, they are index linked. The tenant retains responsibility for internal repairs.

Car-parking spaces in central Madrid are at a premium, and office rentals rarely include any parking space. Spaces will be rented separately at a cost of between Pta 16,000 and 25,000 per space per month.

Finance

Compared with the UK, Spain is not a sophisticated banking market. Its financial vehicles tend to be straightforward overdraft facilities and variable loans. Although so-called fixed-rate loans can be negotiated in the markets, they tend to be subject to review every thirty days! As in the UK, loans are granted at various points over the inter-bank rate, which is itself based on the yield on Spanish Treasury bills. The banks' caution about fixed-rate loans is easy to understand: in early 1987, the inter-bank rate was 22 per cent but by January 1988 it had fallen to 14 per cent. Interest rates bottomed out in June 1988 at 10.5 per cent, but by September 1988, although the daily inter-bank rate remained at 11.5 per cent, the yearly rate was 13 per cent – a clear indication of the banks' view of the future. By January 1989, the inter-bank rate stood at 13 per cent and in May 1989 at 13.75 per cent, with the banks quoting an annual rate of 15.25 per cent. This suggests that there will continue to be a steady increase in the cost of finance.

As is the case in the UK, finance can be raised against property, with Spanish banks traditionally lending up to 65 or 70 per cent of valuation. In the recently booming property market, however, it has not been difficult to find 100 per cent funding.

The exceptionally high interest rates of recent years have led borrowers to seek foreign currency loans, but the government has discouraged this with legislation which requires foreign currency loans or commercial loans from a parent company to be for a minimum of three years and for a maximum of Pta 1.5 billion. Thirty per cent of the value of the loan must also be deposited with the Bank of Spain at 0 per cent interest. This goes some way towards correcting the imbalance between Spanish interest rates and the European average. Companies are, however, permitted to bring the necessary funds into the country as 'capital' rather than as a loan.

Registering a charge on land can take up to a year, depending on the willingness and efficiency of the local office, and as a result some foreign banks prefer to rely on parent company guarantees.

By the end of March 1988, forty-two foreign banks had been established in Spain. Increasingly, with the liberalisation of the system, the commercial banks are facing competition from the saving banks, the largest of which (the Caixa and the Caja de Ahorros de Madrid) are included on the basis of deposit.

Taxation

Taxes on purchase

VAT or Property Transfer Tax (PTT)   In all cases, the purchaser pays the tax.

1. *New property*
plots of land:	6% PTT (for private transfer)
	12% VAT (for business transfer)
housing:	6% VAT
business premises:	12% VAT
parking lots:	6% PTT (if attached to a dwelling)
	12% VAT (if independent)

2. *Second-hand property*
plots of land:	6% PTT
housing:	6% PTT
business premises:	6% PTT

Municipal Capital Gains Tax (Arbitrario de Plusvalia)   Although the vendor is supposed to pay this tax, in practice it is often the purchaser who pays. The taxable base is roughly the difference between the sale price and the official value indices of the land on which buildings have been constructed. These indices change every three years, and the tax rates vary between 5 and 23.5 per cent. In view of the potentially high sum due, it is advisable to ascertain the level of tax before making a commitment to buy.

Taxes on ownership

Contribución Territorial Urbana This tax, payable annually, is assessed on a given income derived from the official value of the whole property as fixed by the government. The tax rate varies between the different provinces, but cannot exceed 20 per cent.

Wealth tax This tax on property is applied on an increasing scale with (currently) two levels:

Pta 0–25,000,000:	0.20%
Pta 25,000,000–50,000,000:	0.30%

Taxes on rental income

Indirect taxation on rental income

- *Business premises:* 12% VAT

- *Housing:* PTT via the officially approved lease contract form

Direct taxation on rental income

- *Non-resident companies:* 20 per cent withholding tax on gross rent. (No reduced treaty rate is available for UK companies despite the UK–Spanish convention to avoid double taxation.)

- *Non-resident individual:* 20 per cent withholding tax on gross rent.

Capital gains tax

- *Non-resident companies:* 35 per cent withholding tax on the difference between the acquisition cost (as determined pursuant to current regulations) and the market value. (The sale price stated in the deed will be accepted if it equals or exceeds the market value.)

- *Non-resident individuals:* from the beginning of the fiscal year 1988, 35 per cent withholding tax on the difference between the acquisition cost (i.e. the total of the sale price, expenses and taxes paid at purchase as updated according to official co-efficients) and the market value (as assessed by the revenue service) or the sale price if it matches or exceeds the market value.

Grant aid and investment incentives

Since 1985, Spain has brought its system of central and regional government grant aid into line with Community requirements. The new legislation establishes two new categories of zone:

- *Zonas Industrializadas en Declive (ZIDs)* – Where industrial restructuring has severely affected employment, ZIDs are established for an eighteen-month period and may be eligible for the maximum permitted level of regional aid (50 per cent).

- *Zonas de Promoción Economica (ZPEs)* – Assessed by a mixture of criteria including income and employment levels, ZPEs have no time limit. They are divided into four sub-categories in which investment is eligible for a maximum state subsidy of 50 per cent, 40 per cent, 30 per cent and 20 per cent respectively.

There are currently four ZIDs, each consisting of a specifically limited area: Galicia, Asturias, Cantabria and the Basque region. All autonomous regions of Spain are ZPEs except for Madrid, Rioja, Cataluña and Valencia, which do not qualify for regional economic incentives from central government.

Economic incentives are usually in the form of cash grants provided by central government through regional governments. The maximum percentage is based on the value of the investment in a project which has been officially approved and the purpose of which is to set up a new establishment or to expand, move or modernise an existing one. Legislation also permits the granting of subsidies on the cost of interest on commercial loans, as well as credits of up to 50 per cent of the employer's contribution to health and social security payments.

In 1988, the Spanish government provided some Pta 8,000–9,000 million towards regional incentives, and the 1989 budget raised this sum by 24 per cent. There are, in addition, much larger sums of public money invested in regional development. The plan for 1989–93 indicates a total planned expenditure of Pta 8,020,000 million, 18 per cent of which will be financed by the Community. The 1989 budget is Pta 167,365 million, of which 90 per cent is for new transport links.

Although the central government's aid scheme is controlled by the Directorate General for Regional Economic Incentives at the Ministry of Economy and Finance, there is unfortunately no central source of information on regional and municipal incentives, both of which are subject to frequent change.

Planning regulations

Madrid

The Plan General del Municipio de Madrid (1984) governs the administration of the town-planning system and applies a land-use classification which covers the entire city area. Prepared within the framework set by the *Ley sobre el Régimen del Suelo y Ordenación Urbana* (Land Use and Urban Development Law, 1956), the Madrid General Plan has the status of a local master plan and the force of a statutory document. It is essentially a development control vehicle, operating in conjunction with a series of *normas urbanisticas* (planning standards) which also have statutory force and have been formally adopted by the City Council.

Within its area of coverage, the Madrid General Plan identifies development sites, land to be protected from building, and existing urban land, including infill sites. This urban land is divided into zones, each of which is subject to a pre-determined set of regulations specifying the permissible use or mix of uses and the height of new buildings. Applied with almost total inflexibility, these regulations also indicate whether existing buildings may be redeveloped or whether the conservation regime (*conservación ambiental*) applies. Much of Inner Madrid (with the exception of specified development sites such as Azca, Cuzco and Plaza Castilla) is subject to the *conservación ambiental*. The overall effect of these regulations is to stifle developer initiative in the assembly of suitable sites.

As regards development land (*suelos urbanizables*), the Madrid General Plan distinguishes between programmed and non-programmed sites. As a site can be developed only after it has been programmed and included in the plan, the system effectively creates phasing. Even so, non-programmed sites may provide the best opportunity for constructive negotiation with the planning authority, in that neither the development content nor the density will yet have been fixed.

Outside Madrid

Regulations outside Madrid are generally less restrictive, varying substantially from one municipality to another. Any property owner must prepare proposals and submit them to the City Council. The Council's discussions and negotiation with the owner's architect may take as long as six months, although, because no action is taken during the summer, applications made in late Spring will take substantially longer.

There is a right of appeal against refusal but, as it is almost unprecedented for such an appeal to succeed, the system is rarely used. It is better to spend the extra time in continuing negotiations with the local authority.

Conveyancing

As a general guide, the total expenses involved in purchasing property in Spain (i.e. notarial fees, transfer taxes and registration expenses) amount to approximately 7 per cent of the purchase price. In addition, legal fees will be payable according to a scale, and a minimum of Pta 100,000 should be anticipated. Depending on the nature of the purchase, the time required to complete the formalities will be (on average) between four and six months.

Brokerage

The law of 18 June 1981 seeks to organise the profession of real estate agents. It provides for the title of 'Real Estate Property Agent' but, in order to obtain this legally protected title, the candidate must have a university diploma, albeit in any one of a number of subjects, including engineering, law, architecture, economics, diplomatic or commercial science. The candidate must also establish his professional competence by passing an examination and will need to produce evidence that his financial affairs are in order.

The maximum level of fees is prescribed by the government. In March 1989, the sale fee was increased from the traditional 3 per cent to 5 per cent of the value of the transaction. This percentage generally holds for modest transactions, but on larger deals it can be negotiated down to between 2 and 3 per cent. The fee for letting used to be the equivalent of one month's rent, but it has now been increased to 10 per cent of the first year's rent.

The construction industry

The construction industry in Spain is well established. Several Spanish companies offer excellent technical and administrative organisation as well as the expertise necessary to compete in the international market.

In terms of turnover, Spain's leading contractors are:

Dragados y Construcciones	Pta 134,905 million
Entrecanales y Tavora	Pta 85,000 million
Agroman	Pta 71,814 million
Focsa	Pta 71,883 million
Cubiertas y Mzov	Pta 65,000 million

General state of the industry

The annual percentage increase in construction activity in Spain has risen significantly from 2 per cent in 1985, to 6.6 per cent in 1986, 10.5 per cent in 1987 and 12 per cent in 1988. Having suffered badly nationwide between 1975 and 1985, with the loss of 550,000 jobs out of the total 1,290,000, the market's recovery has brought employment back to 1,050,000 in 1988.

Both turnover and buoyancy vary from region to region – the major expansion is in Madrid and Barcelona. The selection of Barcelona to host the next Olympic Games and work on the Expo '92 Fair in Seville have necessitated major infrastructure works throughout Spain. At Pta 490,000 million, the Ministry of Public Works' 1989 budget showed a 55 per cent increase over the previous year. The construction target of 2,355 kilometres of main roads in 1990 and 1991, for instance, compares favourably with the 1989 target of only 364 kilometres.

The main referencing of the contractors is by way of a national contractor ranking, and in order to participate in government project bidding it is necessary to be classified – a process which takes account of the nature of the contractor's business and its financial capacity.

Trends in the market

With demand strong in the middle and upper sectors of the housing market and with the construction of tourist housing likely to maintain its current level of activity, a 10 per cent increase was forecast for 1989. The lower end of the housing market has traditionally been protected – projects are overseen by the Ministry of Housing at government-controlled sale prices. (It should be remembered that in Spain, rented housing accounts for only 20 per cent of the market, compared with a European average nearer to 50 per cent.)

Office and related developments will have a firm future in the main commercial centres, and there is likely to be a growth in the number of office developments on the outskirts of the major cities.

The crisis of previous years and the construction boom since 1986 has led to a shortage of skilled labour, particularly in Madrid and Barcelona. The upturn in activity has given the trade unions an opportunity to improve terms and conditions for their members, most of whom are employed on a temporary contract basis. The industry experienced random strikes in Cataluña throughout the Spring and Summer of 1988, and the continuing high level of activity could give rise to industrial action in other regions in future years.

There are no significant problems in terms of the availability of plant and materials. The majority of materials are home-produced, and reinforced concrete design is predominant in multi-storey structures.

Current market conditions indicate a likely increase in tender levels of around 12 per cent in 1990, with the official cost inflation at 7 per cent.

Structure of the industry

Within the industry, three professions take responsibility for design: civil engineers for major civil engineering works, industrial engineers for plant and manufacturing installations, and architects for all building projects. Legal responsibility for the design and supervision of a project remains with these professionals for ten years.

Despite Spain's recent years of democratic reform, these professional bodies still follow traditionally rigid procedures. Each architect or engineer, for instance, has to be a member of the local college (i.e. Institution), and this body has to approve his appointment for a particular project. Approval can be refused if another architect or engineer has already been appointed or if there are fees outstanding. All fees paid to the architects and engineers are accounted via the college. The architect or engineer is responsible for the concept and general design, while the responsibility for the working design details are left to the contractor. Contractors employ professionally qualified architects and engineers themselves as part of their own general resource.

Each building project will also have an *aparejador* – a technical architect who shares responsibility with the architect or engineer for on-site supervision. The *aparejador* handles the accountancy side of the project. Though a member of a separate college, the *aparejador* is regarded as a secondary consultant on the project and will often work under the architect in the architect's office. The structure of the profession is such that the architect or engineer is regarded as the project leader. He or she will not readily accept management control by the client or the client's representative.

Increasingly, on major projects, quality control offices are being engaged, while building guarantee insurance for structure and weatherproofing, subject to the control office involvement, is also now available.

The majority of projects are executed on the basis of there being a general contractor, although it is not uncommon for the major specialist sub-contractors (such as M&E) to be appointed directly by the employer and co-ordinated by the *aparejador*. The contractor is legally responsible for ten years for the execution of the work and for aspects such as safety. Providing that an organisation is properly registered for tax and company purposes, there is nothing to prevent it from acting as a contractor in the private sector of the market. For public works and protected housing projects, the contractor must be registered with the government.

Design considerations

Government building regulations are increasingly exacting as they move gradually towards a level comparable to UK standards. The legal regulations cover all aspects of construction, and all projects must be approved by government agencies.

All materials used must be ratified by an official testing body, and should carry their respective seals. The standard dimensioning of products, however, is still not fully organised and can create difficulties in detailing.

Approvals

The approval procedure is technical and political, and long delays are not uncommon. Once the architect or engineer's appointment has been approved by the college, a building licence must be obtained for the basic project. But the basic project dossier will be considered by the local authority hall only after the college has received payment of the architect's or engineer's scale fees.

Basic project

Each site has a planning use defined by the local authority and the basic project must comply with it. The use will be updated and modified from time to time and such modifications can, unfortunately, delay consideration and approval for years. The minimum period in which a building licence can be obtained is three months, although a more realistic six months' minimum should be allowed.

Execution project

Prior to construction, the execution project must be approved by the local authority, and on completion the architect is obliged to certify to the authority that the project is complete. There then follows a legal inspection and, subject to any qualifications, the granting of an opening licence.

Programme considerations

The main programme consideration during the pre-construction period is the time required to obtain the building licence for the basic project. From the time the licence is obtained to the on-site start-up, a period of five months is needed for the execution project and for bidding by the contractors. The construction timetable itself is marginally faster than in the UK, partly as a result of the less rigid regulations.

Placing the building contract

The bidding of a construction project is based on specification, drawings and a bill of quantities prepared in a brief form. Often the bill is remeasured as the works proceed, but on major projects it is usual to establish a lump-sum bid with the contractor warranting the quantities. The complaint most frequently made by clients is that the architect's project has not been thoroughly prepared and co-ordinated, and, in the absence of a client's representative to oversee the performance of the consultants, claims and variations do occur.

There is no standard building contract, and the terms and conditions are usually specifically negotiated and concluded after bids have been received. Payments to the contractor are usually made on a monthly account verified by the *aparejador* and certified by the architect. On projects of up to eighteen months' duration, there is no difficulty in establishing firm price contracts. Where a fluctuations contract has been entered into, there are no sophisticated indices or formulae, and it is usual to refer to one or two of the national cost indices.

Cost comparison

Professional fees are significantly lower than in the UK. For a new project with a value of Pta 1,000 million (£5 million) excluding VAT, the architect or engineer will charge 5 per cent, with a further 1.5 per cent for the *aparejador*.

Construction costs are also lower than in the UK. An air-conditioned office building on the outskirts of Madrid, for example, will cost approximately only Pta 90,000 per square metre (about £45 per square foot) excluding VAT.

The retail market

Estimated value of retail sales	
1985	Pta 9,677bn (£48.9bn equivalent)
1986	Pta 10,118bn (£52.7bn equivalent)

Estimated number of retail outlets	
1987	119,000 food outlets
	145,000 non-food outlets
	72 hypermarkets

Shop hours	
Major department stores, hypermarkets and large supermarkets:	Mon. to Sat. – 08.00 to 18.00/20.00
Most small and independent outlets:	Mon. to Fri. – 08.00/09.00 to 13.00
	15.00/16.00 to 19.00/20.00
Sunday trading is generally permitted.	

VAT rates		
Lower rate	6%	
Standard rate	12%	
Higher rate	33%	

Source: Corporate Intelligence Research Publications Ltd

Retail premises do not change hands with the regularity of the UK market largely for two reasons: first, the security of tenure and low historic rentals enjoyed by tenants occupying premises on leases entered into before 1985; and second, the dominance of independent traders and the resulting lack of the active market which normally develops through multiple retailers and their determination to maintain and enhance profitability. The market is further inhibited because the landlord is not allowed to sell the freehold without the tenant's agreement and because the tenant has the right of first refusal; this situation puts a severe restraint on the redevelopment of individual properties to provide modern retail accommodation.

The widespread designation of areas as subject to the statutory *conservación ambiental* further limits the scope for small scale development initiatives, particularly in the city centres where, traditionally, most of the retail trade tends to be concentrated.

By North European standards, retail development is immature, although, where comprehensive schemes have been developed, they are invariably successful. The major examples of decentralised development are Madrid 2 (La Vaguada) and the Nuevo Centro at Valencia. Other schemes will certainly emerge in due course, including those planned at Palma and to the east of Madrid. Opportunities also exist in

Barcelona, Malaga and Zaragoza, and although some city councils are unsure of the desirability of this form of development, there seems little doubt that the pressure of increased purchasing power will ensure that Spain follows the pattern of the rest of Europe.

The retail market in Madrid

Retail provision in Madrid reflects its role as a residential city, densely populated even at its commercial core. A general resistance to living at ground-floor level in apartment buildings has led to shopping and associated commercial use being spread almost continuously across the city. The main exceptions to this pattern are the prime office areas, especially Paseo de la Castellana and its southward extension, Paseo de Recoletos. Even so, the extent of ground-floor commercial activity gives a false impression of the level of retail provision: most is, in fact, fairly marginal. It tends to be convenience-orientated, serving small and localised catchments, or else service business rather than true retailing.

There is no discernible retail pattern, except where a concentration of shopping appears, as it does in the traditional city centre around Puerta del Sol and in the purpose-built developments at Azca and La Vaguada.

Madrid city centre   The principal shopping streets – the Calle Carmen and Calle Preciados, which link the Puerta del Sol to Gran Via – are the city's only significant attempt at pedestrianisation, and in terms of pedestrian volume the benefits are evident. These streets also benefit from the presence of the Corte Ingles and Galerias department stores, the latter store occupying two separate buildings and providing over 200 metres' frontage. The extent of this department store frontage means that the two streets together contain no more than fifty or so shops, mainly in old buildings and, with a few exceptions, none has a depth exceeding 20 metres. With an average depth of between 8 and 12 metres, they tend to offer trading areas of less than 100 square metres.

The majority of traders are in the fashion sector, but they tend to be traditional rather than modern-style retailers. The Calle de Serrano has overtaken the central area as a favoured location for aspiring Spanish retailers and international traders. Although Gran Via is no longer a major force in shopping terms (having become largely dominated by tourist and entertainment facilities), there are among the gift shops some beautiful, if rather dilapidated, buildings: Charles Jourdan has a beautifully appointed shop, Loewe a magnificent corner unit and Damart a huge shop with a frontage of around 20 metres.

Calle de Serrano

As Madrid's high fashion centre, the Calle de Serrano has attracted international names such as Christian Dior, Gucci, Rodier and Stefanel, as well as Spanish design houses such as Adolfo Dominguez and Alfredo Caral. In addition to numerous jewellers, gift shops, shoe shops and some high quality furniture, antique and carpet stores, the street has over fifty fashion shops.

The Multi-Centro scheme (one of three such developments in Madrid) adds another forty or so small shops, almost all of them in the fashion business. The retail area extends a short distance eastwards from Serrano towards Calle de Velazquez and includes the lower sections of streets running east–west, such as Goya and Ayala.

Rental values now reach Pta 10,000 per square metre per month on the main east side frontage between Juan Bravo and Goya. Even so, the antique rents (*renta antigua*) created by the old landlord and tenant legislation have left greengrocers rubbing shoulders with *haute couture*, and when you look at the many dilapidated buildings, it is hard to believe that this is Madrid's prime retailing centre.

Goya/Princesa/ Quevedo

These three shopping centres, built at major traffic intersections, tend to serve the areas of the city closest to them, in spite of their accessibility from the city centre. As a result, rental values are significantly lower than those in the centre and around half the price of those in Serrano.

By far the most important of the three centres is Princesa, with its 1970s-built Corte Ingles department store, which trades on nine large floors, with a comprehensive range of goods and a strong middle market appeal. On the opposite side of the street is the largest of Madrid's three Multi-Centro developments, containing about sixty shops arranged on two main levels with basement parking. As on Serrano, the shops are small – typically offering as little as 30 square metres – and almost all sell fashion clothing or accessories.

Azca/Orense

The way in which Madrid is dominated by department store trading to the detriment of unit shopping is exemplified by the Azca development, where the Corte Ingles store is a complete shopping facility in its own right. It stands as an independent entity and makes no attempt to link with the adjacent Calle Orense, which offers numerous specialist shops and the third of Madrid's Multi-Centro fashion schemes.

At the opposite end of the Azca site stands the Moda shopping centre – a two-level scheme of approximately 10,000 square metres containing around eighty shop units, mostly in the fashion sector and of varying size, including some no more than 30 square metres. Although it has no main anchor traders, Moda tenants include Etam,

Benetton and Alain Manoukian, and, with the exception of Madrid 2 (La Vaguada), the Moda development is the only centre so far to incorporate current design features, such as plants, water and a glazed roof.

Madrid 2
(La Vaguada)

A purpose-built development by Société des Centres Commerciaux and opened in 1983, Madrid 2 is the only centre which provides a truly comprehensive range of goods, including food. It is designed for the pedestrian with enclosed malls and integrated car parking, and includes many standard size units with a sales area of around 200 square metres on a frontage of approximately 7 metres. The retail element consists of 320 shop units including one large Alcampo super-market, a C&A department store and a Galerias Preciados store. Out of its 82,000 square metres' (gross) space, 20,000 square metres are set aside for office use.

Madrid 2 has four floors of underground parking for 10,000 vehicles, a nine-screen cinema complex, a bowling alley and other sports facilities, but the scheme unfortunately uses a quality of finishings which are in need of (but do not receive) constant maintenance and, as a result, has a somewhat downmarket feel.

Madrid 2 is the focal point of the Barrio del Pilar, an extensive area of unfashionable modern apartment housing. It is situated at the intersection of two main roads and is on several bus routes. Madrid 2 has no direct access to the metro, but is only a short distance from Barrio del Pilar station on Line 9. Even so, the development is a success, with rents approaching the level of those in the traditional centre – around Pta 6,000 per square metre per month – largely as a result of the absence of any comparable facility either in the city or in its suburbs.

The retail market in the rest of Spain

As in Madrid, the department stores play the major role in the retailing sector in the rest of Spain. The most important chain is Corte Ingles, which tends to be surrounded by the best of the other shopping, with rentals ranging from Pta 2,000 to Pta 4,000 per square metre per month. Galerias Preciados and single units play a secondary role in cities such as Seville, Bilbao and Zaragoza.

Barcelona

In the centre of Barcelona, the principal shopping areas are Diagonal, Gran Via and Plaza Cataluña (near the Corte Ingles store). Although prime rentals have reached Pta 5,000 per square metre per month, the market here is also dogged by *renta antigua* and resulting premiums of up to Pta 150 million. A number of shopping halls specialising in luxury goods have recently been developed downtown. The rent for a small unit in one of these halls will be between Pta 8,000 and Pta 10,000 per square metre per month.

There are several important shopping centres on the outskirts of the city, and further development is under way close to the Olympic Stadium. Average incomes in Barcelona are higher than in Madrid and the communication systems are superior.

Malaga

The best retail zone in Malaga is the Avenida del Generalisimo, Alameda and the surrounding streets, close to the Corte Ingles and to the central business district. Retail units range from 600 square metres to 1,500 square metres, with an average frontage of between 10 and 12 metres. Prime rentals are Pta 3,000 per square metre per month.

Bilbao

The principal shopping areas in Bilbao are Alameda, Urquijo and Alamedo Recalde.

The office market

Madrid

No new planning consents over the past five years means that central Madrid is at present suffering from an acute shortage of office space. Only 100,000 square metres is on the market, of which 87,000 square metres is in the Torre Picasso. With recorded demand currently exceeding 200,000 square metres, the volume now being refurbished (13,000 square metres) or under construction (80,000 square metres) will leave a significant shortfall for some time to come.

The office market in the capital is becoming increasingly popular both with Spanish and international developers and with international investors. The demand for development opportunities has pushed property prices to an all-time high; much of the increase is attributable to the change in 1985 to the landlord and tenant legislation which now enables an investor or developer to receive a market return. The increase is also, to a significant extent, the result of increased activity following release from the restrictions of the Franco years.

**The central
business district**

Traditionally, the central business district of the capital was in and around Alcala, close to the Bank of Spain and other banking headquarters. Although some banking headquarters have remained in this area, the emphasis has shifted during the past twenty years towards the Paseo de Recoletos and its more northerly continuation, the Paseo de la Castellana. This extraordinary boulevard, with its five lanes of traffic in both directions, extensive grass verges, access and slip roads running parallel on either side, is perhaps 100 metres wide. Running south–north from the old centre of Madrid to the Plaza Castilla, the Castellana is lined with a mixture of modern banking headquarters, old period villas, hotels and apartment blocks. During the 1950s and 1960s, many of the older buildings were demolished and replaced by some quite uninspiring development. The new planning regimes prevent any further demolition and activity is limited to high quality refurbishment. One recently undertaken by Redanco has been let to Madrid City Council at a record rent of Pta 5,500 per square metre per month.

Ultimately, however, the continuing success of the office market in central Madrid is being threatened by that perennial problem: traffic congestion. With traffic moving at a snail's pace for much of the day and night, local office workers seem resigned to taking perhaps an hour and a half to travel the 15 to 20 kilometres to and from work. A journey from the city centre to the airport, which in the absence of traffic would take no more than twenty minutes, can take two hours or even longer.

The combination of traffic congestion and the highly restrictive planning regime is directing increasing attention to out-of-town development opportunities. Rentals in central Madrid range from Pta 4,000 per square metre per month in the old business district to a peak of Pta 5,500 per square metre per month in Castellana.

Azca

The Azca development, on the Paseo de la Castellana just to the north of the city centre, was conceived by General Franco as Madrid's answer to La Défense in Paris. The first buildings were constructed some fifteen to twenty years ago on a large site bordered on the east by Castellana, on the west by Orense, by Avenida General Peron to the north and Villaverde to the south. The development includes, in the south, the largest Corte Ingles department store in Madrid, as well as a variety of office towers, among them the Torre Picasso – Spain's tallest building (completed in March 1989). Rents in Azca now exceed Pta 4,500 per square metre per month, although very little space remains for further development.

Tres Cantos

Tres Cantos, 24 kilometres to the north of Madrid, was designed in the 1960s as a dormitory town for the overspill from the capital, but for a long period during the recession the early phases stood empty. The original scheme provided for 100,000 residents, but this has now been reduced to 30,000 while the commercial and industrial content has been substantially increased.

The success of the project is due largely to the presence of AT&T who, under a joint venture with Telefonica in 1984, agreed to locate a plant for the design and manufacture of integrated circuits at Tres Cantos. An industrial estate and high-technology park were created on the back of this major presence, with very substantial financial incentives and subsidies on offer to overseas companies. As a result, almost all of the park's forty-two sites, with surface areas of between 2,600 square metres and 10,400 square metres, have now been sold.

Work on the housing project has now restarted, and it is envisaged that Tres Cantos will eventually have a population of 40,000, and 150 companies providing 10,000 skilled jobs.

Campo de las Naciones

Although details have yet to be finalised, this site of 4.3 million square metres to the north-east of the city centre and close to the airport at Barajas is to be developed as a national exhibition centre. The centre itself will occupy a little over 20 per cent of the total site, with up to 150,000 square metres of offices planned, in addition to retail and recreational facilities.

Barcelona

It is very difficult to find high quality office space in Barcelona, and rental levels in the prime areas have risen to Pta 3,000 per square metre per month. Very little of the land around the city is suitable for expansion, but the local authority has designated ten zones within Barcelona as areas for redevelopment. These zones could together provide a total of 500,000 square metres of new office space by 1994.

The industrial market

Although the market for industrial property is responding slowly to the rapidly expanding economy, UK developers have taken a keen interest in the opportunities for developing business space.

Most of the larger cities have industrial estates (*poligonos*) on the outskirts where the premises are predominantly freehold. In the past few years, however, there has been some development of industrial warehousing which is available on a leasehold basis. In Madrid, rents can be as high as Pta 1,700 per square metre per month. In Barcelona, there has been no new development of industrial property. This has created a scarcity of supply and current rental levels are Pta 800–1,000 per square metre per month.

The fact that Spain does not yet have a major, speculatively built, business park is not due to lack of tenant demand or development expertise, but to the fact that planning authorities are unclear about the approach they should take. The local planning authorities have still to recognise that high-tech is not simply a style of building which supplies cheap office accommodation, but that it has a highly specific function which falls somewhere between office and industrial use. Once the planning authorities recognise this, the advantages of speculatively built schemes where occupiers have the flexibility to expand will be apparent. The influx of foreign expertise will help accelerate the learning process. Already, in the past year, the local authorities in Madrid and Barcelona have begun to promote schemes of their own, even though these are mainly based on the sale of land to owner–occupiers.

The United Kingdom

Geography

Land area	244,000 sq. km.
Population (mid-1987 est.)	56,930,000
Density	233 per sq. km.
Main cities	Population
Greater London	6,770,400
Birmingham	998,200
Glasgow	715,600
Leeds	709,000
Sheffield	532,300
Liverpool	476,000
Edinburgh	438,700
Belfast	303,800
Cardiff	281,500

The UK comprises England, Wales, Scotland and Northern Ireland. It has the third largest population and the fourth highest density in Europe. England is predominantly lowland with upland regions in the North and in Devon and Cornwall. The greatest concentrations of population are in in London and the Thames valley, the conurbations of the Midlands and the North East, the industrial cities of West Yorkshire and the North West, and the Channel coast. Wales, by contrast, is a mountainous country with low lying land restricted to a narrow coastal belt, and a number of river valleys which contain one-third of the total population. The main urban centres are Cardiff, Swansea, Newport and Wrexham. Scotland can be divided into three areas; the sparsely populated Highlands and Islands, the central lowlands containing three-quarters of the total population and the main industrial centres, and the southern uplands bordering on England. The main urban centres are the capital, Edinburgh, the main industrial centre, Glasgow, and two regional centres, Aberdeen and Dundee. Most of Northern Ireland's principal towns lie in

THE BRITISH ISLES

valleys leading from Lough Neagh, which lies in the centre of the country.

England and Wales are divided for administrative purposes into a two-tier structure of counties and districts. In addition, there are thirty-three London boroughs and thirty-six metropolitan districts. Scotland is divided into nine regions and three islands, with the regions being further sub-divided into fifty-three districts. Northern Ireland is divided into twenty-six districts.

Transport and communications

Britain's road network covers 376,100 kilometres (1987), and the volume of motor vehicle traffic is 316,800 million per square kilometre. The motorway network carries 33 per cent of all road traffic, and 60 per cent of all heavy-goods vehicle traffic.

A rail network of over 16,000 kilometres services both passengers and freight. 727 million passenger journeys were made in 1987/8 on a network of inter-city, local and commuter services. Rail freight, which is in decline, now consists mainly of coal, coke, iron/steel building materials, and petroleum. Recent developments, however, include the introduction of high-speed 'speed link' services between major industrial centres, on a central computer-based monitoring system of all freight traffic.

The UK has over 300 ports, which handled 457 million tonnes of traffic in 1987. The shift from conventional port handling to container traffic and the growing importance of European trade has seen the decline of Liverpool, London and Manchester, and the growth of Dover, Felixstowe and Southampton, although some North Sea ports have grown considerably in response to off-shore oil developments.

Britain is a partner in the Channel Tunnel scheme, which aims to provide a rail link between the UK and Continental Europe. The venture will require significant improvements to existing road and rail networks in south-east England, especially in Kent.

In *Trade Routes to the Future*, the CBI estimated that the present level of congestion on the UK infrastructure is costing the country as a whole around £15 billion per annum, and that the situation looks like getting worse. The costs are felt in such things as increased maintenance of vehicles, increased number of distribution outlets, lost time due to delay, lost time from sickness due to stress from traffic congestion, etc.

A comprehensive road and rail network is needed in any aspiring economy, and since business in the UK must compete from the

geographic periphery of the EC it is even more vital if foreign investment is to be encouraged. The problem is centred in the South East,
and especially the London area, the financial heart of the country. If
the UK is to operate competitively, a solution must be found, whether
through private or public investment.

General economic

Current macro-economic policy is aimed mainly at curbing inflation,
while micro-economic policies are directed at encouraging enterprise
and efficiency within the economy. To improve the supply capacity of
the economy, it is vital that government provides an economic climate
in which companies are encouraged to invest. While not taking risks
with inflation, which itself is damaging to business confidence and
investment, government policy needs to reduce the burdens on business and lower interest rates to promote investment over the longer
term and tackle the root causes of inflationary pressures in the UK
economy.

Since the early 1980s the average rate of economic growth in the
UK, at around 3 per cent, has been faster than in the majority of
industrial countries. Manufacturing output has also been rising since
1982, but by the end of 1989 slowed to a virtual standstill in response
to high interest rates and weakening domestic demand. This slow-
down in the growth of demand has also been reflected in some
improvement in the balance of payments – in relation to non-oil trade
– and on inflation.

Retail price inflation has been on a downward trend since 1981, but
picked up during 1988 and 1989. The 'headline' rate peaked at just
over 8 per cent in mid-1989, while the underlying rate of inflation –
annual increase in RPI excluding mortgage interest – has steadied at
around 6 per cent since May 1989 after increasing markedly from 3.7
per cent per annum in early 1988.

Unemployment has been falling steadily since mid-1986 and towards
the end of 1989 averaged 1.6 million, the lowest level since 1980.

Industry

The basis of the Government's overall economic strategy is to create a
climate in which business activity can flourish across the whole
economy. Efforts to achieve this are centred around the control of
inflation, but also involve measures which lower tax rates and reduce

the regulatory burden on business. Competition is stimulated and markets are broadened by privatising nationalised industries wherever possible. These policies are designed to improve the business environment for all sectors, including industry. The Department of Trade and Industry has concentrated on opening up markets and on encouraging enterprise, particularly through consultancy initiatives which spread best practice.

The main industrial trends in the UK include:

- The growth of off-shore oil and gas industries, which has had a particularly strong impact on Scotland

- The rapid development of electronic and micro-electronic industries

- A shift in emphasis from heavy manufacturing industries to service industries, especially financial and business services

Forms of tenure

The principal forms of tenure in the UK are freehold (feuhold in Scotland) and leasehold. Commercial leases are granted either on a full repairing or internal repairing basis. Occupational leases are commonly granted for terms of twenty-five years and usually contain provisions for the rent to be reviewed to the open market rental value each fifth year of the term. The normal institutional lease provides for the tenant to be responsible for the maintenance and repair of the buildings, although where buildings are let in suites or parts, internal repairing leases are the norm with tenants paying a service charge to cover the cost of repairs to the common parts, structure, etc.

In general, most tenants of commercial properties in England and Wales are entitled to security of tenure under the provisions of the Landlord and Tenant Act of 1954. The Act, which does not apply to properties in Scotland or Northern Ireland, lays down the basis of entitlement to a new lease on expiry as well as the grounds on which a landlord may obtain possession of a commercial property on expiry of the lease. Landlords and tenants may, by agreement, contract out of the provisions of the Act, thus waiving tenants' entitlement to security of tenure and to the obligation of the landlord to pay compensation to the tenant in the event that the lease is not renewed.

A Central Land Register is maintained which is not open to public inspection except in Scotland and Northern Ireland but in which all interests in land are registered as and when the disposal of an interest occurs. The Land Registration Act 1988 will open to the public information about the title to freehold and leasehold land in England and Wales. Preparations for public access to the register are expected to be completed next year.

Finance

There is an active and sophisticated investment market in the UK with institutions, banks and property companies all prepared to provide capital for development or for investing in property. The most common of the traditional methods of finance are: mortgage, whereby the property is used as security for a loan; sale and leaseback, where an owner of property transfers the freehold interest in return for a capital sum and takes back a lease of the property at a rack rent (the occupier thus retains possession of the property although disposing of the freehold ownership for a capital sum); and debenture. In recent times, the financing of property has become much more sophisticated, with innovative methods of finance being used to raise substantial capital sums secured on the underlying property assets.

A new form of property finance which is, as yet, almost untried is securitisation and unitisation. Under these methods, investors have the opportunity to own shares in the income and capital growth of a property. An important element of this form of finance is the necessity of tax transparency (avoidance of double taxation). It remains to be seen whether these forms of financing will prove popular.

The UK property investment market is sophisticated and mature and offers many innovative ways of raising finance for property investment or development. These can be tailored to take advantage of tax concessions and also to enable owners of property to participate in future capital growth.

Grant aid

Grant aid in the UK falls under the auspices of the DTI's Regional Initiative and consists of two types of assistance. The first and most common is known as a Project Grant, and is based on the fixed capital costs of a project, and on the number of jobs the project is expected to create or safeguard. The second form of assistance is the Exchange Risk Guarantee: the Government may offer cover against the exchange risk on low interest foreign currency loans from the European Coal and Steel Community (ECSC). A regional enterprise grant may also be awarded to firms of twenty-five employees or less in certain designated areas.

Direct corporate taxes and incentives in the UK

Principal rate	35%
Local rate	—
Tax description	reducing balance
Basis	fixed rates
Losses:	
Carry forward	indefinite
Carry back	1 year
Capital investment tax	—

Deductions exist on the following:

> Royalties
> Interest
> Bad debts (restricted to specific bad
>   debts/provision only)
>
> Interest payable – paid or accrual

Planning

The district and borough councils administer the planning system and all applications for planning permission to carry out a development should be submitted to them. Appeals against a refusal of planning permission or the failure to make a decision within the statutory prescribed limit of eight weeks are made to the Secretary of State for the Department of the Environment in England, the Secretary of State for Wales, the Secretary of State for Scotland or the Secretary of State for Northern Ireland.

The statutory period in which local authorities are expected to make a decision is eight weeks or any longer period agreed with the applicant, after which the applicant has the right of appeal. In practice, applications sometimes take longer but about half of all planning applications in England are decided within eight weeks. Appeals can be dealt with either by written representation or at a public enquiry heard by an Inspector appointed by the Secretary of State. Depending upon the complexity of the issues, written representation appeals take about twenty-three weeks from the lodging of an appeal with the Department to the issue of the decision. Enquiries take about twenty-eight weeks from the lodging of an appeal with the Department to the opening of the enquiry and about another nine weeks from the opening of the enquiry to the issue of the decision. It usually takes between six and nine months for the appointment of an Inspector and between three and six months for a decision following the enquiry.

Simplified planning procedures are adopted in Enterprise Zones and in Simplified Planning Zones.

Brokerage

The principal professional body representing surveyors in the UK is the Royal Institution of Chartered Surveyors. The other major professional society is the Incorporated Society of Valuers and Auctioneers. Proposals to merge the Institution and Society are under consideration at this time. Fee scales have been abolished and fees are now a matter of negotiation and agreement between the client and the surveyor.

Conveyancing

It is normal practice to employ the services of a solicitor to handle conveyance, assignment and the granting of a lease. Different legal systems apply to England, Wales and Scotland. Fee scales have been abolished and are now the subject of negotiation.

Stamp duty is payable on all acquisitions of freehold interests over £30,000 and on a premium paid on grant or assignment of a lease. It is payable at the rate of 1 per cent of the consideration. The stamp duty on rents reserved on grant of leases is as follows:

- Leases up to 7 years: 1%
- Leases of less than 35 years: 2%
- Leases of between 35 years and 99 years: 12%
- Leases of over 99 years: 24%

The construction industry

In 1988, the UK construction industry had an overall growth of 9 per cent, with the lion's share contributed by the private sector, which had a growth of 14 per cent. The private sector accounted for all the growth of new work. In the first quarter of 1989, the industry experienced a 6 per cent growth, but a slow-down was seen in the second quarter of the year when no growth was shown. Total new work in the second quarter of 1989 was 2 per cent lower than in the previous quarter, but 5 per cent higher compared with the same period a year earlier.

Construction output (£ millions at 1985 prices)												
1978	1979	1980	1981	1982	1983	1984	1985	1986	1987	1988	1989	1990
All work 28,746	29,178	27,830	25,131	25,471	26,648	27,537	27,851	28,757	31,022	33,800	34,905*	34,830*
Growth (+7%)	(+0.5%)	(−5%)	(−10%)	(+1.5%)	(+4%)	(+3.5%)	(+1%)	(+2.5%)	(+8%)	(+9%)	(+3%)	no change

*Forecast

Design considerations

Building regulations are published by HMSO, but there are numerous independent bodies covering various different topics with regard to the construction industry, such as the British Standards Institute and the Building Research Establishment.

Contracts

Contracts in the UK come under the Joint Contract Tribunals 1980 and can take various forms.

The retail market

Estimated value of retail sales (1980 = 100.0)	
1985 (HDE)	150.4
1987 (HDE)	176.4
1986	162.9

Estimated volume of retail sales (1980 = 100.0)	
1983	107.4
1984	111.3
1985	116.4
1986	122.6
1987	129.8

Estimated number of retail outlets
1980 = 368,253
1982 = 356,590
1984 = 349,728
1986 = 343,387
1987 = 345,467

Source: DTI Business Statistics Office

The 'market place' and the high street are still the prime location and the fundamental anchor of UK shopping throughout the nation. At local, district, regional or national levels, shopping has been focused on the town centre. And only since the mid-1970s have moves to promote out-of-town or edge-of-town opportunities met with any measure of success. Nowadays the multiple chain has replaced the department store as anchor. The UK is unique in this approach, although other areas of Europe have followed suit to a degree but predominantly by franchising rather than by direct expansion.

The first generation shopping centres emerged in the 1960s as a result of a growth in consumer demand and product awareness. At the time, they represented a bold new step eagerly anticipated and well received by the shopper and retailer alike. They offered 'focus' shopping and were the forerunners of what is today termed 'destination' shopping.

In the 1970s shopping-centre development came into its own. Developers concentrated on town centre redevelopment – i.e. building on what was known to be the core shopping area and maximising the back land available (the Whitgift Centre in Croydon; Victoria Centre, Nottingham; the Bull Ring, Birmingham; Corporation Square, Birmingham; and St David's Centre, Cardiff are examples of the development of the established shopping zone). The 1970s also saw the first tentative moves towards out-of-town or rather edge-of-town development: Brent Cross is an example. Lambasted in early days, its success is apparent in the fact that Hammerson are now looking to build a second phase.

As consumer spending grew and the public became more aware of shopping choice, there was tremendous evolution in shopping-centre design and format. Recently, the retailer has shifted from department store/multiple chain orientation towards a renaissance of speciality and niche retailing. The latter came about when the retail community, or rather the hard core of the retail community, recognised the need for change; redesign and innovation in shopfitting and layout then became the order of the day.

The 1989 market shows the retail sector poised on the brink of further development and change. The first major regional mall (140,000 square metres at the Metro Centre, Newcastle) has proved to be a success and there is room for perhaps four or five such schemes in the country. Central areas (which now include refurbishments of the early 1960s and 1970s schemes) are favourite targets for retail redevelopment because their very location fits with the whole background of UK retailing. Specialisation and diversification by all retailing concerns, and particularly by the multiples, have thrown a more competitive edge into the market place.

The daily shopping trip for fresh foodstuffs is not predominant in the UK, as it is in most of the rest of Europe. Thus shopping is more destination orientated, and shoppers have specific purchases in mind. The next decade will begin to see greater definition of shopping patterns: more emphasis on design, accessibility and comfort, and, in particular, attempts to accommodate the demographic shifts in shopping patterns, especially through age groupings.

The UK has one of the greatest concentrations of retail floor space her head of population in the world. At January 1989, there was in excess of 12 million square metres of new shopping floor space proposed for the UK (either at construction or at planning stage). While curtailments on consumer spending may reduce the amount of retail space being developed, the retail market still dominates the construction industry.

A peculiarity of the UK retail market is the use of Zone A to lay down high shop rents. Zone A is the first 6 metres' depth of the shop unit and the rental value of the shop unit is apportioned as follows:

Zone A = 6 metres × width (charged at Zone A rent)
Zone B = next 20% depth × width (charged at 50% Zone A rent)
Zone C = remainder of the depth × width and all other areas,
          e.g. lower ground floor sales area (charged at 25% Zone A rent)

Cardiff

Cardiff acts as the regional centre for the entire South Wales area. Its shopping core is focused around Queen Street and is fully pedestrianised. Cardiff's socio-economic profile is above the UK average and as a consequence the majority of traditional high street multiple retailers have secured representation and achieve strong trading performance. All major UK store groups are represented within the prime location, including Debenhams, Howells (House of Fraser), Marks & Spencer, British Home Stores, C & A, Littlewoods and Boots.

The city's major scheme is the St David's Centre developed by Heron in 1982, and its main mall is almost as strong as Queen Street. Queen Street is generally perceived as being worth £150 Zone A, with the main mall of the St David's Centre approaching that level. The scheme merges well with the city's existing pedestrian patterns, linking Queen Street with the traditional shopping in St Mary's Street and also the main car park.

Various further developments are under way, including Guardian Royal Exchange's Capital Exchange development, at the eastern end of Queen Street. It is due to be completed in Spring 1990 and to offer some 14,000 square metres of new accommodation. In a somewhat better location is the Queen Street Centre, situated at the opposite end of Queen Street but linking into the prime pitch and also into the St David's Centre. Scheduled to open for trading at the end of 1991, the scheme consists of 15,800 square metres over two levels and will be predominantly targeted at the multiple market.

London

The West End

The West End houses some of the most famous retailing streets in the world, including Oxford Street, Regent Street, Piccadilly, Bond Street and South Molton Street.

Oxford Street (£3,750 per square metre Zone A), anchored by Selfridges, John Lewis, Debenhams, House of Fraser and a myriad of mainstream multiple retail organisations, achieves an annual turnover in excess of £3 billion and is probably the premier shopping street of Europe. Regent Street (£2,150 per square metre Zone A) offers up-market retail shopping, including Liberty's, Austin Reed, Acquascutum and Burberrys. Piccadilly (£1,600 per square metre Zone A), once predominantly showrooms and travel organisations, is now seeing a retail revival that is promoting fashion and speciality shopping to complement the existing stores of Simpsons and Fortnum and Masons. Just to the rear, Jermyn Street (£1,050 Zone A) is a truly speciality street with an emphasis on shirt makers.

Bond Street (£2,150 per square metre Zone A) and South Molton Street (£2,370 per square metre Zone A) concentrate on fashion and top quality retailing but with a subtle shift of emphasis between the two. Bond Street is firmly in 'international jet-setting' retail, whereas South Molton Street, pedestrianised since the late 1970s, brings the young fashion name to the market place. Cartier, Tiffany, Boucheron and the like are all found in Bond Street. Joseph Butler and Wilson, Jean Paul Gaultier and Katharine Hamnett are typical of South Molton Street.

Covent Garden

Unlike Les Halles in Paris, this former fruit and vegetable market was refurbished and converted to speciality shopping in the early 1980s. A selected blend of tenants gave variety and a definite non-fashion emphasis and within two years Covent Garden market and surrounding piazza have become established tourist draws. Prime position is the market place (£2,150 per square metre Zone A) but James Street (£2,150 per square metre Zone A) links the market place with the underground station and the natural draw is northwards. This has benefited Long Acre (£1,950 Zone A).

Chelsea

Westwards from Sloane Square and the John Lewis department store is the King's Road – mecca of the fashion designers of the 1960s and 1970s and still retaining its popularity. Prime retail position is at the Sloane Square end (about £2,370 Zone A) with a gradual falling off as one moves west along the road to £100 Zone A approaching Worlds End.

Knightsbridge

The Brompton Road (£4,035 Zone A) is anchored by Harrods and Harvey Nichols department stores and has major national and international organisations represented, including Graff Diamonds, Charles Jourdan, Stefanel, Fiorucci, Russell and Bromley and, more recently, Laura Ashley and the Body Shop.

The top of Sloane Street, to the east of Knightsbridge, experienced tremendous rental growth between 1987 and 1989, from £1,240 Zone A to a maximum achieved of £4,100 Zone A. Sloane Street is like Bond Street in trading style, and representation here now includes Louis Vuitton, Chanel, Etienne Agner, Valentino and Esprit. Joseph have recently announced a 1,020 square metre emporium to be opened in early 1990 and, in Brompton Road, Giorgio Armani recently opened his emporium in 2,400 square metres of accommodation.

The City

A five-day retail market with intensive retailing between the hours of 12.00 and 15.00, the City was long forgotten as a retail centre. The high spending power of the City worker, boosted by events following Big Bang, have all contributed to retail growth and the main thoroughfare and prime retail position, Cheapside (£2,370 Zone A), has shown 400 per cent growth in three years. However, retail viability in rental performance terms has lagged well behind office value, and only limited retail development is occurring.

Kensington

Kensington High Street is anchored by Barkers department store (4,600 square metres). Prime position (£2,150 per square metre Zone A) adjoins the underground station and is accessed through a retail arcade which was developed in the late 1970s and which includes a

3,500 square metres Boots. Kensington High Street enjoys a strong domestic market but also has tourist draw. Leading national retailers as well as specialist retailers (particularly fashion) have outlets, and Jigsaw, Mark O'Polo, Stefanel, Benetton, Next, Hennes and Mauritz emphasise its core retail activities.

The Midlands

Birmingham

For many years Birmingham relied heavily on the traditional prime retailing areas of High Street, New Street, Corporation Street and Union Street – four thoroughfares which almost form four sides of a square. Rental value is in the region of £1,450 Zone A. Until the mid-1980s, the only covered shopping centres were the Bull Ring (one of the first shopping-centre developments in the UK), which is generally perceived as providing down-market shopping, and Norwich Union's Pallisades scheme, situated above New Street station and recently refurbished.

In the last two years, Royal Life has developed the Pavilions shopping centre, located in the High Street and comprising over four levels three variety stores and forty-three standard and specialist units, predominantly let to fashion retailers. Rental levels have achieved in excess of £1,450 Zone A, but the market response in consumer terms has yet to fulfil retailers' expectations.

Birmingham's future seems bright, with an international convention centre currently under construction, and a proposed £250 million development of the Bull Ring shopping centre by LET, which will provide approximately 93,000 square metres of retail space.

Nottingham

With a catchment population of about 270,000 people, Nottingham is the principal shopping centre for the East Midlands and its proximity to the M1 and other good communication networks makes it instantly accessible to a wide catchment area. The Broadmarsh (40,400 square metres) and the Victoria (46,500 square metres) shopping centres are the principal retail locations, and both have been developed out of the traditional street thoroughfare locations, such as Listergate, Albert Street, Exchange Walk, Bridalsmith Gate and Clumber Street. Clumber Street has been fully pedestrianised and achieves approaching £2,150 square metres Zone A. Major refurbishment works have improved Zone A value in the Broadmarsh shopping centre from about £430 (1982) to £810 plus in 1989 and in the Victoria from about £540 in the mid-1980s to £1,100 plus in 1989.

Two speciality schemes, Corn Exchange and Flying Horse Walk have brought a number of distinctly up-market and specialist trading names into the city centre retailing arena, including Mondi, Alexon, Le Pew, Wires, Out Set and Rodier.

The North

Leeds

The major regional centre for West Yorkshire, Leeds' prime shopping area, Briggate, has been extended to include Bond Street Centre and Boar Lane in the south, the Merrion Centre in the north, and from Albion Street in the west to Kirkgate Market in the east. The pedestrianised areas of Commercial Street and Lands Lane have emerged as *the* focus of retail activity and, as a consequence of recent lettings, Zone A values now stand at around £1,900 per square metre. The opening of the 23,200 square metres Schofields Centre, anchored by Schofields Department Store and Marks & Spencer, is seen as reinforcing the central core and largely absorbing unsatisfied retail demand.

Newcastle upon Tyne

The commercial and shopping capital for the north-east of England due to its geographical location and excellent communications, Newcastle upon Tyne benefits from a catchment in excess of 3 million people. The prime retailing area is to the north of the city centre on the recently refurbished 69,700 square metre Eldon Square development and the largely pedestrianised Northumberland Street, where Marks & Spencer, Fenwick, British Home Stores, C & A and Littlewoods are all represented.

The 140,000 square metre Metro Centre in Gateshead, only a short ride from Newcastle's city centre, is one of Europe's largest covered shopping complexes. The development is anchored by Carrefour and Marks & Spencer, along with stores for House of Fraser, C & A, BHS and Littlewoods.

Manchester

Manchester is the North West's premier commercial and retail centre. It has excellent communications, which partly account for the tremendous growth seen in its commercial sector over the last few years.

The prime retail area is generally acknowledged as being the pedestrianised thoroughfare, Market Street. Rents currently stand at about £1,400 per square metre Zone A. The Arndale Centre, which runs parallel to Market Street, provides over 92,000 square metres of retail floor space and forms the nucleus of the town's retail area. Externally, prime Zone As are approaching £1,700 per square metre but this is the effect of Market Street rather than the scheme itself, where the interior is ripe for refurbishment.

Recent retailing trends have been instrumental in increasing the popularity of Manchester's quality fashion retailers, predominantly relocated in King's Street, St Anne's Square and the Royal Exchange. Demand for representation in these locations is high and this competition has pushed rents upwards of £650 Zone A.

Glasgow

Glasgow is Scotland's premier fashion enclave. The city has a lively approach to development, and bold schemes like the Prince's Square and the St Enoch's schemes are the result. Prince's Square (13,940 square metres) opened in 1988 on a turnover leasing basis and is a major retail success. St Enoch's opened in mid-1988 and boasts 46,500 square metres over two levels. Anchored by Lewis's, Storehouse and Boots, the scheme achieved £950 Zone A on first lettings and is already demonstrating its retail strength.

Prime Glasgow is Argyll Street at £1,500 Zone A (department stores include Lewis's and Arnott's). Major multiple representation is found supplemented by secondary locations like Buchanan Street (£860 Zone A) favoured by specialist retailers.

Out-of-town retailing

This market sector continues to expand in areas of food and non-food use. Food store operations are able to provide large new facilities, with extensive car parking, at strategic locations, accessible to a large number of customers. Food stores tend to range between 4,600 and 7,500 square metres, with 500 or more car parking spaces on site. Sites tend to cover about 8 acres.

The non-food market remains buoyant, although, after the rapid growth of the mid-1980s, retailers are now more discerning about their requirements and want quality before quantity. The preference today is for retail parks averaging 9,300 square metres to 14,000 square metres. Ninety retail parks were open and trading by the end of 1988, providing more than 1,022,300 square metres' space.

Rents have continued to show consistent rises throughout the country. Today the £110 per square metre barrier has been broken in the South East and figures in excess of £85 per square metre have been achieved in the West Midlands. Disparity between operators is beginning to appear as markets reach saturation point in certain areas (e.g. furniture). DIY operators continue to offer premiums on prime locations, particularly in areas where representation has historically been difficult or where there may be planning embargoes.

Overall, the market in non-food is beginning to reach saturation. Developments either in planning stage or under construction will double the existing floor-space within the next two to three years, leaving certain areas over-supplied, and other areas, particularly in the South East, continuing to be in demand. Institutions are today becoming more discerning and prime sites continue to be fought over, leaving many poorer locations unsold. Yields vary from 7.25 per cent to 9 per cent plus.

Trading hours

Shops generally trade six days a week, between 09.00/09.30 and 17.30/18.00, but the heaviest shopping day is Saturday. Local shops have early closing days (Tuesday or Wednesday afternoons) but city centre retailing tends to operate all six days. Late night shopping (in London until 19.00/21.00 on Thursday) is gaining in popularity.

There is currently a restriction against trading on Sunday. Many retailers ignore the law and face the consequences of the fine because the fine is a pittance compared with the trading returns. Legislation is continually being sought to allow Sunday trading.

The office market

London:

The West End

The West End is made up of two main areas – Mayfair and St James's. Each has its own distinguishing features although both have similar tenant mixes. Both are characterised by small to medium-sized ornate period buildings. This has restricted redevelopment, because many are 'listed' by the local authority and cannot therefore be demolished or altered to make way for new construction. While new development is on the increase, it generally takes place behind the original façade, so the emphasis is on restoration and refurbishment to the highest specification possible, given the physical constraints of a period building.

The last two years have seen an enormous increase in the demand for office space in the West End. The increasing strength of the UK economy, reductions in the level of inflation and the deregulation of the financial market in 1986 have resulted in unprecedented tenant demand from both UK and foreign organisations. Areas such as Covent Garden, Holborn and Victoria, which are outside the immediate central core and traditionally less valuable, have increased enormously in value in recent years as they have been able to provide the sites necessary to cater for demand for large new buildings with first-class specification.

Over the last two years overseas occupiers have played a major role in central London. 1992 and the arrival of the single market may well result in a further increase in demand for office space.

The City
    The City fathers have, for a number of years, had to balance the desire to conserve the architecture and street pattern of the City with the need to provide quality office accommodation. The deregulation of the financial markets has stimulated the demand for new office accommodation to unprecedented levels, as has London's status as one of the three major financial capitals of the world.

    The area around the centre of the City, the Bank of England, is unsuitable for large-scale development due to fragmented land ownerships and restrictive planning policies. Banks and finance houses are now prepared, in the interest of efficiency, to move to new, large developments on the fringe of the City, approximately one kilometre from the Bank of England, to London Bridge City on the south bank of the River Thames, and to the new Broadgate development.

    The success of Broadgate (approximately 465,000 square metres of offices located on the northern boundary of the City) has been the result of the developers' ability to create an integrated financial community on a large tract of virgin land, thanks to a few land ownerships and planning policies which were relaxed to enable the large office developments required after deregulation. At Broadgate floorplates of 2,800 square metres are common.

    There is still a demand for smaller, self-contained buildings, which can be satisfied in the central core of the City. Addresses in the major thoroughfares such as Moorgate, Lombard Street, Threadneedle Street, Bishopsgate and Cornhill are still regarded as enhancing the identity of the occupiers.

    Leasing is on the basis of twenty-five-year leases, with five-yearly upward only rent reviews. The tenant takes full responsibility for the maintenance and upkeep of the building. 'Clean' leases of this kind are attractive in the investment market, as moves towards a more active management of property assets by landlords are only just emerging.

    The total costs of occupation are likely to rise in the next three years. The reform of the rating system in April 1990 will lead in the vast majority of cases in the City of London to an increase in the rates paid by occupiers. Although these increases will be phased in, it is likely that the full rate burden will rise to approximately 50 per cent of rents.

    VAT has been applied to property since April 1989. It is not yet clear how this will affect the market – approximately half the occupiers in the City of London, especially banks, finance houses and those involved in the insurance industry, are unable to reclaim VAT payments. The increased payments on rates and VAT is likely to affect the level of rents which tenants will offer.

Following the substantial rental growth that has taken place in the City of London market in the last five years, landlords are unlikely to see substantial rental growth within the next two to three years. Rents have now stabilised to approximately £540 to £645 per square metre in the central core, with £375 to £485 per square metre being sought for similar modern, high specification offices on the fringes of the City.

Virtually all new buildings include variable air volume air-conditioning, raised floors with underfloor trunking, suspended ceilings with inset lighting and double glazing. In addition, entrance halls now tend to be an imaginatively designed feature to aid the marketing of buildings and to project the image of the occupier. Service charges, which include air-conditioning, heating, maintenance, insurance, window-cleaning, lifts, lighting of the common parts and security, are in the region of £55 per square metre.

City tenants tend not to have the same rigid location preferences as formerly. EC3 is dominated by insurance underwriters and brokers, but nowadays there are few commodity traders and shippers. The legal and accountancy professions prefer EC4, partly because this is midway between their clients in the City and the West End and partly for proximity to the Royal Courts of Justice and the Old Bailey. EC2 remains the haven of banks and finance houses. Smithfield, in the northern sector of EC1, seems set to become a new centre for companies associated with the media as they are priced out of Covent Garden.

The office market outside London

Outside Central London, office development has been largely confined to the home counties and the larger provincial cities. Within the home counties, suburban centres such as Croydon in the south and Harrow in the north-west saw a large amount of office development during the 1960s when the first decentralisation from London took place. More recently, with the opening of the M25 motorway which surrounds the capital, occupiers began to move further out to take advantage of the improved transport links. This phase of development took place largely during the early 1980s although it continues today.

The attraction of the M25 area for international companies has been particularly strong between London's two major airports, Heathrow and Gatwick. International companies involved in computer or high technology businesses have established offices in this area particularly along the line of the M4 motorway. Centres such as Watford and Uxbridge have outstripped the suburban centres in terms of rental level and their attraction for national and international companies shows no sign of abating.

Established office markets are found in a number of major cities, principally Birmingham, Bristol, Leeds, Manchester and Liverpool, although these cities have suffered from an over-supply of accommodation in the past. The boom in demand of the last 12 to 18 months, coupled with the lack of new construction, has led to rapid rental growth. A number of major office schemes are in progress in most provincial cities.

A recent phenomenon has been the growth of the business park, which has been further encouraged by changes in planning controls allowing companies to use these buildings either purely as offices or for research and development. The principal differences between business parks and city or town-centre offices are the availability of large amounts of car parking and low rise buildings. The lack of public transport does not appear to deter potential occupiers who treat this as a small price to pay for the improved working environment.

Rental levels outside Central London in June 1989 were:

- Suburban centres
  Northern suburban locations: £290–£320 per square metre
  Southern suburban locations: £215–£270 per square metre

- M25 locations
  Northern M25: £215–£270 per square metre
  Western M25: £320–£380 per square metre
  Southern M25: £215–£270 per square metre

- Provincial cities
  Prime central business district: £130–£160 per square metre

The industrial market

South-east England

Industry in the South East is generally confined to light industry, service industry and, more recently, electronic or high-tech industry. There have been few major industrial plants in the South East, the most notable being Ford's at Dagenham.

Major industrial estates have been centred around the main trunk roads and airports: Park Royal Industrial Estate, the closest to London, is situated along Western Avenue (A40); Slough Estates is close to Heathrow Airport; Purley Way Industrial Estate, Croydon, is on the A23 London to Brighton trunk road; the Barking & Dagenham Estates are on the A13 adjoining Ford's Dagenham plant. These old industrial estates still have a major influence on the London industrial property scene, although warehousing, distribution and retail warehousing are playing a larger part than hitherto. These older estates are gradually being transformed and, to some extent, form the basis for more modern high-tech industry, especially in areas such as Slough and Park Royal.

There is considerable demand for service industry and warehousing along the main arterial roads and close to the motorways (A4, A40, A13, A23, A2 and M1, M2, M3, M4 and especially the M25). Green belt policy, however, especially around the M25, means that there is a shortage of development land. This is fuelling demand for industrial and commercial property and, together with the 1988 Use Classes Order, it means that today very little land is being developed for ordinary shed industry or even high-tech industry in the South East.

Building costs   Industrial sheds: £290–£380 per square metre
High-tech buildings: £485–£645 per square metre

Rental values   The best rentals obtainable are in the north-west and west segments (Acton to Heathrow and Slough) where industrial sheds reach £97 to £119 per square metre and high-tech premises reach £162 per square metre.★

Site values   Industrial sheds: up to £2,470,000 per hectare
High-tech buildings: up to £4,940,000 per hectare

There is considerable demand for large industrial and warehouse building (over 9,300 square metres) and no supply because developers have steered clear of building large units.

The Midlands

Formerly the location of major engineerng companies, the Midlands has suffered considerably in recent years from a major over-supply of industrial and warehouse properties, most of it second-hand and of poor quality. Much of this property has now been redeveloped for other uses and demand for the area is considerable, especially around the Coventry and Birmingham areas close to the M1 and M6 motorways.

★ In all cases, rental values quoted apply to new buildings only. Second-hand buildings can have rental values considerably lower than those for new buildings.

Rental values Industrial property: between £38 and £65 per square metre
High-tech buildings: between £86 and £110 per square metre

Site values Industrial shed: £617,500 to £864,500 per hectare
High-tech buildings: £864,500 to £1,358,000 per hectare

Other major areas

There has been considerable over-supply in Manchester, Leeds and Newcastle, but demand is now beginning to show through and much of the surplus accommodation is being taken up or redeveloped. Rental values are similar to those in the Midlands, or perhaps a little lower. The major industrial estates are Team Valley at Gateshead (originally a government-sponsored development) and Trafford Park Industrial Estate in Manchester. Trafford Park was one of the earliest industrial estates, started around the turn of the century.

Site values Industrial shed: £494,000 to £741,000 per hectare
High-tech buildings: £741,000 to £1,235,000 per hectare

Nursery-type units

The market is rather distorted, as a larger number of small nursery-type units have been made available in the last year or two on a purchase only basis. Prices far in excess of capitalised rental values above have been obtained for example for small industrial properties of up to 90 square metres. In the Greater London area up to £1,900 per square metre have been obtained and up to £1,345 in the Midlands area.

West Germany

Geography

Land area	248,709 sq. km.
Population (1987)	61,143,000
Density	246
Main cities	Population (1986)
West Berlin	1,950,000
Hamburg	1,620,000
Munich	1,290,000
Cologne	940,000
Frankfurt	640,000
Essen	630,000
Stuttgart	600,000
Dortmund	590,000
Düsseldorf	580,000
Hannover	550,000

The area of the Federal Republic and West Berlin is 248,709 square kilometres. The north consists of a large plain with few elevations, the central part has wooded uplands, rivers and reservoirs; in the south-west are mountain ridges with the Alps in the south-east.

West Germany can be divided into five main areas:

- The maritime north, with ports such as Hamburg, Bremen, Bremerhaven, Emden, Lübeck, Kiel and Wilhelmshaven, is the principal importing region

- The Ruhr, served by Duisburg – the largest inland port in Europe – contains a quarter of West Germany's consumers

- Frankfurt and the surrounding area is the centre for banking, finance and many important industries

- Bavaria and Baden-Württemberg in the south

- West Berlin

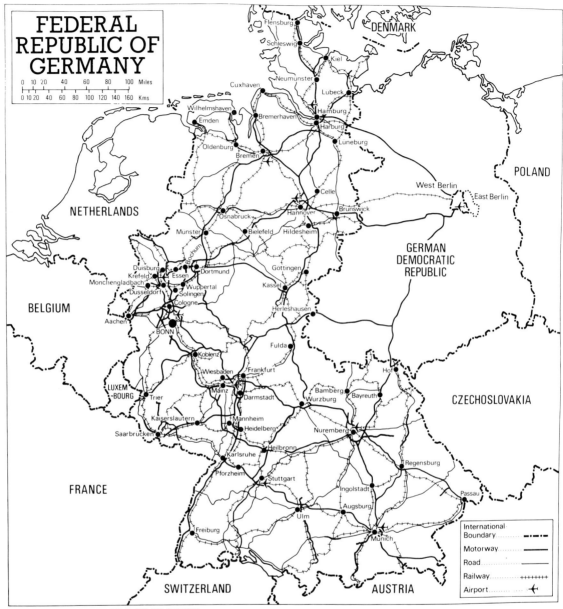

FEDERAL REPUBLIC OF GERMANY

0 10 20 40 60 80 100 Miles
0 10 20 40 60 80 100 120 140 160 Kms

DENMARK

Flensburg
Schleswig
Kiel
Neumunster
Lubeck
Cuxhaven
Wilhelmshaven
Emden
Bremerhaven
Hamburg
Harburg
Luneburg
Oldenburg
Bremen

NETHERLANDS

Celle
West Berlin
East Berlin
POLAND

Osnabruck
Hannover
Brunswick
Munster
Bielefeld
Hildesheim

GERMAN
DEMOCRATIC
REPUBLIC

Duisburg
Krefeld
Monchengladbach
Bochum
Essen
Dortmund
Dusseldorf
Wuppertal
Solingen
Cologne
Gottingen
Kassel

BELGIUM

Aachen
Herleshausen

BONN
Koblenz
Fulda

Wiesbaden
Frankfurt
Hof

LUXEM-
BOURG
Trier
Mainz
Darmstadt
Bamberg
Bayreuth
Wurzburg

CZECHOSLOVAKIA

Kaiserslautern
Mannheim
Saarbrucken
Heidelberg
Nuremberg

FRANCE

Karlsruhe
Heilbronn
Pforzheim
Regensburg

Stuttgart
Ingolstadt
Passau
Augsburg

Freiburg
Ulm
Munich

International
Boundary
Motorway
Road
Railway
Airport

SWITZERLAND
AUSTRIA

Department of Trade and Industry CDO No.1809,1987; 7084,1988

Transport and communications

West Germany's comprehensive and efficient rail system linking most urban centres extends for more than 30,000 kilometres, and over a third of it is electrified.

There are 173,000 kilometres of classified roads, including 8,300 kilometres of *Autobahn*. All major cities are served by airports with frequent domestic and international connections.

General economic

The distinguishing feature of the West German economic structure is the high ratio of foreign trade to GNP. Currently, exports account for 35 per cent of GNP, a fact which has helped West Germany to earn a reputation as 'the locomotive of the European economy'. A small and declining agricultural base accounts for only 1.5 per cent of GNP, while manufacturing contributes approximately 33 per cent and other production sectors add around 8 per cent. Distribution, private services and an 11 per cent contribution from government operations make up the remainder.

The historical fear of high inflation has led to tight fiscal and monetary policies. As a result, over the past ten years, inflation in the retail price index has exceeded 5 per cent on only three occasions and in 1988–9 was running at 2.5 per cent. Economic growth has, however, been slow.

Industry

Although now of less importance in terms of GNP than the service sector, manufacturing remains the backbone of the economy. The Ruhr is still both the centre of iron and steel production and the principal industrial area, although, as in other developed economies, there has been a decline in traditional smokestack industries. The industrial emphasis is now shifting towards the south, particularly to Hessen and Bavaria where the country's high-tech industries have located, many of them in the vicinity of the Isar River. The country's major industries are: engineering, vehicle building, electrical engineering, precision instruments, food, chemicals, iron and steel, textiles and clothing.

Forms of tenure

The most common form of legal estate in land is absolute ownership (*Eigentum*), under which the owner has complete control of land and buildings owned by him. His rights are, in most respects, identical to those of an owner in fee simple in the UK.

Under the Condominium Act (*Wohnungseigentumgesetz*), it is possible to have separate absolute ownership of a self-contained unit, in the case either of residential property (*Wohnungseigentum*) or of commercial property (*Teileigentum*). Under these provisions, each condominium owner has absolute ownership of his or her self-contained unit together with ownership in common of the structure, common areas and so on.

Title is registered with the Land Register (*Grundbuch*), the style and operation of which is similar to that of the Land Registry in the UK.

Leases

The Civil Code (*Bürgerliches Gesetzbuch* or BGB) sets down standard terms for leases and, in principle, there are no special requirements as to the form they take. Only leases of more than one year have to be in writing and the longest permissible term for a lease is thirty years. Though it is not compulsory, most leases are entered into by way of detailed written agreements because the general provisions of the BGB lay down terms which are not as favourable to lessors as those which can be obtained in the open market. With standard commercial leases, it is not necessary to use the services of a lawyer.

Business leases are generally agreed for terms of five, ten or twenty years, with renewal and option clauses often inserted in short-term leases.

Traditionally, leases have imposed very limited repairing obligations on tenants, and the BGB does not even provide for an obligation on the tenant to redecorate. More recently, however, the trend has been towards increased obligations upon the tenant. As companies have realised the potential benefits of freehold and leasehold sale-and-leaseback transactions, there has also been a shift towards more onerous repairing liabilities and, in some cases, towards full repairing obligations.

Rents are frequently linked to the cost-of-living index although (except in certain circumstances) such provisions are subject to State approval, which is generally given where the lease is granted for a term of ten years or more, and where the provision allows adjustment both upwards and downwards.

Taxation

Corporate income tax

Rental income	Retained profits			50%
	Distributed profits			36%
Realised gains	Rate			56% or 36%
	Basis			Excess of proceeds over cost
	Indexation relief			No
Relief for rentals				Yes
Relief for capital expenditure	Land			Nil
	Factories and warehouses	Constructed by taxpayer/ acquired in year of completion	In year of construction/ acquisition and following 3 years	10% p.a.
			Next 3 years	5% p.a.
			Remaining 18 years	2.5% p.a.
		Other purchases		4% p.a.
	Other buildings (offices)	Constructed by taxpayer/ acquired in year of completion	In year of construction/ acquisition and following 7 years	5% p.a.
			Next 6 years	2.5% p.a.
			Remaining 36 years	1.25% p.a.
		Other purchases	Completed before 1.1.1925	2.5% p.a.
			Completed after 31.12.1924	2% p.a.
		Buildings in West Berlin (in year of construction/acquisition and next 4 years)		75% over the 5 years
		Companies investing in buildings in West Berlin that remain in business use for 3 years can claim a cash investment grant		10% of cost

VAT

Land*	Exempt	
New buildings*	Exempt	
Old buildings*	Exempt	
Construction services	14%	
Professional fees	14%	

* Purchaser and vendor may opt for sale to be subject to VAT

Transfer taxes

Transfer tax	2% of value

Other national/federal taxes

Trade tax on income (deductible for corporate income tax purposes) at rates set by local authorities	Effective rates range generally from 12% to 19.4% (West Berlin 9.1%)

Local taxes

Net assets tax (includes land and buildings usually valued at between 30% and 40% of current market value)	Effective rate 0.45%
Real estate tax (based on assessed value of local property multiplied by municipal multiple)	Effective rates range up to 1.4%

Grant aid and investment incentives

In West Berlin and certain designated development areas, including areas bordering the German Democratic Republic and Czechoslovakia, a number of investment incentives are available at both federal and state level in the form of direct cash subsidies, tax incentives, special financing and guarantees of loans and export accounts receivable.

Planning and building law

No new erection, demolition or change of use may be undertaken without building permission (*Baugenehmigung*). *Baugenehmigung* is provided in the form of a statement from the relevant authority that the proposed structure and its intended use are not contrary to the law. This permission will be given when it has been established that the proposed project complies with both the planning law (*Bauplanungsrecht*) and the building law (*Bauordnungsrecht*).

The federal planning law covers use, volume, density and aesthetics, while building law is similar to UK building regulations in that it deals with technical standards. There may also be local by-laws covering such matters as car parking, trees and landscaping.

Although the local authority is responsible for town planning, it is also controlled by federal planning policy as laid down in the Federal Regional Policy Act. A preliminary land use and development plan (*Flächennutzungsplan*) prepared by the local authority shows in general terms how the land within its area is to be used. From this area plan, detailed local plans (a *Bebauungsplan*) will be drawn up showing in detail the uses proposed for the land. Once such a local plan exists, a landowner can assume that any development within the specified use will be permitted. Not all land will, however, already have a detailed plan and, in order to protect its planning aims, a local authority has the power to freeze all development within a given area while the local plan is prepared. This development freeze expires after two years although it may be renewed twice for further periods of one year. During such a freeze, a landowner can request an exception to be made and, very occasionally, a development may be permitted. Compensation can only be claimed if the freeze lasts longer than four years. Where no detailed plan exists, building may take place in built-up areas provided it does not interfere with the existing layout and development and is not contrary to the public interest.

A local authority is entitled to pass by-laws designating an area 'built-up' but, if no such designation has been made, the question is asked as to whether, in spite of there being individual undeveloped plots of land, the existing structures give an impression of homogeneity and the plot of land on which a building is proposed forms part of such a homogeneous unit. Understandably, the decision is often a matter of dispute between the authorities and the landowner. For 'white' land (i.e. land outside a built-up area), permission is generally granted only for buildings which are typical of the area, such as farm buildings and public utilities.

Before permission can be granted, the owner must have provided the necessary services for the site, including roads, sewerage, electricity, gas and water. The necessary services are deemed to be provided when the authority can be assured that the services will be ready for use when the building work has been completed. Only at that stage can the land actually be regarded as building land. The provision of services (*Erschliessung*) can be the subject of negotiation with the local authority, and detailed conditions have been established to cover such matters as the obligations of the local authority, compensation and the transfer of land for road building.

As for building law, it is generally the case that all buildings must be designed and constructed in accordance with accepted building practice. The supervision of building work is the responsibility of the administration of the federal state (*Land*), exercised either through the rural district authorities or the urban authorities.

Brokerage

Estate agents (*Immobilienmakler*) generally offer no service beyond that of introducing parties who wish to sell, purchase or lease property. As in the UK, the agent's fees are generally payable only when an introduction is effective, although in West Germany these fees are generally paid by the purchaser. The level of fees is by negotiation and can range from 1.5 per cent of a large transaction to a high of 5 per cent of the purchase price. The agent's commission on a letting varies between 1.8 and 2.4 times the gross monthly rental (i.e. between 15 per cent and 20 per cent of the annual rent passing). Although frequently paid by the lessee, in some regions this fee is shared by the two parties and, in the case of large properties, paid by the lessor alone.

Conveyancing

Since all land in West Germany has been registered for many years and since these registers are available for public inspection, it is a simple matter to check on title and on any restrictions or encumbrances. Indeed, such is the level of confidence in the real estate register, that title insurance is not even available in this country.

Having agreed the basic terms of the contract, both parties will take this agreement, together with a recent copy of the real estate register, to a notary. Acting independently and advising both parties equally, the notary will prepare the contract and arrange the settlement of any unpaid taxes or charges. Copies of the finalised deed will then be sent by the notary to the tax office for assessment of the real estate transfer tax (currently at 2 per cent) and to the local authority, which has a statutory right of pre-emption contract for a period of four weeks.

The notary's fees are charged on a sliding scale based on the value of the contract and the extent of the notary's involvement in the transaction, although on average the charge is between one third and one half of one per cent of the value.

It should be noted that any transfer of real estate as well as any mortgage or easement prepared other than by way of a notarial deed is invalid.

The construction industry

Capacity

The industry is well represented in the international league table of construction companies and several West German companies are capable of executing the largest projects worldwide. The leading companies in terms of turnover are:

Philipp Holzmann A.G.	DM5,800 million
Hochtief A.G.	DM4,700 million
Bilfinger Berger A.G.	DM2,600 million
Strabag Bau A.G.	DM2,300 million
Dyckhoff & Widmann A.G.	DM2,100 million

Although there is no national referencing system for the industry, it is possible to find competent contractors in each sector throughout the country.

The majority of multi-storey buildings are constructed in reinforced concrete and 'system' building is particularly often used.

General state of the industry

The industry has recovered from the recession of the mid-1980s and the market is currently buoyant. As yet, there is no shortage of labour or materials, nor any difficulty in establishing a list of selected contractors for competitive tender. With the upturn in the market, both margins and costs have increased; the annual increment in the price of construction tenders in the Frankfurt area, for example, currently runs at about 11 per cent, compared with the officially published cost inflation which runs at 3 per cent.

Although the workload is spread through the major conurbations, the shift of high-tech industry to the southern part of the country means that there is proportionately more construction activity in Frankfurt and in southern cities such as Munich and Stuttgart. Even so, with no less than six major international and commercial centres, West Germany enjoys a far greater spread of wealth and business activity than any other European country.

The outlook is good for the immediate future, although the growth of new political groups (particularly the Green Party) will inevitably slow down the availability of planning approvals and of projects.

The structure of the industry

Invariably, the client enters into separate contracts with each professional consultant (architect, structural engineer, mechanical and electrical engineer). It is usual for the consultant to have full responsibility for design and for on-site supervision, but once the building contract has been placed the contractor accepts liability for detailed design. The cost control function is part of the architect's role.

The high cost of general contracting means that most projects are carried out using separate trades, whether restricted to major work categories or fragmented through the project. The development of system building, together with the demands of international owner-occupiers, has lead to an increase in the number of main contractor 'turn key' operations.

Co-ordination of the various work packages is usually the responsibility of the architect and only on very large projects will an independent co-ordinator be engaged. All projects have an officially appointed proof engineer, who is responsible for quality control. The proof engineer's fees are borne by the client and the client's requirements as regards structure must legally be complied with. The proof engineer may also oversee weatherproofing and technical installations, although this is not mandatory. It is the contractor's responsibility to ensure that these quality requirements are complied with.

The duration of legal liability for construction projects varies, although five years is the norm. The building fabric is not usually covered by insurance.

Design considerations

The general codes and regulations (the *Verdingungsordnung für Bauleistungen* or VOB) apply throughout West Germany, although the mandatory regulations vary from town to town and can result in differences of interpretation and standard. It is, therefore, important to consult the local authority responsible for controlling the particular project. The codes and standards for materials and workmanship (*Deutsches Informationszentrum für technische Regeln*) are also applicable nationwide.

Approvals

Obtaining planning approval is a notoriously slow process, with no legally fixed period for the determination of an application. The approval, which – under the building contract – it is the contractor's responsibility to obtain, is handled by the local authority's technical officials and, other than on very major projects, is not subject to a political committee, as it is in the UK.

Upon completion of the structural works, the proof engineer must certify acceptance of the structure. When the entire construction is completed, an official inspection will provide a certificate of conformity with the planning approval.

Programme considerations

The major factor in the establishment of a pre-construction programme is the length of time it takes to obtain planning approval (which includes building regulations). Even the most optimistic programme would need to allow six months for obtaining planning approval. The construction project then needs to be finalised and bids obtained.

The construction timetable in West Germany is generally shorter than in the UK, thanks in part to the use of system structures.

Placing the building contract

Although the bidding and placing of building projects is usually carried out in accordance with the VOB, the extensive use of separate trades contracts makes it unusual for all trades to be bid at the same time. As a result, the client's overall financial commitment is not usually known until some way into the project.

The co-ordination of the separate trades and inter-related responsibilities is not as specifically defined as in France. The basis of the building contract is the specification and drawings; the contractor's priced build-up only becomes relevant in the event of variations arising.

Cost comparison

The level of professional fees is similar to the level in the UK. For a new build project of DM9 million (approximately £3 million) excluding VAT, the total fees for the architect, engineer and so on would be in the region of 12 per cent. It is possible to obtain a commercial agreement with a consultant at a level below fee scales, but the proof engineer's office must also be paid.

Construction costs are lower in West Germany than in the UK: for example, an air-conditioned speculative office building on the outskirts of a major city will cost approximately DM2,600 per square metre (£75 per square foot) excluding VAT. In comparing the unit cost, however, it is important to remember that the requirements of an office user in West Germany are different from those of the UK office user. A significant proportion of the space, for instance, will be taken up by associated activities such as welfare, social and sporting facilities. It is also usual for the owner of the building to provide partitions and amenities which, in the UK, would be deemed as in addition to the 'Landlord's Works'. The prestige features of a building – the entrance and core facilities – also tend to be rather less ambitious than in the UK.

The retail market

Estimated value of retail sales:	
1985 (HDE)	DM 476bn (£158bn equivalent)
1987 (HDE)	DM 530bn (£171bn equivalent)
1986	DM 20bn total hypermarket sales
	DM 34bn total department store sales
	DM 15bn total co-operative outlet sales
	DM 24bn total mail order sales

Estimated volume of retail sales (1980 = 100)		
	1983	95.6
	1984	96.1
	1985	96.8
	1986	100.2
	1987	102.3

Estimated number of retail outlets	
1979 (Census)	413,000 total outlets
	116,000 food outlets
	297,000 non-food outlets
1987 (HDE)	370,000 total outlets
	87,000 food outlets
	283,000 non-food outlets
1987 (ISB)	6,965 free-standing supermarkets (+332 in department and variety stores)
	55,922 self-service food stores

Shop hours
Mon. to Fri. — 08.00/09.00 to 18.30
Saturday — 08.00/09.00 to 14.00
(Compulsory early closing except on first Saturday in each month, when opening is permitted until 18.00)
No Sunday opening.

VAT rates		
	Lower	7%
	Standard	14%

Source: Corporate Intelligence Research Publications Ltd

Before the Second World War, retailing was focused mainly in department stores and this continued in the post-war era. Over the past fifteen years, the retail market has undergone a significant structural change, with department store trading declining and a substantial increase in the number of regional and national retail chains, shopping centres and edge-of-town/hypermarket developments. Nevertheless, the German public still wishes to shop daily, and places great emphasis on fresh food; this supports the traditional corner shop and means that the suburban high street retains its importance.

Shopping centre development, still in its infancy by comparison with the UK, is growing in importance, and the German public is adapting to the idea of combining shopping with leisure activities or of shopping being a leisure activity in its own right.

Hamburg

Hamburg, West Germany's second largest city, has two main retail centres – the principal downtown centre at Mönckebergstrasse and the more upmarket speciality shopping district half a kilometre away at Neuer Wall/Grosse Bleichen and its surrounding streets.

Mönckebergstrasse

Mönckebergstrasse runs eastwards and gently uphill from the Rathausmarkt to the junction of Glockengiesserwall and Hauptbahnhof Nord. There is a large Dyckhoff department store at the western end, with Karstadt and Eichmeyer further along on opposite sides of the street. At the top end, close to Hauptbahnhof Sud station, Peek & Cloppenburg and Kaufhof face each other, and Horten occupies an island site immediately beyond them. In between, a variety of large and small units include C&A (with a 30 to 40 metre frontage), Benetton, Hennes and Mauritz. A Romanesque detached building at the junction of Mönckebergstrasse and Spitalerstrasse is occupied, rather incongruously, by Burger King. Rentals have dropped from their 1986 high of DM250 per square metre per month to stabilise at DM230 per square metre per month.

Spitalerstrasse

Running out of Mönckebergstrasse at Gerhard-Hauptmann-Platz and continuing behind the main street for its remaining length, Spitalerstrasse is a pedestrianised street with a lively market atmosphere. Apart from the fruit, flower and vegetable stalls, the street contains a selection of smaller fashion units and other traders, as well as the rear frontage of some of the larger department stores on the north side of the main street (including Peek & Cloppenburg and Karstadt).

Neuer Wall/ Grosse Bleichen

On the other side of the Rathausmarkt and over the canal, a series of shopping streets – Neuer Wall, Grosse Bleichen and Poststrasse – are linked not only by narrow cross-streets but also by small shopping arcades.

Neuer Wall, perhaps the most fashionable of these streets, contains traders such as Gortz, Rodier, Benetton, Rosenthal, Laura Ashley, Villeroy & Boch and Louis Vuitton.

A number of small shopping arcades run from Neuer Wall through to ABC Strasse:

- **Kaufmannshaus:** a small development of speciality shopping beneath a four-floor office building, it leads through to Grosse Bleichen close to a shopping centre now under construction.

- **Hanse Viertel:** a cross-shaped development beneath a new hotel, with shopping at ground-floor level and a Moevenpick food court at a lower level beneath the central atrium. The best of the arcade developments, Hanse Viertel leads through to Poststrasse.

- **Neuer Gänsemarkt:** a small development, running from Poststrasse to ABC Strasse, with speciality shopping anchored by a large restaurant unit.

In this same district, on the corner of Grosse Bleichenbrücke but a considerable distance from the city's prime shopping area, a new centre now under construction (the Bleichenhof) will provide 3,500 square metres of shopping and 12,000 square metres of offices.

Frankfurt

Zeil

A wide pedestrianised street planted with avenues of plane trees, Zeil is the main downtown shopping centre in Frankfurt and reputedly the busiest in West Germany. Beginning at Goetheplatz, Zeil contains a large number of department stores, including Kaufhof, Woolworth and Peek & Cloppenburg. The majority of the buildings have seven floors, most of top six floors being used for retail or storage. The smaller units have 8- to 10-metre frontages and depths of between 30 and 35 metres.

Where Zeil opens out into a large piazza at the junction with Gross Friedberger Strasse, the square, too, is pedestrianised. But here the shopping falters – a number of banks and other outlets break the retail frontage.

Beyond the square, Zeil resumes with a large C&A department store, although beyond this the shopping is of a poorer quality and soon ceases. Rental levels were static between 1986 and 1988 at around DM200 per square metre per month, but they have now shown some growth. At present they are in the region of DM260 per square metre per month.

Goethestrasse

On the west side of Goetheplatz, in Goethestrasse and a few surrounding streets, an area of upmarket and speciality shopping provides a pleasant pedestrianised route through to the Opera and to the adjoining park. Traders in this area include Laura Ashley, Louis Vuitton, Cartier, Stefanel, Guy Laroche, Rolex, Benetton and Gianni Versace.

Kaiserstrasse

At the top end of Kaiserstrasse, close to Goetheplatz, there is a mixture of fashion retailers, leather goods shops and restaurants, and – around the Hotel Frankfurter Hof in Kaiserplatz – a number of smaller speciality retailers selling jewellery, leather goods and silver-ware. As it continues towards the station, Kaiserstrasse becomes a two-way street with wide pavements and a mixture of secondary retail units, travel agents, airline offices and restaurants.

Düsseldorf

Königsallee

Königsallee, the most important shopping street in Düsseldorf, runs north–south from Theodor Korner Strasse to Karl-Theodor Strasse, with the shopping on the west side and the canal on the east. Traders include Rodier, Burberry, Louis Feraud, Ciro, Benetton and Gucci. Nearly halfway along the street is the Koe-galerie, a speciality shopping mall with three main arms running out from a central atrium, a Moevenpick foodcourt at lower ground-floor level and shopping on two floors above. This centre is occupied principally by German multiples and a large number of private German traders.

**Schadowstrasse/
Klinger Passage**

To the east of Königsallee, and on the other side of the canal, runs Schadowstrasse, a pedestrianised street on the corner of which stands a large Horten department store. The lower level of this store has been converted to create approximately twenty small, in-store units for speciality food traders. This very pleasant and effective gourmet foodcourt is reached directly by escalator from the pedestrianised street. The remainder of the area contains downmarket fashion, music and other such shops.

As in Hamburg, rental levels fell back from a 1986 peak of DM280 per square metre per month but have recovered to approximately DM300 per square metre per month.

The office market

Whereas previously the office market was evenly spread between the major cities, there has recently been a visible shift of emphasis towards the south. The north and the Ruhr area have suffered from the decline in the traditional smokestack industries, while the south and the region around Frankfurt has been able to attract the new high-tech sectors.

It has been suggested that the credit is due to the local authorities in the southern states for their active pursuit of a policy designed to capture new industry. Consequently the bulk of investment interest is now concentrated in the southern part of the country and around

Frankfurt, with cities such as Munich and Stuttgart experiencing an office boom, and Frankfurt itself, the undisputed market leader in the office sector, continuing to strengthen its position as the world's fourth most important financial centre. Over 370 domestic and foreign banks have now located in Frankfurt, creating an enormous demand for office space which the city is unable to meet.

Some of West Germany's largest cities, including Hamburg, Munich, Cologne, Frankfurt, Stuttgart and Düsseldorf, are major centres for the service industries. By comparison with the national average of 9 office employees per 100 inhabitants, Frankfurt has 37 per 100 and Cologne 18 per 100. Office work already represents 47.5

Population and employment in West Germany

Population (January 1987)	Total employment (January 1988)	Office employees per 100 inhabitants
Hamburg 1,571,300	Hamburg 723,800	Hamburg 18.4
Munich 1,274,700	Munich 664,100	Munich 22.1
Cologne 914,300	Cologne 420,000	Cologne 18.1
Frankfurt 592,400	Frankfurt 462,300	Frankfurt 37.1
Stuttgart 565,500	Stuttgart 370,200	Stuttgart 27.5
Düsseldorf 560,600	Düsseldorf 339,200	Düsseldorf 26.9

Source: Müller International Immobilien

per cent of total employment in Frankfurt and 39.5 per cent in Cologne, but informed opinion suggests that the number of jobs in the service and administrative sectors will continue to increase in all eleven major cities and that the demand for office space will continue to rise through to the year 2000.

Frankfurt

The office market in Frankfurt is characterised by the lack of available space and of new development opportunities in the traditional central business district and in the West End, the first of the overspill areas and one which was extensively developed during the early 1970s, prior to the imposition of strict planning controls. At that time, the authorities decided to develop a new business centre at Niederrad, to the south-west of the city centre, and this has proved popular with computer and high-tech companies.

Although there is some development in other areas, such as the western and southern districts, strong demand for space in a prime location continues. The authorities are keen to accommodate the demand for fear that the city will lose its jealously guarded status as the world's fourth financial centre to Paris or Amsterdam.

Two new towers on Mainzer Landstrasse in the city centre will be completed in the early 1990s, but this will not meet the demand for 500,000 square metres over the next five years. Of eleven new office schemes proposed, the Messeturm – a development by Tishmann Speyer Properties – will, when completed, be Europe's tallest building (at 254 metres).

These developments are part of a total of 750,000 square metres of office space planned for the western districts, a figure substantially higher than for the rest of Frankfurt put together and one which underlines the importance of the areas to the west of the central business district.

The fact that in 1989 total absorption amounted to 250,000 square metres compared with the 1986 peak of 205,000 square metres shows the absence of suitable space for office development. Over the same period, prime rents have risen from DM43 per square metre per month in 1986 to DM70 per square metre per month in 1989. Given the length of the development period for the construction of high-rise blocks, demand will continue to outstrip supply until the mid-1990s.

Düsseldorf

With more than 300 Japanese companies now represented in Düsseldorf, this city is second only to New York in the size of its Japanese business community. A further sixty companies from other Far East countries have also opened offices here.

Although the office supply is centred around Königsallee, the banking quarter, the city centre and the area around the railway station immediately to the east, the lack of new development opportunities in these areas has increased attention on overspill areas such as the left bank of the Rhine, Ratingen and Neuss.

The largest of the new developments planned are in the office district known as Am Seestern, on the left bank of the river, where the 140,000 square metre development proposed is to include an 85,000 square metre office park. The absorption in 1989 of 180,000 square metres of space set a new record and left the city with its lowest vacancy rate since 1983. Rents in 1989 have remained stable at DM36 per square metre per month.

Hamburg

Hamburg's traditional business district is centred along the banks of the River Alster at the southern end of the Aussen Alster, a huge lake in the heart of the city. The river continues alongside the Rathaus (the town hall) and through to the docks. With no new development opportunities in this area, the City-Sud and City-Nord developments have become increasingly important locations for office tenants looking for modern buildings with large floor areas and sufficient car-parking spaces.

The area around the Fuhlsbüttel airport is also being developed, and the local authority is now considering a scheme to privatise the Speicherstadt – an island on the River Elbe 15 square kilometres in area.

The total office supply in Hamburg is now approximately 279,000 square metres. During 1988 130,000 square metres were taken up, compared with 101,000 square metres in 1987 and the 1986 peak of 140,000 square metres. The 1989 vacancy rate (214,000 square metres) was the lowest recorded since 1982, and rents are stable at DM35 per square metre per month.

The industrial market

Despite the fact that industrial property is traditionally owner-occupied in West Germany, there is a growing move towards an investor-led rented market. During 1988, the pace of rental growth in the industrial sector quickened to between 5 and 7 per cent.

There is a trend towards good quality premises, and the demand for high-tech developments (*Gewerbepark*) is certainly very strong. With a rise in rental levels for high-tech premises of 10 per cent in 1988, new projects now tend to concentrate on this sub-sector.

Hamburg

Heavy industry is concentrated in the industrial zones Hamburg–Billbrook, Rothenburgsort, Veddel and Peute and in the harbour area. Norderstedt, close to Hamburg, is the centre for mixed/light industry and warehousing. Rents range from DM10 to DM12 per square metre per month for storage space, and from DM12 to DM15 per square metre per month for production space.

Munich

There is no heavy industry in the Munich area, and the centres for light industry, warehousing and trading companies are: Puchheim, Germering, Karlsfeld, Haar, Ottobrunn, Gräfelfing and Neufahrt. Rentals for new warehouses in and around Munich are in the region of DM 10 per square metre per month; rentals for production space range from DM10 to DM14 per square metre per month and for office space DM14 to DM18 per square metre per month.

In the past five years, high-tech industry has developed into a major market in Munich (the silicone valley of Bavaria). Although it has now slowed down somewhat, Munich still leads all other West German towns in this sub-sector.

Index